Cultivating Charismatic Power

Tiffany Cone

Cultivating Charismatic Power

Islamic Leadership Practice in China

Tiffany Cone
Asian University for Women
Chittagong, Bangladesh

ISBN 978-3-030-09072-2   ISBN 978-3-319-74763-7   (eBook)
https://doi.org/10.1007/978-3-319-74763-7

This Palgrave Macmillan imprint is published by the registered company Springer International Publishing AG part of Springer Nature.
The registered company address is: Gewerbestrasse 11, 6330 Cham, Switzerland

PREFACE

At the age of 12, I lived in Indonesia for one year. Being immersed in a culture outside of my own instilled in me a deep curiosity about how human beings imbued the world with meaning and understood their place within it. Years later, I came to realise just how deep an impression this experience left on me. In particular, I was struck by the interplay of Buddhist and Islamic practice in daily life. During my undergraduate degree in anthropology, I first visited China and over the subsequent years became involved in a number of film projects there. After completing a study of Sufism at the end of my first degree, I directed a film project titled Living Chinese Philosophy. This film explored the central tenets of Confucianism and Daoism in the context of daily life in China. These collective experiences inspired me to undertake a deeper study of Sufism in China from the perspective of philosophical anthropology. Specifically, I was interested in the processes that fostered the emergence and flourishing of esoteric Islam in China. To borrow here from the French philosopher Gilles Deleuze, at heart I was interested in the assemblage and re-assemblage of the world— that is, in the 'complex constellations of objects, bodies, expressions, qualities and territories' that ceaselessly create and re-create the world anew (Parr 2010, p. 18).

ACKNOWLEDGEMENTS

This project would not have been at all possible without the generous support and practical assistance from numerous people. In China, profound thanks must go to Professor Ding Shiren at Lanzhou University in

Lanzhou, Gansu Province, who hosted me as a student and has continued to provide support during the writing process. Thanks must also go to Professor Hu Long and Professor Yang Wenjiong for their assistance, advice, and encouragement. To the many students and leaders at the *gongbei* for being generous with your time and knowledge and to local families in Linxia who took me into their homes, fed me delicious food, and poured me endless cups of hot tea during a very cold winter—my deepest thanks. For their warm friendship and support in Lanzhou, my sincere thanks and love goes to Alice, Eric, Asma, and Madina. In Xi'an, I also want to thank Shannon, Rebecca, and Johnny.

In Australia, many thanks must go to all of the faculty and fellow gradu-ates at the Australian National University who offered their advice, support, and friendship. In particular, generous thanks must go to Professor Andrew Kipnis for his wonderful guidance from the very beginning of this project and right throughout the journey. It would not have been possible without your support. Special thanks also to Dr Philip Taylor for his generosity of spirit and time in engaging with this project. I also want to give thanks to Kathy Robinson, Andrew McWilliam, Alan Rumsey, Francesca Merlan, Ashley Carruthers, Sverre Molland, Antje Lubcke, Roger Casas, Li Geng, Francesca Mosca, Saskia Lillepuu, Lina Jakob, Jean Kennedy, and Darja Hoenigman.

In Bangladesh, I want to thank colleagues and students at the Asian University for Women who have been a great support and inspiration over the last two years. It's been an honour and a privilege to teach and learn from such a diverse student body. In all of my classes, I have been able to further deepen my knowledge and understanding of the world in dialogue with young women from a wide range of cultural contexts. Outside of the classroom, I want to especially thank my dear colleague and friend Rebecca Dawson for her unwavering positivity and support throughout my time in Bangladesh, for finally getting me to Nepal, and for inspiring me to return there during the last stages of this project. I also want to give special thanks to Raihana Raha, Azmina Karim, and Sharmin Rahmatullah for offering such warmth, care, and laughter during my time in Bangladesh.

At Palgrave Macmillan, many thanks to Mireille Yanow who responded enthusiastically to my initial proposal and subsequently to Alexis Nelson, Kyra Saniewski, and Mary Al-Sayed who carried it through all of the various stages to publication. Thank you for your time, support, and guidance in this process. Generous thanks must especially go to Professor Jonathan Lipman for his incisive and helpful comments on the manuscript. Thank you also to Associate Professor Jackie Armijo for sharing forthcoming research and to Associate Professor Matthew Erie for his assistance on the finer details. Thank you also to Zhu Yayun, Li Geng, Rebecca Gao, and Muhammad Adlin Sila for feedback on translations and proofreading.

In New Zealand, many thanks must go to my close friends and family. Firstly, to Jane McCabe—for your faith, support, and care throughout this long journey—from my initial imaginings, through significant shared travels, and to the words in this book. I will always be grateful to you. To my friend Monique Patterson—thank you for your presence and support from afar throughout these long years. To my wonderful siblings—Julian, Jared, and Hannah—and their respective families, thank you for your support, patience, and encouragement through so many years of comings and goings. I am lucky to have you all. To Chris Edwards—thank you for the many hours spent, often at a great distance, helping to 'build' this project. Your endless patience and attention to detail have been invaluable.

Finally, to my parents. Thank you to my father Malcolm—the conversations I shared with you as a youngster planted the seeds of my deep interest in anthropology, religion, and philosophy. I will forever be grateful to you for sharing your knowledge with me, for exposing me to the magic of travel, and for teaching me the importance of an examined life. To my mother Marian—your creativity, humanity, and intuitive sense of the world continue to inspire me. I hope traces of these qualities find some expression in this work. I dedicate this book to you both. Thank you for everything.

Notes on the Text and Use of Images

Throughout the text, Chinese terms are italicised in the standard pinyin form. Proper nouns (place names or personal names) are not italicised (e.g. Guo Gongbei). The glossary provides definitions, the pinyin, and the character equivalents for key Chinese terms used many times in the book. When analysing particular Chinese characters, quoting an important Chinese phrase, or referencing important dates according to the Chinese lunar calendar, the characters have been left in the main body of the text. Similarly, Arabic terms are also romanised and italicised throughout (except for proper nouns). Important terms, phrases, and names are written in the glossary with all diacritics. If the term, phrase, or name is not in the glossary, diacritics are also used in the main text when the terms are first mentioned but not consistently thereafter. This is in order to both simplify the text and sustain consistency of style with cited sources. I have chosen to use the 'Qur'an' transliteration, but have retained 'Koran' if used within a published citation. All translations are my own unless otherwise indicated. Likewise, all images used throughout the book are my own. Maps were created by the CartoGIS unit at the College of Asia and the Pacific, Australian National University, and are used with permission. Some primary ethnographic data in Chaps. 6 and 7 was previously published in a book chapter in *Religion and Mobility in a Globalising Asia: New Ethnographic Explorations* by Routledge, UK. It is used with permission in this book (Lau and Cao 2014).

ORGANISATION OF THE BOOK

This book is organised into eight chapters. Chapter 1 provides background information on Islam and Sufism in China, summarises the key concerns of the study, and lays out the theoretical and methodological foundations. Chapter 2 introduces the exemplary model of charisma in the context of Guo Gongbei through considering stories and narratives about the saints. Chapter 3 discusses the daily bodily disciplines within the Sufi site that lead to the generation of individual charismatic power. Chapter 4 moves on to explore the emulation of this particular set of charismatic practices amongst students and members of the Qadiriyya community. Chapter 5 considers social proximity and distance in relation to the generation of charisma. Chapter 6 considers the role of mobility (and in turn, education) in the generation of religious authenticity and authority and how this strengthens the charismatic reputation. Chapter 7 explores the various voices in the contentious debates surrounding this charismatic practice. It does so with reference to a set of metacultural categories—that of 'orthodoxy', 'integrity', 'unity', and 'stability'. The final chapter, Chap. 8, offers some conclusions and reflections.

Chittagong, Bangladesh   Tiffany Cone

REFERENCES

Lau, S., and N. Cao. 2014. *Religion and Mobility in a Globalising Asia: New Ethnographic Explorations*, ed. by S. Lau and N. Cao. London: Routledge Press.
Parr, A. 2010. *The Deleuze Dictionary*. Boston: Edinburgh University Press.

CONTENTS

LIST OF FIGURES

Map

Location map of Linxia, Gansu, China

CHAPTER 1

Introduction: Islam, Sufism, and China

I believe precisely that at the bottom of all our mystical states there are body techniques which we have not studied, but which were studied fully in China and India, even in very remote periods. I think there are necessarily biological means of entering into "communion with God". (Mauss 1979, p. 122)

This is an ethnographic study of Islamic leadership in the contemporary world, located at the Western edge of East Asia. Islamic leadership is specifically explored in the context of a Sufi community in Northwest China, through an in-depth study of charismatic power and its cultivation by Sufi disciples at this site. Islam and China are, in and of themselves, topics of significant relevance and contention in today's economic, political, and religious climate. At present, there is a global concern about both the rise of a militant Islam and of an ever increasingly assertive Chinese state. A study of this kind is thus both timely and relevant.

The effective transmission or cultivation of this 'charisma' amongst disciples is vital to the maintenance and continuity of Sufi genealogies around the world. This is even more important for the Chinese Qadiriyya Sufi network at the centre of this study. The disciples of the three other Sufi networks in China are able to have families and can thus pass leadership on to their sons or related male members of the extended family. But

© The Author(s) 2018
T. Cone, *Cultivating Charismatic Power*,
https://doi.org/10.1007/978-3-319-74763-7_1

1

the disciples of the Qadiriyya cannot have families. Their Chinese name *chujiaren* literally means 'people who have left home or the family'.[1]

Succession to leadership (to the position of leader or *dangjiaren*) is thus based solely on religious merit, not blood inheritance (Gladney 2004, p. 135). As a result, the successful embodiment of 'charisma' by disciples is even more crucial for the continued existence of the order—crucial because of the religious authority that the embodiment of this charisma ensures.[2] The successful embodiment of this charismatic power is also at the heart of debates amongst the wider Muslim community in Northwest China that continue to question the orthodoxy and integrity of the Qadiriyya charismatic practice and, in turn, their religious authority.

Furthermore, the Chinese Qadiriyya network at the centre of this study has been described as relatively withdrawn from 'worldly' involvement in politics and the local community around them. However, the site of Guo Gongbei, the main focus of this project, maintains a very open connection to the networks beyond their walls. They house orphans, teach and provide lodgings for both male and female Muslim students, support chujiaren (disciples) and students to study overseas, and provide support and guidance for both Muslim and non-Muslim members of the community on a daily basis. Perhaps most significantly, Guo Gongbei has a particularly strong relationship with Iran and has a well-established system of sending chujiaren (disciples) and students there to study. This is notable in light of the fact that China is also now Iran's largest trading partner. Most recently, the two countries signed an agreement to bring Iran fully into the emerging strategic New Economic Silk Road and Maritime Road blueprint known as 'One Belt, One Road'.

Against this background, this study is guided by three underlying concerns. Firstly, what is the nature of charismatic power in this context?

[1] It should be noted that there are apparently two different styles for 'seeking the Way' in the Qadiriyya. One is to leave the family, practise austerities, and remain celibate (the *gongbei* systems that I studied acted this way). The other group marries, does not leave the family, and practises austerities (at home); this group is a minority and I had no contact with groups of this sort. The Gaoshan Gongbei in the Dongxiang acts in this way (Ma 1983, 2008).

[2] While I stress here the importance of charismatic embodiment in the case of the Qadiriyya, I do not deny that varying degrees of charismatic cultivation would exist in both systems of succession (by descent and by mystical recognition). It would however require a comparative study to determine to what degree and in what ways 'charismatic' cultivation differed amongst different Chinese Sufi orders.

Secondly, why is it considered contentious by some in the wider community? Finally, what can this study contribute to global understanding amidst the virulently contentious debates about the role of religion in the contemporary geo-political landscape? By exploring the ways in which this Chinese Sufi institution is interacting with—and is influenced by—religious sites in Iran, this study affords a glimpse into the ways in which Islamic communities throughout the world are linked not only economically and politically but culturally. Moreover, though the study focuses on a specific religious community, in so doing, it contributes important insights that could enhance and deepen understandings of the religious, political, and economic concerns that are relevant to not just the Muslim community but to the global community. These concerns include narratives of unity and disunity amongst different religious factions, cultural syncretism and resulting questions of religious legitimacy (orthodoxy and unorthodoxy), materialism and desire and their impact on religious integrity, and perhaps most importantly the stability of religious institutions within rapidly growing economies.

STUDIES OF ISLAM AND SUFISM IN CHINA

In the past 30–40 years, there has been a growing academic interest in the Chinese Muslim community within the English-speaking world. In the 1990s and early 2000s, this was reflected most notably in the work of Jonathan Lipman, Maria Jaschok, Dru Gladney, Maris Gillette, and Elisabeth Alles. In the past two years, a significant number of new studies have also been published exploring various facets of the Hui Muslim community. Some notable examples include studies of Islamic law (Erie 2016), of the shifting definitions of Islam in China (Tontini 2016), of ethnic identity and Muslim networks in Hong Kong (Ho 2016), of Islamic revival and ethnic identity in Qinghai Province (Stewart 2017) and of Muslims in Amdo Tibet (Hille et al. 2015).

In relation to the Sufi orders in China, as far as this author is aware, only a small number of related works have been published. Gladney, Lipman, and Dillon have depicted how Sufi orders have disseminated new ideas and established networks of solidarity amongst Muslim communities (Gladney 2004; Lipman 1997; Dillon 1999). In doing so, they often refer to the pioneering work of the Chinese scholar Ma Tong in the 1980s. Gladney in particular focuses on the importance of Sufi tombs to Hui communities.

While the tombs may not necessarily be relevant to all Hui, Gladney asserts that 'they continue to serve as powerful frameworks for personal identity and social action, which both distinguish Hui communities from one another and provide important charters for their corporate identity' (Gladney 2004, p. 121). As has been noted in other parts of the world, the Sufi tombs are also a source of conflict (Marcus 1985, p. 456). Gladney has noted that discussion of membership in an order based on descent is often the basis for conflict and criticism of inferior orders (Gladney 2004, p. 137). Historically, the Qadiriyya have not been involved in political feuds or activism, and perhaps as a result little research attention has been paid to them (Lipman 1997, p. 89).[3] They have however been subject to criticism and debate for a number of distinctive reasons, and it is an intention of this research to examine these criticisms and their relation to charisma.

Western studies of Islam in China from the 1980s onwards have focused on socio-historical or political issues to do with the 'phenomenon' of Islam in China (demographics, distribution, public policy, national identification, ethnic conflict) rather than looking at the beliefs and practices of Chinese Muslim groups themselves, Sufi or otherwise (Gladney 1995, p. 373). In such studies, Islam as a tradition is often generalised into the background (Gladney 2004, 120). Similarly, while Chinese scholarship since the 1980s about Islam in China has proliferated, few works have addressed the beliefs and practices of Sufi orders deeply. The work of Ma Tong was seminal in providing detailed historical, political, and socio-economic accounts of the practices and institutional structures of the various Islamic orders. Other scholars of his generation such as Yang Huaizhong, Ma Qicheng, and Mian Weilin provided further detailed accounts of Sufi orders in terms of social structures. In the next scholarly generation, the works of Jin Yijiu, Gao Zhanfu, Yu Zhengui, and Wu Wanshan all provided further historical material (Ma 1983; Gao 1991; Yang 1992; Mian 1997; Yu and Lei 2001; Ma 2006; Jin 2008). A number of shorter research papers produced in the last ten years specifically focus on the history of Sufism in Northwest China and in particular on the disciple system of the Qadiriyya order (Ma 2008; Han 2009; Ding 2009; Ha and Ma 2014; Ma and Ma 2014). However, most of this material either continues to speak of Chinese Sufism in terms of

---

[3] Unlike the Jahriyya who practised a more 'transformationist' and 'militant' Islam, the Qadiriyya sought resolution between the dictates of Chinese society and their practice of Islam through 'ascetic withdrawal from the world' (Gladney 1996, pp. 61–62).

structures, institutions, leaders, and economics or discusses philosophical ideas of Chinese Sufism at a remove from actual local practice, often relying solely on textual analysis.

In 2009, Han Zhongyi and Ma Yuanyuan reviewed the Chinese scholarship of Sufism over the last 30 years and highlighted the lack of studies concerning everyday practice and belief and the repetitive content of some of the research. They state that 'the research of scholars in our country is still in an exploratory stage, no theoretical system has been formed. Detailed studies of Sufism are still lacking and although many books have been published, very little detailed research is conducted and [most researchers] are still at the stage of introduction'. They hoped to

strike an accurate balance between religious emotion and academic principles. Sufism is an Islamic school with a strong experiential element. It is very hard to understand the essence of it by just reading articles. So [we] need to deepen our understanding of it through understanding real life. In order to understand the Sufi doctrines of folk believers, and practitioners, we need to watch and study its practice rituals, which is very challenging (Han 2009, pp. 104–105).

A study was published in 2010 by a student at Lanzhou University, perhaps in response to this perceived need for more grounded studies of religious activity. In this study the author tries to adopt an anthropological approach to the study of daily life amongst Hui Sufi women in the Huanghe county of Gansu (Ma 2010). This study adopts a similar approach by focusing on daily life in a Sufi order and attempting a genuine engagement with their beliefs and practices.

RESEARCHING SUFI CHARISMA IN LINXIA

The focal point of my research was the Guo Gongbei Qadiriyya Sufi complex located in Linxia City (formerly known as Hezhou), the capital city of Linxia Hui Autonomous Prefecture, Gansu Province. To undertake the research, I was formally enrolled at Lanzhou University in the Institute of Islamic Studies for one year from September 2011 through to September 2012. The Guo Gongbei complex included a worship hall that was connected to the main tomb of the first founder, two classrooms for language lessons, housing for *chujiaren* and students, an office and meeting room, a kitchen, bathroom, store rooms for food and wood, and conservatories containing the tombs of past deceased saints. While those living at the *gongbei* were all male, the Arabic and Persian classes run by the *gongbei* were open to both men and women. In the class that I attended, there were 15 boys and three girls, all between 15 and 19 years of age. While there were female religious adherents of the order in the community, there were no women that practised the life of a *chujiaren*.

The primary informants in the study were the leader (*dangjiaren*) of Guo Gongbei (and two other *dangjiaren* at adjacent *gongbei*), seven *chujiaren* who were based at Guo Gongbei and 15 students (12 boys, three girls) who were students at the *gongbei*. In the community I also came to know nine families connected to the *gongbei*, five of them very well. Each family included two sets of grandparents, parents, between two to four children and their grandchildren (one to two). My secondary informants included ten Hui students (male and female) who were not at the *gongbei* but studying at mosque schools or at a tertiary college, Hui in the community of varied age and occupation (taxi drivers, food sellers, bank tellers), four scholars based in Lanzhou (either at Lanzhou University or religious research institutions), and Han university students and families. The names of two local scholars mentioned in this book have been changed for the purposes of privacy. Three primary data collection methods were used in this research: semi-structured interviews, participant observation, and the analysis of text. Primarily I was interested in daily practice in the *gongbei* space and the community surrounding it. In the end this included daily and weekly worship (individual and group, formal and informal), public and private ceremonies (weddings, funerals, commemorations), language and Qur'anic classes, physical exercise, and cooking and cleaning (in both public and domestic spaces).

ISLAM AND SUFISM IN CHINA: BRIEF HISTORY

Amongst the 56 official *minzu* or nationalities of the PRC, there are now 10 Muslim minority nationalities totalling close to 26 million people (Wang 2016, p. 570). The Hui are the largest and most dispersed minority, with approximately 9.2 million religious adherents, followed by the Uyghur, whose population is 8.6 million (Armijo-Hussein 2006, p. 2). There is tremendous cultural and linguistic diversity amongst the Hui population with a variety of Islamic orders to which one can belong. The orders that exist in China are the Gedimu, the Qadiriyya, Jahriyya, Kubrawiyya, and Khafiyya Sufi orders, the Yihewani, and the Salafiyya (Gladney 2004,

p. 128).[4] Linxia is the capital of Linxia Hui Autonomous Prefecture, in Gansu Province, Northwest China. It has historically been known as the 'Little Mecca' of China and has been a very important site in the development and establishment of different Islamic teachings (Gladney 2004, p. 134). In Linxia City, the majority of the Muslim population identify as Yihewani or Gedimu. The next largest majority identify as belonging to the Qadiriyya Sufi order (approximately 10,870 religious adherents), the Khafiyya Sufi order (approximately 10,195 religious adherents), and the Jahriyya Sufi order (approximately 1200 religious adherents) (Li and Jing 2011, p. 384).[5]

Sufism was said to have arrived in China in the late seventeenth century with shaykhs—both Chinese and foreign—who brought new teachings from the cities of Medina and Mecca (Gladney 2003, p. 454). Over time, Sufi institutions were established by descendants of these early Sufi saintly leaders, which later became known as *menhuan* or the 'leading or saintly descent groups' (Gladney 1996, p. 41).[6] Lipman suggests that the term *menhuan* probably derives from *menhu* ('great family'), 'but it has come to refer exclusively to Northwestern Chinese Sufi solidarities whose leadership remains within a single lineage' (Lipman 1997, p. 70).

The founder of the Qadiriyya in China was Qi Jingyi, also known in Arabic as Hilāl al-Dīn (1656–1719). He was buried in Linxia's 'Great Tomb' (Da Gongbei) shrine complex, which became the centre of Qadiriyya Sufism in China. The Guo Gongbei site neighbours Da Gongbei

---

[4] Bashir has argued that in describing Sufi solidarities, 'network' is a better term than 'order' because of its relative neutrality: 'In my view, the use of order has led scholars to misapprehend the type of internal cohesion and discipline than can be attributed to the Sufi communities in question. Resisting this usage opens up the space to try to understand Sufi networks on their own terms, as examples of a form of sociality contingent on the particulars of the histories of Islamic societies' (Bashir 2013, p. 11). While I note this important point, to sustain consistency and clarity between the work of others in this field and my own, I have decided to use 'order' throughout my discussion.

[5] While these are the four main Sufi orders, there are 'myriad smaller *menhuan* and sub-branches due to ideological, political, geographical and historical differences' (Gladney 2004, p. 128).

[6] Though not unusual elsewhere in the Muslim world, Lipman notes that the idea of 'hereditary succession to religious, social and political authority fell on particularly fertile ground in China [...] As a unique blend of Chinese and Sufi forms, the *menhuan* combined the appeal of prophetic descent with Chinese notions of family structure and socioeconomic competition' (Lipman 1997, pp. 70–71).

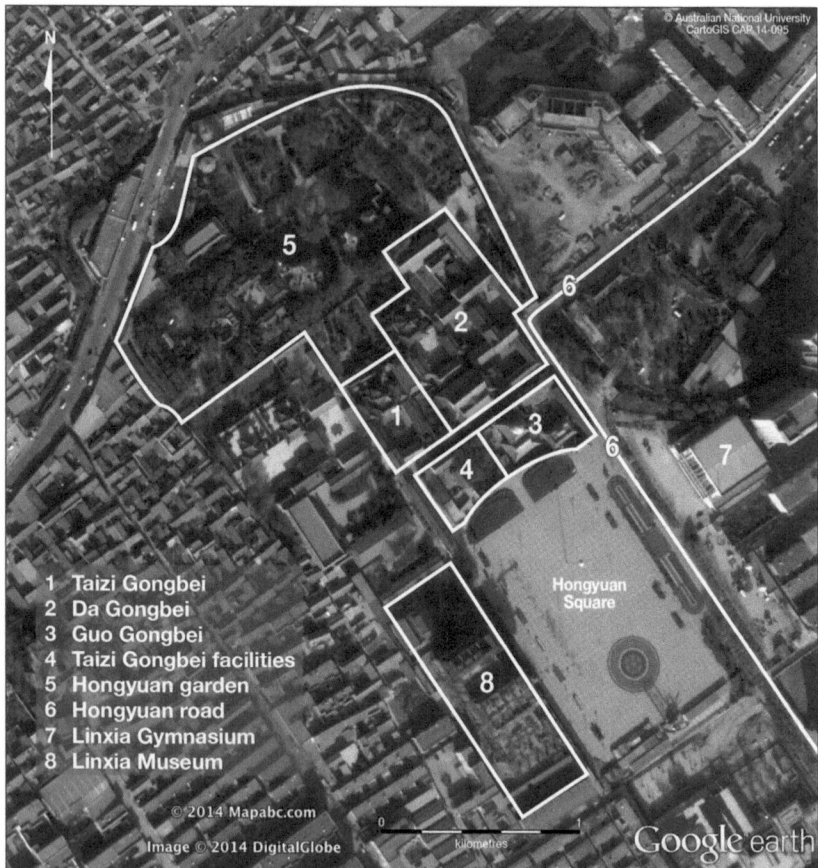

Fig. 1.1   Layout of main Qadiriyya Gongbei sites in Linxia

and is the burial site of another Qadiriyya founding saint named Chen Yiming (Fig. 1.1). The term *gongbei* is the Chinese transliteration of the Persian word *gunbad* or *gunbaz* meaning 'dome'. In China, it refers to the tombs of Sufi teachers and the shrines that have developed around them. According to a 2009 survey, there are 35 active *gongbei* sites in the Qadiriyya network: 6 in Sichuan, 13 in Shaanxi, and 16 in the prefecture of Linxia, Gansu (Wang 2009, pp. 12–13).

The Qadiriyya Sufi order derives its name from the founder 'Abd al-Qādir al-Jīlānī (1077–1166 CE, also transliterated as 'Gilani') who was a native of the Iranian province of Gilan.[7] He was a pupil at the school of the Sufi Abu Sa'īd al-Mubārak Mukharrami and became the leader of this school after Mukharrami's death in 1119 CE. He and his family lived in the school (*madrasa*) until he passed away in 1166. At this time, his son, 'Abd al-Wahhāb, succeeded him as *shaykh*. In the fourteenth century Abd al-Qadir's sons played an active role in the propagation of the order, and Sufi *shaykhs* in different countries acted as representatives of the prestigious Qadiriyya. By the fifteenth century, the Qadiriyya had branches not only in the Arab countries of the Middle East but also in Morocco, Spain, Turkey, India, Ethiopia, and Somalia, as well as amongst the Tuareg in present-day Mali. In the sixteenth century it reached China and Malaysia, and from the seventeenth century it came to have religious adherents also in the European territories of the Ottoman Empire (Abun-Nasr 2007, pp. 86–96).

Nowadays, the order is widespread, particularly in the Arabic-speaking world. As well as the countries mentioned above, it can also be found in Afghanistan, Bangladesh, Pakistan, the Balkans, and parts of Europe and the Americas (Abun-Nasr 2007, pp. 86–96). In a cursory survey of succession amongst Qadiriyya orders in other parts of the world (Afghanistan, Iraq, Kurdistan, Northern Caucasus, Pakistan, and Indonesia) lineage was overwhelmingly hereditary (Abu-Manneh 2000, 115; Bruinessen 2000, 131; Gammer 2000, 275; Buehler 2000, 339; Bruinessen 2000, 361).[8] However—as mentioned—lineage amongst the Chinese Qadiriyya group discussed in this work is not. This practice of celibacy, of being a *chujiaren*, points to the influence of Buddhism on this order—an aspect of their practice that will be discussed further throughout this work.

CHALLENGES FOR ISLAMIC LEADERSHIP

Religious leaders within the Sufi community in China face a number of important challenges. These challenges, though of course unique in their particularities, are shared to varying degrees by diverse Muslim

---

[7] Matthew Erie has noted that Abd al-Qadir al-Jilani followed the Hanbali school of Sunni Islam, while the Qadiriyya in China followed the Hanafi school (Erie 2016, p. 136).

[8] The practice of *dhikr* amongst Qadiriyya has also varied, ranging from the ecstatic 'loud' and shaking versions to the silent (such as Qadiriyya in China).

communities throughout the world. The first challenge is perhaps one of the most crucial in thinking about the continued practice and flourishing of Islam; that is, on what basis can unity in the Islamic community be achieved in the face of divisive factions?

Ever since the death of the Prophet Muhammad in 632, uncertainty and conflict related to leadership within the Islamic community have animated Islamic history. Despite the egalitarian spirit promoted by Muhammed himself, after his passing the community now lacked a leader, and it became essential to establish some form of succession in order to regain stability (Esposito 1998, p. 40). While the majority of Muslims accepted the initial decision to elect Abū Bakr (a companion of the Prophet) as the first successor, there were some who supported 'Ali ibn Abī Thālib , the Prophet's cousin and son-in-law. Those who supported Ali later became known as 'Shī'a', while those who opposed succession based on bloodline to the Prophet came to be known as 'Sunnī', meaning 'followers of (the Prophet's) customs *sunna*)' (Esposito 1998, pp. 41–44). The Sufi movement that began during the Umayyad Caliphs (661–750) consisted of ascetic devotees, 'whose pious ideals implicitly condemned the worldliness that prevailed in the Muslim community under the Umayyad Caliphs' (Abun-Nasr 2007, p. 7). By the late ninth century, this movement had developed a system of mystical tenets that challenged the orthodoxy of the beliefs that religious scholars had developed. These tenets also constituted a challenge to the institutionalised system of religious leadership at the time. Abun-Nasr notes that 'the development of Sufi beliefs since this time paralleled the growth of the Sufi *shaykhs*' influence as spiritual guides at the expense of the holders of religious offices in the caliph's system of government' (Abun-Nasr 2007, p. 7).

In China, as well as introducing a more esoteric practice of Islam, Sufism also introduced new forms social organisation. Gladney has explained that the leaders of Sufi shrines throughout their order owed their allegiance to their *ahong*, the founder of the order. This in turn required them to stay in particular communities for extended periods of time, 'unlike the Gedimu *ahong* who were generally itinerant, not well connected to the community, and less imbued with appointed authority' (Gladney 1996, p. 41). In other words, the arrival of Sufi orders provided a 'means of mobilisation, a network of solidarity, that had never been present among Chinese Muslims before' (Lipman 1997, p. 64). However, Sufis also debated with non-Sufis over Islamic practice, calling for a more 'immediate experience of Islam through the rituals of remembrance and meditation, and the efficacy of the Saint, instead of the daunting memorisation and recitation of Koranic texts' (Gladney 1999, p. 114). Fundamentally, their focus was less textual and more 'experiential', emphasising the power of the saints and Allah to perform miracles and acts of healing (Gladney 1999, p. 114).

Non-Sufis, on the other hand, accused Sufis of heterodoxy and conspiracy (Lipman 1996, pp. 104–105). Ma Dexin, a prominent Hui Muslim scholar (1794–1874), criticised the branches of Sufi orders in China, whom were deeply influenced by Shi'ism, as heretical sects (Wang 2014, p. 74). His criticisms were that they should not worship Ali, but rather Allah only; that they should follow the Hanafi Islamic school of jurisprudence; that they (the shaykhs) should not 'declare themselves sacred'; and that they should not glorify or emphasise miracles (Wang 2014, pp. 74–76). Conflicts also occurred between Sufi factions themselves, with Khafiyya Sufis characterising Jahriyya practices as 'superstitious, heterodox, and sometimes—as in the case of rhythmic motion during vocal *dhikr* recitation—downright immoral' (Lipman 1997, p. 90).

In relation to this question of unity and disunity, and in light of the significant ties between Guo Gongbei in China (where the majority of Muslims identify as Sunni) and religious schools in Iran (where the majority identify as Shi'a), it is worth noting here the question of identification by the gongbei as Sunni or Shi'a.[9] Iran is an Islamic republic with a Shi'a majority population. It has an uneasy relationship with its Sunni minority. In China, apart from a small number of Shi'ites amongst the Tajik of Xinjiang and amongst some Uyghur in the Khotan region, the majority of the Muslim population identify as Sunni. However, the continuing influence of aspects of Shi'a culture on Islamic practice in China has been noted by some scholars—most easily evidenced in the ongoing popularity of personal names associated with the family and followers of Ali (Zang 2016, pp. 48–49). Several scholars have also highlighted the profound impact of Persian Shi'ism on the Sufi orders in China specifically (Israeli 2002, pp. 147–167), (Wang 2014, p. 78). Jianping Wang explains this connection as follows:

---

[9] Nearly every Sufi order throughout the world, whether identifying as Sunni or Shi'a, traces its lineage to the Prophet Muhammad through Ali ibn Abi Talib (599–661 CE), the cousin and son-in-law of the Prophet.

Because Islam came to China through Persia along traditional travel routes (such as the Silk Road and the Spice Route), Persian Islam was bound to have a strong impact on Islam in China. The coming of the Sufi orders into China certainly bore the features of Iranian Shi'ism, not surprising given that the closest region connecting China to the Islamic world from the sixteenth to seventeenth centuries—Central Asia—was both Persianized and influenced by Sufi mysticism. (Wang 2014, p. 78)

He goes on to say that many Sufi orders or suborders in China trace their origins to Iran (Wang 2014, p. 78) and that notably the Qadiriyya in China are heavily influenced by Shi'ism (Wang 2014, p. 78). Though the Qadiriyya order in China identifies with the Hanafi school of Sunni Islam, in a locally produced text—*A Brief History of Ancestral Sages*—it is stated that 'the true path (of Qadiriyya) originates from the Shi'a' (Qi 1982, p. 22).[10] Interestingly, perhaps in the interests of maintaining harmonious relations with the Sunni-majority Muslim community in China, the leader in Guo Gongbei (Ma Yufang) downplayed the schism between Sunni and Shi'a. Specifically, he did not see this schism as problematic in terms of sending his students to Iran to study, seeing it not as a religious divergence, but a political one: 'Shi'ite and Sunni are political factions but not religious factions. Islam was divided into different sects with the aim of internal differentiation; they appeared as political factions after the Prophet (Muhammad) died. In Iran, although Shi'a is the mainstream, it does not affect our children learning over there, because we believe that Islam was not sectarian, we believe that it all comes from the same master, the same letters, as set down in the Qur'an'. Today, some scholars and students within the Chinese Muslim community have said that there are 'too many *paibie*' (Islamic factions) and that this is leading to disunity. Some spoke of a returning to a time before the existence of factions and drawing on Sufism to re-establish a sense of unity within the Islamic community in China. This is an interesting observation given that in the past, Sufi shaykhs were sometimes criticised for weakening the unity of the Chinese Muslim community due to their tendency to generate factionalism (Wang 2014, p. 76).

[10] In Shi'ism, Ali is seen as an intermediary between man and God and necessary for salvation. He had exclusive, divine right to the Caliphate. Moreover, Ali and the *imams* who 'descend from him are beings of superhuman virtue possessing miraculous gifts and absolute spiritual and temporal authority' (Glassé 1989, p. 34).

Relatedly, a central impetus in the generation of new factions within the Islamic world has been the continual 'contestation over orthodox discourse' (Gladney 1999, p. 116). This, in turn, has continued to pose a challenge to the maintenance of effective leadership. Which philosophical and practical orientation is deemed orthodox and which is not? How can conflicts between different factions be managed? This is another challenge to be discussed. As elsewhere in the world, in China the variety of factions (*paibie*) that exist within Hui Islam have been understood as a product of a history of reforms and Islamic movements that have occurred as a result of both interaction with and isolation from the Islamic world outside of China. Each new movement that came to China sought to portray itself as more loyal than others 'to the original ideals, the spirit as well as the texts, of Islam' (Gladney 1999, p. 116). Gladney illustrates this contestation over orthodoxy in reference to the labelling of each successive group as 'New Teachings' (*xinjiao*) and 'Old Teachings' (*laojiao*), terms which in themselves have had shifting meanings over time[11]:

> It was often the case that those who regarded themselves as maintaining the established traditional beliefs of Islam in China portrayed the reformers, who were their critics, as 'new' and thus, suspect, while they presented themselves as 'old', or more true to their traditions. The reformers, on the other hand, generally thought of themselves as the more orthodox, based on a more informed, sometimes esoteric, interpretation of Islam due to more recent contact with movements in the Muslim heartlands (Gladney 1999, p. 116).

Lipman identified that the tensions that were established during the Qing Empire, between a revivalist and militant Islam (such as that advocated by the Jahriyya order), and at the other extreme a syncretic and adaptive Islam (represented by the use of the adaptive and syncretic Han Kitab texts that blended Islam and Confucianism), 'continue to enliven Sino-Muslim life to the present day' (Lipman 1997, p. 92). Today, while there is a rhetoric of tolerance amongst Chinese Muslims communities, these contradictions continue to exist at a deeper level and form part of a later discussion.

Another challenge to be explored is the importance of sustaining a level of moral 'purity' so as to sustain religious authority and integrity. In the

[11] Amongst all of my informants, *xinjiao* referred to the Yihewani and Salafiyya movements, while *laojiao* referred to the Sufi orders or Gedimu.

Chinese context, this refers specifically to the notions of *suzhi* (personal quality) and *qingzhen* (literally 'pure' and 'true', or purely Islamic codes of conduct). The sociologist of Islam, W. Montgomery Watt, argued that there is a feeling amongst Muslims (across the world) that they are 'in danger of losing their Islamic identity because of its erosion by Western intellectual attitudes [...] Modern Islamic fundamentalism [Wahhabism] is a collective response to this intellectual and emotional crisis because of its promise that a return to the 'true Islam' of the earliest period will solve all of the social problems that face Muslims and their societies' (Hassan 2001, p. 133). From the perspective of a person who identifies as Chinese and Muslim, the threat of the West could be equated to the perceived threats from non-Muslim populations in China in lowering their *suzhi* (personal quality) through encouraging, for example, the fulfilment of sexual desire and materialistic wealth and thus challenging their ability to uphold *qingzhen* or Islamic values.

At the level of spoken discourse, local characterisations of the minority and majority 'other' went both ways and were prevalent within the wider Chinese Muslim community that were the focus of this study. Value judgements that related to education levels (*wenhua*) and *suzhi* came up frequently in discussions. During a taxi ride in Lanzhou city in February of 2012, I asked the driver to take me to a Sufi tomb complex known as Lingmingtang. He didn't recognise the name of the site itself, but he knew the Muslim area where it was located (Qilihe). He commented that Qilihe was a very poor area and asked me why I was going there. After explaining that I was a student studying local Islamic culture, he began to share some of his opinions on the subject with me. 'You know', he began, 'They (the Hui Muslims) have no "education/culture" (*tamen meiyou wenhua*)'. I replied asking why he thought so. 'Well, their education levels are very low, they marry very young, have many children. They also receive many privileges and dispensations from the government.' He identified himself as being a Han Chinese. This perception by 'Han', that 'Hui' were somehow without 'culture' or 'education', was a view that did not go unnoticed by the leader of the Qadiriyya Sufi shrine, Ma Yufang; 'Muslims are viewed as being of low "quality" (*suzhi di*)', he explained, 'but we are not'. Indeed, for many Hui and Han converts alike, Islam was seen as the way towards cultivation and education.

One afternoon I was sitting in the square outside the Qadiriyya Sufi temple, talking to an 18-year-old Hui student from Yunnan, Ding Yong, and his younger classmate, who were between classes. During this conversation, an older man came to sit down near us. He introduced himself as Wang Wen. He was a taxi driver and identified himself as a Hui. He spoke of himself as being of low cultural quality (*suzhi hen di*), but was enthusiastic in telling me what he knew about Islam. In particular, he stressed the idea of cleanliness, 'You must keep yourself clean in Islam (*zishen qingjie*)'. While he talked, he puffed away on a cigarette. At one point, I asked them all, 'Is it okay for Huizu (Muslim minority) to smoke?' Wang Wen said yes, but Ding Yong criticised him stating that 'Islam doesn't condone drinking and smoking'. Wang Wen retorted, 'In Islam (in the Qur'an) there are no rules against smoking'. Ding Yong replied, 'Ah, but there is a hadith that says smoking is bad for your health'. He explained how he himself used to smoke as a younger boy, before he started studying Islam properly—a decision he now regrets. 'If you understood Islam properly', he said to Wang Wen, 'you wouldn't smoke'. Wang Wen stared quietly at the ground, and after a moment, the topic of conversation shifted. After about an hour, another man, Mai Xiao Ming, sat down with us. He was a Hui, in his 50s, and ran a travel booking business in Linxia. He also criticised the taxi driver for smoking. He then spoke of how the *suzhi* of the Muslim (Huizu) in the Northwest (Xibei) region was not as high as those in the South of China (Nanfang). Later in the conversation I indicated that I needed to go and meet a Han friend. Wang Wen quickly exclaimed, 'Ah, Hanzu (Han people) are no good! Don't hang out with them!' Mai Xiao Ming replied calmly, 'Nono, they are fine. Every *minzu* (ethnic group) is fine. Isn't that right? It makes no difference'. When I asked him what the biggest difference was between Han and Hui, he replied, 'belief (*xinyang*)'. The young student chimed in and said 'Han eat pork, the Hui don't eat pork. They are not *qingzhen* (pure and true)'.

Maris Gillette has written of the labelling of the Hui as being of 'low *suzhi*' (low quality), by the local government in Xian. She found that officials 'institutionalised the Hui race's inferiority by ensuring that Hui "nationality" practices continued, even while the government castigated them as "feudal", "backward" and "superstitious". She connects this labelling of the Hui back to the projects undertaken between 1950 and 1956 by the Chinese Communist Party (CCP) in which Chinese anthropologists, historians, and sociologists gathered information on the Chinese people so that ethnic groups (*shaoshu minzu*) could be classified, in ascending order of modernisation, according to Marx's evolutionary model as either primitive, slave, feudal, bourgeois-capitalist, socialist, or communist societies.

This process of classification often employed the terms *wenhua* and *suzhi*. These two terms were, and are still, central to the discourse of evolutionary development advanced by the CCP. The character *wen* (文) can be translated as 'writing' or 'language'. As an adjective it can mean 'refined' or 'civil'. The character *hua* (化) means to 'change' or 'dissolve'. Brought together, *wenhua* refers to 'education' or 'civilisation'. The term has also been translated as 'culture', referring both to 'ways of life' and the transformation, the refinement of life. The cultural geographer Tim Oakes argued that when '*fazhan*' (meaning 'development') was added to *wenhua* in socio-political discourse, the result was a

'modernised manifestation of the centuries-old "civilising project" of imperial China. As a post-Mao modernisation ideology, *wenhua fazhan* implies the attainment of literacy (in standard Chinese), an education in science and technology, an understanding of modern commerce, expertise in enterprise management, and even an entrepreneurial spirit. But it also implies the enlisting of selected and invented cultural traditions to be paraded both as markers of progress and as local delegates to the national assembly of symbolic cultural diversity' (Oakes 1998, p. 136) (Fig. 1.2).

The two characters in the word *suzhi* are *su* (素) and *zhi* (质). In his etymological investigation of the word, the anthropologist Andrew Kipnis explains:

Zhi means "nature, character or matter," while su has many meanings, including unadorned, plain, white and essence. Before the late 1970s, *suzhi* most often meant the "unadorned nature or character of something" [...] As modern nature/nurture dichotomies influenced Chinese thought during the 20th century, *suzhi* became more closely associated with inborn characteristics (Kipnis 2006, pp. 296–297).

During the economic reforms that began in 1976, the term became conjoined with the idea of population, and since then *suzhi* has taken on a new 'discursive power' (Anagnost 2004, p. 190). *Suzhi* now marks 'hierarchical and moral distinction between the high and the low' (Kipnis 2006, p. 297) and has become an important concept in the endeavour to (re)produce 'citizens of the highest mental and physical quality' (Gillette

Fig. 1.2 The text reads: *Fazhan minban jiaoyu, tigao minzu suzhi* meaning "Develop private education, improve the quality of the nation"

2000, p. 46). In addition, as Kipnis (2006) notes, *suzhi* discourse, though state-led, taps into long-standing traditions of self-cultivation.

The State Commission for Nationality Affairs that led the classification project of minorities in the 1950s (described earlier) relied on Stalin's four criteria for defining a nationality. That is to say, the population in question had to possess a common language, territory, economic life, and psychology. But, as Gladney noted, these criteria were problematic as the Hui do not share a common language, do not live in a common locality, do not share a common economic life, and, finally, do not share a 'common psychological makeup or culture, as there are Hui who maintain traditional Islamic customs, Hui who are atheist Communist Party members, and many young urban Hui who have ceased to follow any Islamic customs traditionally associated with being Hui' (Gladney 1996, p. 70). As Professor S. at Lanzhou University informed me, 'the label "Hui" was just one

Fig. 1.3 The characters 'qingzhen' adorn an Islamic restaurant in downtown Linxia. The crescent moon also depicted has come to be associated with Islam, but has no direct theological connection. It was a symbol for the Ottoman/Turkish Empire and came to be adopted in the 1950s and 1960s by some Muslim nations as an emblem for Islam

of convenience for the government—of course we are not all the same'. In the absence of these commonalities, I follow Gladney in his assertion that *qingzhen* is 'the "sacred symbol" marking "Hui", or at least, Muslim identity in China' (Gladney 1996, p. 35) (Fig. 1.3).

The character *qing* (清) can be most simply translated as purity and the character *zhen* (真) as truth.[12] Gladney posits that purity (*qing*) reflected a concern with ritual cleanliness and moral conduct, 'a way to be morally

---

[12] Lipman has translated *zhen* as both 'True' and 'Real' (Lipman 2016, p. xvii). In a translation of Wang Daiyu's *Zhengjiao zhenquan* published in 2017, Sachiko Murata consistently translates *zhen* as 'Real' rather than 'True', translating the work as 'The Real Commentary on the True Teaching' (Murata 2017, p. 1).

legitimate in a Confucian society preoccupied with moral propriety and order' (Gladney 1996, p. 15); and 'truth' (*zhen*) reflected a concern with belief in the 'True Lord' (*Zhenzhu*) which allowed the Hui to distinguish themselves as monotheists in a land where polytheistic belief and practice predominated. In his study of *qingzhen*, he observed: 'there is clearly a subtle irony here, as in China the Han have typically looked down on the Hui as dirty, larcenous, and immoral, while the Hui, by their very choice of translation, portray their ethnoreligious identity as more 'pure and true' than the Han' (Gladney 1996, p. 15). *Qingzhen* is sometimes translated directly into the Arabic word *halal*. *Halal* literally means 'released' (from prohibition), and refers to that which is lawful, particularly food and meat from animals which have been ritually slaughtered. However, the wider meaning of *qingzhen* goes beyond this term, for it involves much more than food that has been ritually prepared. *Qingzhen* is a concept that 'governs all one's life' (Gladney 1996, p. 35).

Professor L., a Hui scholar working at a Research Institute for Minorities in Lanzhou, told me that *suzhi* is derived from one of the important works in the Confucian canon, the Great Learning (*Daxue*). In this work, Confucius describes the cultivation of virtue (*de*) at the level of person (being sincere in thoughts, seeking knowledge, rectifying the heart) which in turn cultivated the family, which then allowed the State to rightly govern, and in turn the whole kingdom to be tranquil and content. 'Virtue' (*de*), is a term that from ancient times was employed to mean goodness, strength of character, and worthy conduct. The Chinese philosopher Chen Chun explained that virtue, in contrast to the Way of heaven and earth, 'is concerned with human effort. In general, the Way is what is common, while virtue is what is achieved in the self, thus becoming one's possession' (Chen 1986, pp. 114–115).

Professor L. then pointed out a connection between *suzhi* and *qingzhen*, referencing in his explanation the work of the Chinese Muslim scholar Wang Daiyu.[13]

---

[13] In the process of legitimating and familiarising Islam to Muslims and non-Muslims in the Chinese world during the Qing Dynasty, several Chinese Muslim scholars found deep resonance with this Confucian discourse of self-cultivation. These texts became known as the Han Kitab. Notable scholars included Wang Daiyu (mid-seventeenth century), Ma Zhu (late seventeenth century), Liu Zhi (early eighteenth century), Yuan Guozuo (late eighteenth century), and Ma Dexin (mid-nineteenth century) (Lipman 2016, p. 5). Liu Zhi, in his introduction to *The Nature and Principle of Islam* first published in 1704, said 'I suddenly

Firstly, *qingzhen* refers specifically to Muslims. Muslims believe that *suzhi* refers to external factors, *qingzhen* is the internal factor. In other words, *qingzhen* is belief (*xinyang*), *suzhi* is self-cultivation (*gongxiu*), as the Muslim scholar Wang Daiyu stressed, "first return to the body, then return to the heart (*shen hui, xin hui*)." By maintaining a Reverence for God, following the moral and virtuous example of the Holy Prophet Muhammad, and cultivating morality in the profession of *qingzhenyan* (Shahāda) and also in practical action, he or she is a quality person/a 'virtuous' person (*suzhi ren*). To be a *suzhi ren* in the Muslim context was explained by the Hui scholar Ma Zhu in the following way: "the fundamental virtue is to take care of one's blood kin; the extended virtue is to take care of one's religious fellows; the public virtue is to be kind to those outside of this religion; the universal virtue is to be kind to all birds and animals, insects and vegetation."

The discourse of *suzhi* that taps into traditions and thought of Confucian social philosophy in China takes on a different meaning in the Chinese Islamic discourse. In the Hui context, a virtuous person displays an embodiment of the five tenets of Islam: the profession of faith, prayer, charity, fasting, and pilgrimage. These Islamic rituals outwardly indicate a commitment to the Islamic faith. *Qingzhen* Muslim (a 'Pure and True' Muslim) was a term I heard many times in referencing someone who was deemed to be virtuous in the Islamic context. A Hui student, studying anthropology at Lanzhou University, explained it to me that 'the original meaning of *qingzhen* is to do with Islamic belief: you must cultivate a pure character (*chunjie xing*), a genuine character (*zhenshi xing*), a lawful character (*hefa xing*), according to religious morals and standards. So we have the concept of *qingzhen* language, *qingzhen* mosques, *qingzhen* food. But *qingzhen*, first and foremost, means the faith of Islam. *Qingzhen*

came to understand that the Islamic classics have by and large the same purport as Confucius and Mencius' (Murata et al. 2009, p. 73). The broad theme of self-cultivation that was so central to Confucianism found direct parallels in the Islamic tradition. The purpose of the syncretic works of Wang Daiyu (1573–*ca.* 1619) and Liu Zhi (born *ca.* 1617; date of death unknown) was both to make Islam known to non-Muslims in the Chinese context and to write for their 'co-religionists, who did not have sufficient acquaintance with the Islamic languages to master Islamic thinking' (Murata and Chittick 2000, p. 4). In these works, Islam is depicted in a completely non-Islamic idiom—in Chinese. As Murata has noted, 'Anyone who reads these texts with a knowledge of the Chinese ambiance of the seventeenth and eighteenth centuries can see that they are part of the ongoing discussion and debate among Chinese intellectuals concerning the nature of the quest for human perfection' (Murata and Chittick 2000, p. 6).

foods—they must be *halal*. You cannot smoke, you cannot drink, you must act in accordance with Islamic teachings and rules, if you want to be what we would call a *qingzhen* Muslim'. These concerns over 'quality' and 'integrity' and the importance of the *'qingzhen'* 'habitus' for all Muslims within China are challenges that I shall discuss in specific relation to perceptions around the Sufi *gongbei* and their practitioners. I use Bourdieu's notion of habitus here, or deep history, in order to emphasise that the ways in which the 'Hui' have responded to countering 'Han' ethnocentrisms are deeply embodied and partly unconscious.

The final challenge to be discussed is the stability of religious institutions within rapidly growing economies. Islam, as a world religion, is the target of much negativity, misrepresentation, and fear in today's global media landscape. Notions such as 'islamophobia', 'extremism', 'radicalisation', and 'terrorism' saturate our world. The fervent and oft-times violent religiosity of a minority of Muslims has proven very effective in causing nation-states around the world to re-think their treatment of Islamic movements within their borders. In China, the Chinese Communist Party maintains an atheist ideology: it continues to enforce atheist propaganda through the education system, mass media, and numerous party and state organs and carries out frequent crackdowns on religious groups (Yang 2012, p. 158). Most recently, Jianping Wang has analysed China's policy towards Islam in particular (Wang 2016, p. 577). He makes a crucial observation that the close supervision of Muslim communities by the government is 'not only motivated by international pressures to guard human rights and protect religious freedom, but also prompted by the political and economic need for strong ties with the Islamic world and a secure energy supply from the Middle East' (Wang 2016, p. 577).

Relatedly, Wang argues that the government's international strategy might lead to the growth of political Islam in China, increasing the 'influence of precisely those forms of Islam that the PRC might find most difficult to control. Government policy that is intended to prevent the rise of "extremist" and separatist movements might have the paradoxical effect of enabling such movements' (Wang 2016, p. 578). In November 2016, RT News reported that Wang Zuoan, head of the State Administration for Religious Affairs, told religious leaders at the National Congress of the Chinese Islamic Association that 'extremism' is now 'moving to the inland provinces'. He urged Muslim communities to learn 'to use the law to safeguard legal interests, instead of trying to solve problems through illegal actions such as creating disturbances' (RT 2016). In March 2017, multiple media outlets reported that Chinese authorities have imposed a supposed ban on 'abnormal' facial hair and veils in public places in Xinjiang Province—home to the Muslim Uyghur population. This is part of an apparent effort, according to the source, to 'curb extremism and radicalization in the area bordering Kyrgyzstan, Tajikistan and Afghanistan' (RT 2017).

This fear of extremism spreading to inland provinces such as Gansu, where Guo Gongbei is located, has resulted in a renewed wish to somehow stabilise the system of succession within these Sufi sites—in other words, to increase the ability for government bodies to manage them. Specifically, in relation to the gongbei, a 'scholar-official' Ma Hucheng has described a desire to transform the method of religious succession within the Sufi gongbei sites so that it is no longer wholly 'charismatic' and thus 'unstable' (Ma 2011).[14] In his report (published in 2011 by the Institute for Global Engagement), he puts forward a suggestion that religious succession should no longer be performed on the basis of the leader's (what he terms the 'hierarch') 'divine permission', but rather on the basis of 'democratic' election involving not only those within the *menhuan* but also the governing bodies outside of it.

The assumption here seems to be that more formally bureaucratic systems are easier to control and thus more stable, whereas charismatic ('mystical', 'religious') systems are ineffable and inherently unstable. This is very much in line with the thinking of Max Weber. Weber described charismatic authority as being strongly opposed to rational and bureaucratic authority. In his analysis, in contrast to 'bureaucratic organisation, charisma knows no formal and regulated appointment or dismissal, no career, advancement or salary, no supervisory or appeals body, no local or purely technical jurisdiction, and no permanent institutions in the manner of bureaucratic agencies' (Weber and Runciman 1978, p. 1112). Of key relevance here is Weber's observation that because of this, charisma 'cannot remain stable, but becomes either traditionalised or rationalised, or a combination of both' (Weber and Runciman 1978, p. 244). This supposed 'rationalisation of charisma' is directly tied to a broader question about the

---

[14] Ma Hucheng was the former Vice Minister of United Front Work Department of the Gansu Provincial Committee of the Chinese Communist Party (Huang 2016, p. 19).

role of religion within human societies and its ability to oft-times create both stability and instability simultaneously.

CHARISMA AND SUFISM: AN EMBODIED APPROACH

The central theme of this book relies on the use of a ubiquitous term—'charisma'. It is important therefore that its usage is clear. Here, before considering the specifics of charisma in the Sufi context, I want to outline some key orientations towards the term in the social sciences and where this study sits in relation to them. In *Economy and Society* (1913), Weber differentiated three types of authority: bureaucratic, as seen in today's society; traditional, as in feudal and primitive cultures; and something he called charismatic authority:

> The term 'charisma' will be applied to a certain quality of individual personality by virtue of which he is considered extraordinary and treated as endowed with supernatural, superhuman, or at least specifically exceptional powers or qualities. These are not accessible to the ordinary person, but are regarded as of divine origin or as exemplary (Weber and Runciman 1978, p. 241).

While Weber wrote of many different types of charisma, all exhibiting varying degrees of 'rationalisation' (e.g. pseudo-charisma, lineage-charisma, charisma of office, manufactured charisma), it is pure charisma that is most interesting here. In many passages, Weber's concept of pure charisma is very similar to Victor Turner's concept of anti-structure (Turner 2011). For instance, he states that 'in a revolutionary and sovereign manner, charismatic domination transforms all values and breaks all traditional and rational norms' (Weber and Runciman 1978, p. 1113). He also says: 'Since it is "extra-ordinary", charismatic authority is sharply opposed to rational and particularly bureaucratic authority, and to traditional authority [...] It recognises no appropriation of positions of power by virtue of the possession of property, either on the part of a chief or of socially privileged groups' (Weber and Runciman 1978, p. 244).

Studies of charisma since Weber have been motivated by one of two questions—what is the source of charisma? Or, following Weber in keeping an agnostic respect for the mystery of the source, asking instead—what is the locus of charisma? Rather than stressing the antithesis between charisma and bureaucratic or patrimonial domination, Edward Shils argued that institutionalised charisma 'permeates' all walks of life. He maintained that the 'source of charisma was the "contact through inspiration, embodiment or perception, with the vital force which underlies man's existence", a force located at the centre of society' (as cited in Werbner and Basu 1998, p. 15). Shmuel Eisenstadt took this further—seeing it as a universal human predisposition, what he called the 'charismatic dimension of human life'. Charisma was the liminal, in-between transcendent moment and was the source of all religions and civilisations (Eisenstadt 2003, pp. 47–48). Here, rather than charisma being focused on a leader, it was a 'generalised propensity, out of which charismatic movements and groups can emerge' (Feuchtwang and Wang 2008, p. 92).

Stephan Feuchtwang developed ideas from Weber, Shils, and Eisenstadt to arrive at another definition of charisma that focused on the locus rather than the source. For him, Eisenstadt's idea of charisma 'becomes indistinguishable from transcendence and its experience. To be sure, charisma must be about the possibility of transcendence and hope, the questioning of the norms of a current reality. But to be sociologically meaningful this possibility must be embodied in a leader and a following' (Feuchtwang and Wang 2008, p. 92). Feuchtwang then describes charisma as 'a sociological dynamic of embodiment'. He elaborates on this dynamic as follows:

> The liminal sense of community among charismatic followers is established by companionship and joint dependence on a vision and a visionary leader. This fellowship contains a desire to go beyond the boundaries of normal social life and reality. But the journey beyond these boundaries itself requires rules, sanctions and the staff to enforce them. It requires institutionalisation to approximate, if never to achieve, the impossibility of a universal community of trustfulness. (Feuchtwang and Wang 2008, p. 92)

There are several threads I want to draw out here. In this study, I do not use the term charisma in the broad universal sense of Eisenstadt—as the 'source' of all religions and civilisations. In the context of Sufism, like Weber, I remain agnostic as to the divine source of charisma. Rather, I seek to understand the locus of charisma—that is, its location and expression in the social and observable realm.[15]

---

[15] This is not to imply that what is unseen is necessarily untrue. Rather, I follow Lambek, who argues for a shift in the study of religion from Platonic binaries to the Aristotelian focus on the idea of phronesis (moral practice or judgement). Rather than the anthropological

As such, I find Feuchtwang's description of charisma as a 'sociological dynamic of embodiment' particularly helpful. In this study, I use the term charisma in reference to a *culturally specific spiritual power* that is located, embodied, and generated in an individual. Accordingly, I argue that there are very specific disciplines that are generative of charisma in this context which are distinctive from more general practices of submission to religious ritual. For example, disciples participate in a very specific set of practices (detailed in *Chapter Three*) with the aim of generating this particular power. This is different from the daily obligatory prayers carried out by adherents, who do so with no intention or expectation of generating this charisma. This intention is the key difference between the charismatic religious practices of the elites and the everyday religious practices of non-elites.

Secondly, rather than charisma being 'foreign to all rules' (Weber 1968, p. 244), charisma is always dependent on some sense of routine and institutionalisation. This is a crucial idea in my explication of charisma in this context. In the Sufi examples, one continues to find both 'mental and physical exercises, sometimes aided by medicines and always by the hard practice of learning scriptures or performance techniques. They are the groundwork for both creativity and authoritative innovation' (Feuchtwang and Wang 2001, p. 17). Furthermore, routines also include the disciplines that produce mystical or visionary experiences. The many and varied ascetic practices of shamans, diviners, monks, and prophets 'produce trance or meditation states', and they produce 'such states out of standard repertoires of symbols and bodily disciplines' (Feuchtwang 2010, p. 109).

Finally, while I emphasise that charisma is primarily located, embodied, and generated in an individual, I also recognise the ways in which it is then *strengthened, maintained, and reinforced* through relationships with others

study of religion being reconstituted as 'either the study of faulty beliefs about supernatural realms or an idealised mimetic identification with (and appropriation of) the knowledge and practices of our subjects', Lambek argues that, under-scored by Aristotelian notions of morality and practice, it should be 'an investigation of the historically situated, socially constituted imagination and realisation of meaningful ends, practical means, authoritative voice, dignified and virtuous agency, and reasoned as well as passionate submission' (Lambek 2000, p. 318). Following Aristotle provides the opportunity to take an alternative route, 'one which enables us to see the particular conjunction of contemplative thought, reasoned action (*praxis*), and creative production (*poiesis*) characteristic of any given social setting' (Lambek 2000, p. 309).

and the narratives shared amongst them. The maintenance of charismatic integrity relies upon a strong community of 'charismatic followers' who share a 'joint dependence on a vision and a visionary leader'. This in turn relies upon a clear differentiation between what is reverence for charismatic authority and what is more general religious reverence. In this study, reverence to a *charismatic* authority means reverence to an authority symbol or figure who is seen to possess a particular 'charismatic' power. In contrast, general religious reverence is that expressed towards figures who are respected as leaders or teachers but are not known to possess this particular 'charismatic' power (such as an *imam* or Arabic language teacher). The formation of followings as a 'community' around a charismatic authority and its transmission is a process explored most explicitly in *Chapters Four* and *Five* which discuss, respectively, emulation of the exemplary charismatic leader amongst adherents and students and social distance and proximity between charismatic leaders and adherents.

Sufi orders legitimise the authority of the master on the basis of a spiritual lineage linking back to Muhammad himself. Religious adherents seek to benefit from the Master's teaching, advice, and example as well as to receive his blessing or divine grace (*baraka* or *fayd*), the product of his spiritual power.[16] The typical rite of initiation is modelled on the handclasp known as *bay'at al-riḍwān* ('the oath-taking of God's good pleasure') that the Prophet took from his Companions at Hudaybiyyah (referred to in the Qur'an, sections 48:10 and 48:18). The rite is understood to transmit an invisible spiritual force of blessing (Ar. *baraka*) that opens up the disciple's soul to transformation. The primary meaning of *baraka* here is grace—in the sense of a blessing or a spiritual influence that God sends down. *Baraka* may be found in persons, places, and things. Certain actions and circumstances may also be a vehicle for blessing, as other actions and circumstances can dispel grace. Many religious greetings and expressions include the idea of *baraka*, such as *Baraka 'Llahu fik* (May God bless you), the most common and traditional way of saying thanks (Glassé 1989, p. 64). According to Jamil Abun-Nasr, 'divine grace is the central element of the Sufis' system of beliefs. In the Qur'an, God is referred to as the Wali (the Guardian), and walaya is used in the sense of his guardianship of the

---

[16] Buehler more frequently uses the term *fayd* to reference this spiritual force (Buehler 1998, p. 117). However in the local context of this study, *baraka* or *baileketi* in pinyin was the word used and thus why I use it throughout.

believers' (Abun-Nasr 2007, p. 1). Sufis predicated *baraka* not on descent from the Prophet, 'but on the belief in divine grace as a manifestation of walaya (their role as spiritual guardians or spiritual authorities) in the world. Accordingly, Sufi *shaykhs* who claimed descent from the Prophet, were held to be repositories of a special *baraka* inherent in their walaya' (Abun-Nasr 2007, p. 76). In this context, *baraka* (a divine blessing) confers charisma to a person. One who is seen to possess *baraka* is seen to possess, in the Weberian sense, an 'uncanny personal power'.

Anthropologists who have studied this *baraka* have generally equated it with 'charisma' in the sense of Weber and have tended to argue that the meaning of charisma in Sufism was to be found solely in the structure of social relations. Consequently, *baraka*, as a particular spiritual power, was not real. For Clifford Geertz, *baraka* was a doctrine:

> Literally, *'baraka'* means blessing, in the sense of divine favour. But spreading out from that nuclear meaning [...], it encloses a whole range of linked ideas, material prosperity, physical well-being, bodily satisfaction, completion, luck, plenitude, and, the aspect most stressed by western writers anxious to force it into a pigeonhole with mana, magical power. In broadest terms, *baraka* is not [...] a paraphysical force, a kind of spiritual electricity [...] it too is a 'doctrine'. (Geertz 1968, p. 44)

For Akbar Ahmed, in discussing Sufi *shaykhs* of Pakistan's Swat valley, charisma remained 'largely a function of success; its qualities are both inherent in the person and in the social situation. The charismatic leader is convinced of his "mission" or "destiny" but he must convince those around him of his capacity for leadership' (Ahmed 2011, p. 14). As he says, 'Charisma creates following and following creates charisma' (Ahmed 2011, p. 115). But, as Kenneth Lizzio notes, he doesn't explain how one initially acquires this charisma (Lizzio 2007, p. 5). He relies solely on an economic interpretation, asserting the role of money in the formation of charisma: 'Funds and religious adherents go hand in hand with a charismatic leader and are a vital index to his fortunes. There is a circular and cumulative causation between funds, religious adherents, and charisma. The relationship with his religious adherents was based on the same principles of redistributive economies that the Akhund (of Swat) had established' (Ahmed 2011, p. 113).

In studies of Muslim and Christian saints, Donal Cruise O'Brien argued that it was not possible to find examples of Weber's pure type of charisma. Instead, he found what he called NQC or 'Not Quite Charisma' (Cruise O'Brien 1988, p. 6). There were 'procedures of sanctification, of charisma as habit', but more often than not these procedures would erupt into 'rebellious social movements and new lines of succession' (Feuchtwang and Wang 2001, p. 17). As a result, O'Brien posited that religious adherents recognised miraculous powers in a *shaykh* as a result of social crisis (Cruise O'Brien 1988, pp. 1–2). In this instance, the source of charisma lay primarily in the capacity or at least the reputation for performing miracles.

In *Pilgrims of Love: The Anthropology of a Global Sufi Cult*, Pnina Werbner offers a richly detailed description of a 'post-colonial' Naqshbandi Sufi order that is now expanding into the secular space of Britain (Werbner 2003). For her,

> no single factor produces the effect of charisma of a living Sufi saint. It is conditional upon a receptive cultural environment and conventional expectations, and supported by bodily practices, narratives of unique individuality and, in the case of Sufi saints, a theory of transcendental connection to a distant God. Above all charisma is embodied in ritual performance, sanctioned by a newly generated sacred geography, and underpinned by voluntary mobilisation on a vast, transregional and transnational scale (Werbner 2003, p. 282).

Interestingly, despite her recognition that bodily practices are an essential part of the embodiment of Sufi theory (and thus the development of charisma), she says that rather than a 'secret theosophy' being arrived at through practice, in reality, 'in the context of global migration and print capitalism, this esoteric knowledge is widely known through published Sufi texts' (Werbner 2003, p. 287). While she was told that the way to knowledge in Sufism was through the heart, it is Sufi texts rather than revelation 'that may open up for ambitious disciples the realms of gnosis and the religious imagination' (Werbner 2003, p. 209). Nevertheless, what is significant here is Werbner's recognition of the importance of the body in the cultivation of spiritual power.[17]

[17] In her book 'Arguing Sainthood', Katherine Ewing offers another account of the Sufi saint in the context of Pakistan. Her focus however is rather different to that of Werbner. Drawing on the history of religious politics in the region, Arabic and Persian textual sources, and theories from psychoanalysis, she offers a sophisticated and complex exploration of how

The anthropologist Lizzio also recognised the importance of bodily practice. In a study of ritual and charisma amongst a Naqshbandi order in Pakistan, Lizzio posited that charisma is

a dynamic physical manifestation of the spiritually realised person or one in whom the process of awakening has begun. Charisma is intentionally projected and intentionally—and sometimes unintentionally—received. Charisma accounts for the existence of the orders and is the rationale for association with the *shaykh*. In conjunction with prescribed rituals such as *dhikr*, charisma is the catalyst for mystical experience and development (Lizzio 2007, p. 33).

He further adds that charisma can be transmitted over many generations and is not 'necessarily subject to rationalisation over time as Weber believed' (Lizzio 2007, p. 33). This emphasis on the physicality of charisma points to the centrality of the body as a form of knowing, calling to mind the phrase from Thomas Csordas that the 'locus of the sacred is the body, for the body is the existential ground of culture' (Csordas 1990, p. 39). In the context of Sufism, Paulo Pinto has identified a type of corporality or embodied subjectivity that he calls 'the mystical body'. The construction of the religious self amongst members of a Sufi community is achieved through the embodiment of principles of the Sufi tradition, and this is a form of corporality or bodily knowledge (what Bourdieu would call, the operation of bodily hexis). During the performance of *dhikr*, Pinto observes that 'there is a mobilisation of the bodies of participants in order to induce existential states that can be communicated and classified as mystical experiences' (Pinto 2010, p. 465). In the context of a Sufi shrine in India, Arthur Saniotis similarly argues, 'By drawing the Saint's blessedness into themselves through their various sensory perceptions, Sufis come to view their bodies as conduits of mystical power' (Saniotis 2008, p. 25). Furthermore, Pinto argues that these ritual recitations are used as a way of indexing the 'religious quality' of the participants and thus reinforce the 'hierarchical organisation' of the Sufi community. In this sense, the body is

competing ideologies are experienced at the individual level of the spiritual master. She argues that the subject of the master becomes the site of 'conflicting desires and multiple subjective modalities [...] oblivious to its own inconsistencies' (Ewing 1997, p. 35). It is a very nuanced work and in the context of this study serves as a reminder of the multiple, complex, and potentially contradictory factors involved in the generation of Sufi charisma.

'both the main focus of the disciplinary dimension of the Sufi ritual and a performative arena for the communication of mystical experiences and the affirmation and classification of Sufi subjectivities' (Pinto 2010, p. 465).

The notion of 'embodiment' however took some decades to develop within anthropology. Rene Descartes, writing in the seventeenth century, spoke of the body as a mere mechanical object, external to the life of his 'real' self; his 'mind'. For him, the mind, not the body, knows, perceives, and understands. However, as early as 1938, Marcel Mauss shifted from the Cartesian view by emphasising the study of 'techniques of the body', of 'habit', and of the 'self' (Carrithers et al. 1985, p. 3). Similarly, Maurice Merleau-Ponty argued that we come to know the world in embodied ways, and we have many forms of knowledge and understanding which are entirely bodily: that is, abilities such as 'I know how to type, or to drive' (Merleau-Ponty 1962, p. 146).

The real-world reality of 'having and being a body' is what underpins Pierre Bourdieu's concepts of habitus (an extension of the notion of habit from Mauss) and bodily hexis (an extension of the notion of embodiment from Merleau-Ponty). Islam, following Bourdieu, is understood 'not as a state of mind, still less as a kind of arbitrary adherence to a set of institutionalised dogmas and doctrines (beliefs) but rather a state of the body' (Bourdieu 1990, p. 68). The religious habitus for Bourdieu refers to the 'specifically religious dimension of an individual agent's habitus that manifests itself most apparently, though not exclusively, in the religious field' (as cited in Rey 2007, p. 92). Bourdieu offers two definitions of religious habitus: (1) a 'lasting, generalised and transposable disposition to act and think in conformity with the principles of a (quasi) systematic view of the world and human existence' and (2) 'the principle generator of all thoughts, perceptions and actions with the norms of a religious representation of the natural and supernatural worlds' (as cited in Rey 2007, pp. 92–93). This religious habitus is constructed through and manifested in the shapes of bodies, gestures, deportment, and everyday uses of the body. Some have argued that this habitus and bodily memory are fixed or deterministic. However, habitus is 'not the fate that some people read into it. Being the product of history, it is an open system of dispositions that is constantly subjected to experiences, and therefore constantly affected by them in a way that reinforces or modifies its structures. It's durable but not eternal' (Bourdieu and Wacquant 1992, p. 133). This is the process of embodiment, or the operation of bodily hexis, which Bourdieu describes as follows:

Political mythology realised, embodied, turned into a permanent disposition, a durable manner of standing, speaking, and thereby of feeling and thinking, [...] treating the body as a memory, they entrust to it in abbreviated and practiced i.e., mnemonic form, the fundamental principles of the arbitrary content of the culture. (Bourdieu 1990, pp. 93–94)

In relation to the generation of a religious habitus or bodily hexis in the context of Islamic practice, the Arab scholar Farid al-Zahi has attempted to 'reintegrate the many different "bodies" explicated in Western theory, seeing them not as different bodies, as the Western terminology suggests, but as different dimensions of what is, frustratingly, a singular body' (Kugle 2012, p. 16). Drawing from Merleau-Ponty, Foucault, Ricoeur, Eliade, and Lacan, Al-Zahi has stressed the need for a 'phenomenological model upon which we can reflect, as in a mirror, our own sense of being in a body' (Kugle 2012, pp. 16–17). Al-Zahi contends that there are four basic dimensions of bodily experience that are all integrated into a singular body, an idea which Scott Kugle, a religious studies scholar, develops further. While grounded in Bourdieu's idea of bodily hexis, this study will draw specifically from the work of al-Zahi and the religious studies scholar Scott Kugle in understanding the process of charismatic embodiment in this context.

REFERENCES

Abu-Manneh, B. 2000. The Wali Nejib Pasha and the Qadiri Order in Iraq. *Journal of the History of Sufism* 1–2: 115 [Zarcone, T. and Buehler, A., editors. Simurg Press].

Abun-Nasr, J.M. 2007. *Muslim Communities of Grace: The Sufi Brotherhoods in Islamic Religious Life*. New York: Columbia University Press.

Ahmed, A. 2011. *Millennium and Charisma Among Pathans: A Critical Essay in Social Anthropology*. London: Routledge.

Anagnost, A. 2004. The Corporeal Politics of Quality (Suzhi). *Public Culture* 16(2): 189–208.

Armijo-Hussein, J. 2006. Islamic Education in China. *Harvard Asia Quarterly* 10(1).

Bashir, S. 2013. *Sufi Bodies: Religion and Society in Medieval Islam*. New York: Columbia University Press.

Bourdieu, P. 1990. *The Logic of Practice*. Cambridge/Oxford: Polity Press/B. Blackwell.

Bourdieu, P., and L.J.D. Wacquant. 1992. *An Invitation to Reflexive Sociology*. Chicago: University of Chicago Press.

32   T. CONE

Bruinessen, M. v. 2000. The Qadiriyya and the Lineages of Qadiri Shaykhs Among the Kurds. *Journal of the History of Sufism* 1–2: 131 [Zarcone, T. and Buehler, A., editors. Simurg Press].

Buehler, A. 1998. *Sufi Heirs of the Prophet: The Indian Naqshbandiyya and the Rise of the Mediating Sufi Shaykh*. Columbia: University of South Carolina.

Buehler, A. 2000. The Indo-Pakistani Qadiriyya - An Overview. *Journal of the History of Sufism* 1–2: 339 [Zarcone, T. and Buehler, A., editors. Simurg Press].

Carrithers, M., S. Collins, and S. Lukes. 1985. *The Category of the Person: Anthropology, Philosophy, History*. Cambridge: Cambridge University Press.

Chen, C. 1986. *Neo-Confucian Terms Explained: The Pei-hsi Tzu-i*. New York: Columbia University Press.

Cruise O'Brien, D. 1988. *Charisma and Brotherhood in African Islam*. Oxford: Clarendon Press.

Csordas, T.J. 1990. Embodiment as a Paradigm for Anthropology. *Ethos* 18(1): 5–47.

Dillon, M. 1999. *China's Muslim Hui Community: Migration, Settlement and Sects*. London: Curzon Press.

Ding, M. 2009. Xibei Sufei zhuyi menhuan xingcheng yu zuzhi xingtai yanjiu (A Study on the System and Organisation of Sufi Schools (Menhuan) in the Northwest). *Journal of Beifang Ethnic University* 5.

Eisenstadt, S.N. 2003. *Comparative Civilizations and Multiple Modernities*. Leiden: Brill.

Erie, M. 2016. *China and Islam: The Prophet, the Party, and Law*. Cambridge: Cambridge University Press.

Esposito, J.L. 1998. *Islam and Politics*. Contemporary Issues in the Middle East. 4th ed. Syracuse, NY: Syracuse University Press.

Ewing, K.P. 1997. *Arguing Sainthood: Modernity, Psychoanalysis, and Islam*. Durham: Duke University Press.

Feuchtwang, S. 2010. *The Anthropology of Religion, Charisma, and Ghosts: Chinese Lessons for Adequate Theory*. Berlin: Walter de Gruyter.

Feuchtwang, S., and M. Wang. 2001. *Grassroots Charisma: Four Local Leaders in China*. London: Routledge.

Feuchtwang, S., and M. Wang. 2008. Suggestions for a Redefinition of Charisma. *Nova Religio: The Journal of Alternative and Emergent Religions* 12(2): 90–105.

Gammer, M. 2000. The Qadiriyya in the Northern Caucasus. *Journal of the History of Sufism* 1–2: 275 [Zarcone, T. and Buehler, A., editors. Simurg Press].

Gao, Z. 1991. *Xibei Musilin shehui wenti yanjiu (Research into the Question of Muslim Society in the Northwest)*. Lanzhou: Gansu Minorities Publishers.

Geertz, C. 1968. *Islam Observed; Religious Development in Morocco and Indonesia*. New Haven: Yale University Press.

Gillette, M.B. 2000. *Between Mecca and Beijing: Modernization and Consumption Among Urban Chinese Muslims*. Stanford, CA: Stanford University Press.

Gladney, D.C. 1995. Islam. *Journal of Asian Studies* 54(2): 371–377.

Gladney, D.C. 1996. *Muslim Chinese: Ethnic Nationalism in the People's Republic.* Cambridge, MA: Harvard University Press.

Gladney, D.C. 1999. The Salafiyya Movement in Northwest China: Islamic Fundamentalism Among the Muslim Chinese? In *Muslim Diversity: Local Islam in Global Contexts*, ed. L.O. Surrey: Nordic Institute of Asian Studies

Gladney, D.C. 2003. Islam in China: Accommodation or Separatism. *Religion in China Today: The China Quarterly Special Issues New Series* 3: 451–467.

Gladney, D.C. 2004. *Dislocating China: Reflections on Muslims, Minorities, and Other Subaltern Subjects.* London: C. Hurst.

Glassé, C. 1989. *The Concise Encyclopedia of Islam.* London: Stacey International.

Ha, B., and J. Ma. 2014. The Master-Disciple Relationship and the Spiritual Connotation of Chinese Sufism. *Northwestern Journal of Ethnology* (3).

Han, Z. 2009. Zhongguo yisilan Sufei zhuyi yanjiu xueshu zhuzuo zongshu (Reviewing Chinese Studies on Sufism for 30 Years from 1978 to 2008). *Journal of Beifang Ethnic University* 4: 20.

Hassan, R. 2001. Imagining Religion: Self-Images of Islam in the Late Twentieth Century. *Asian Studies Review* 25(2): 131–151.

Hille, M.-P., B. Horlemann, and P. Nietupski, eds. 2015. *Muslims in Amdo Tibetan Society: Multidisciplinary Approaches.* Studies in Modern Tibetan Culture. Lanham: Lexington Books.

Ho, W.-Y. 2016. *Islam and China's Hong Kong: Ethnic Identity, Muslim Networks and the New Silk Road.* Routledge Contemporary China Series. London: Routledge.

Huang, P.Z. 2016. *Yearbook of Chinese Theology 2015.* Leiden: Brill.

Israeli, R. 2002. *Islam in China: Religion, Ethnicity, Culture, and Politics.* Lanham: Lexington Books.

Jin, Y. 2008. *Islam. Chinese Religions and Beliefs - A Series of Contemporary Studies in China*, vol. 1. Beijing: China Minorities Publications.

Kipnis, A. 2006. Suzhi: A Keyword Approach. *The China Quarterly* 186: 295–313.

Kugle, S. 2012. *Sufis and Saints Mysticism, Corporeality, and Sacred Power in Islam.* Chapel Hill: University of North Carolina Press.

Lambek, M. 2000. The Anthropology of Religion and the Quarrel Between Poetry and Philosophy. *Current Anthropology* 41(3): 309–320.

Li, W., and M. Jing. 2011. *Gansu Linxia Menhuan Diaocha (Survey of Menhuan in Linxia, Gansu Province).* Beijing: China Social Sciences Publishing House.

Lipman, J. 1996. Hyphenated Chinese: Sino-Muslim Identity in Modern China. In *Remapping China: Fissures in Historical Terrain*, ed. by G. Hershatter, E. Honig, J. Lipman, and R. Stross. Stanford, CA: Stanford University Press.

Lipman, J. 1997. *Familiar Strangers: A History of Muslims in Northwest China.* Studies on Ethnic Groups in China. Seattle: University of Washington Press.

Lipman, J., ed. 2016. *Islamic Thought in China: Sino-Muslim Intellectual Evolution from the 17th to the 21st Century.* Edinburgh: Edinburgh University Press.

Lizzio, K. 2007. Ritual and Charisma in Naqshbandi Sufi Mysticism. *Anpere E-Journal for the Anthropological Study of Religion*, 1–37. http://www.anpere. net/2007/3.pdf.

Ma, T. 1983. *Zhongguo Yisilan Jiaopai yu Menhuan Zhidu Shilue (A History of Muslim Factions and the Menhuan System in China).* Yinchuan: Ningxia People's Publishing Society.

Ma, Q. 2006. *Huizu lishi yu wenhua ji minzuxue yanjiu (Research on the History and Ethnology of the Hui People).* Beijing: Central University of Nationalities Publishing House.

Ma, Y. 2008. Gadelinye Menhuan Chujiaren Zhidu Tanxi (A Discussion of the Monk System of the Qadiriyya Menhuan). *Journal of the Second Northwest University for Nationalities, Department of Philosophy and Religious Studies, Central University for Nationalities, Beijing, China* 1.

Ma, G. 2010. *Sufei Yujingxia de Musilin Funu Yanjiu (Study of Muslim Women in the Sufi Context).* Ph.D. thesis, Lanzhou University, Lanzhou. http://www. cnki.net.

Ma, H. 2011. The Historical and Present Situation of Islamic Menhuan in China. In *Muslims and a Harmonious Society: Selected Papers from a Three-Conference Series on Muslim Minorities in Northwest China : Gansu Province, 2008, Shaanxi Province, 2009, Xinjiang Autonomous Region, 2009.* Arlington, VA: Institute for Global Engagement.

Ma, C., and Ma, W. 2014. Gadilinye, Wenquantang and Salar: Fieldwork on Northwest Islamic Mysticism. *Journal of Beifang University of Nationalities* (3).

Marcus, M. 1985. The Saint Has Been Stolen: Sanctity and Social Change in a Tribe of Eastern Morocco. *American Ethnologist* 12 (3): 455–467.

Mauss, M. 1979. Body Techniques. In *Sociology and Psychology.* London: Routledge and Kegan Paul.

Merleau-Ponty, M. 1962. *Phenomenology of Perception.* New York: Humanities Press.

Mian, W. 1997. *Zhongguo huizu yisilan zongjiao zhidu gailun (A Survey of China's Hui People and Islamic Religious System).* Ningxia People's Publishing Society.

Murata, S. 2017. *The First Islamic Classic in Chinese: Wang Daiyu's "Real Commentary on the True Teaching".* Albany: State University of New York Press.

Murata, S., and W.C. Chittick. 2000. *Chinese Gleams of Sufi Light: Wang Tai-yu's Great Learning of the Pure and Real and Liu Chih's Displaying the Concealment of the Real Realm.* Albany, NY: State University of New York Press.

Murata, S., W.C. Chittick, and W. Tu. 2009. *The Sage Learning of Liu Zhi: Islamic Thought in Confucian Terms.* Cambridge, MA: Harvard University Asia Center for the Harvard-Yenching Institute.

Oakes, T. 1998. *Tourism and Modernity in China*. London: Taylor & Francis.

Pinto, P. 2010. The Anthropologist and the Initiated: Reflections on the Ethnography of Mystical Experience Among the Sufis of Aleppo, Syria. *Social Compass Journal* 57 (4): 464–478.

Qi, D. 1982. *Qingzhen Genyuan (Origins of Islam)*. Unknown.

Rey, T. 2007. *Bourdieu on Religion: Imposing Faith and Legitimacy*. London, Oakville: Equinox Publishing.

RT. 2016. *Radical Islam Spreading to Inland China – Senior Official*. https://www.rt.com/news/368473-radical-islam-inland-china/.

RT. 2017. *China Bans 'Abnormal' Beards & Veils to Curb Extremism in Muslim Region*. https://www.rt.com/news/382891-china-xinjiang-bans-beards-veils/.

Saniotis, A. 2008. Enchanted Landscapes: Sensuous Awareness as Mystical Practice Among Sufis in North India. *Australian Journal of Anthropology* 19 (1): 17–26.

Stewart, A. 2017. *Chinese Muslims and the Global Ummah: Islamic Revival and Ethnic Identity Among the Hui of Qinghai Province*. London: Routledge.

Tontini, R. 2016. *Muslim Sanzijing: Shifts and Continuities in the Definition of Islam in China*. Leiden: Brill.

Turner, V. 2011. *The Ritual Process: Structure and Anti-structure*. New Brunswick: Transaction Publishers.

Wang, H. 2009. *Linxia Da Gongbei Menhuan xingcheng yu zuzhi yunxing moshi yanjiu (Organization and Formation of Da Gongbei Menhuan in Linxia)*. Masters, Northwest Minorities University. http://www.cnki.net/KCMS/detail/detail.aspx?QueryID=0&CurRec=19&recid=&filename=LXSK198806009&dbname=CJFD7993&dbcode=CJFQ.

Wang, J. 2014. The Opposition of a Leading Akhund to Shi'a and Sufi Shaykhs in Mid-Nineteenth Century China. *Cross-Currents: East Asian History and Culture Review* 3: 518–541.

Wang, J. 2016. Islam and State Policy in Contemporary China. *Studies in Religion* 45 (4): 566–580.

Weber, M. 1968. *Economy and Society; An Outline of Interpretive Sociology*. New York: Bedminster Press.

Weber, M., and W. Runciman. 1978. *Max Weber: Selections in Translation*. Cambridge: Cambridge University Press.

Werbner, P. 2003. *Pilgrims of Love: The Anthropology of a Global Sufi Cult*. Bloomington: Indiana University Press.

Werbner, P., and H. Basu. 1998. *Embodying Charisma: Modernity, Locality, and Performance of Emotion in Sufi Cults*. London: Routledge.

Yang, H. 1992. *Huizu renwu zhi (Biographies of Notable Hui)*. Yinchuan: Ningxia People's Publishing Society.

Yang, F. 2012. *Religion in China: Survival and Revival Under Communist Rule*. Oxford: Oxford University Press.

Yu, Z., and X. Lei. 2001. *Zhongguo huizu jinshi lu* (*A Record of the Chinese Hui*). Yinchuan: Ningxia People's Publishing Society.

Zang, X. 2016. *Handbook on Ethnic Minorities in China*. Handbooks of Research on Contemporary China. Northampton: Edward Elgar Publishing Limited.

CHAPTER 2

Charisma and the Exemplary Saint: Narratives and Names

Charles Lindholm has described both Shi'a Islam and Sufism as 'exemplary religions', meaning a religion in which the prophet is 'the living receptacle of a static, immanent, and abstract essence' (Lindholm 1998, p. 210). This exemplary religion is the 'home of charisma, since it rests upon the recognition of a spiritually gifted individuals' oneness with the sacred' (Lindholm 1998, p. 210). In popular understanding, the exemplary saint of the Sufi is a 'magical being: a God on earth' (Lindholm 1998, p. 210). This is in contrast to Sunni Islam which Lindholm describes as an 'emissary religion', that is, a religion in which 'God is utterly omnipotent and transcendent but nonetheless active and moral, ordering humanity onto the right path. In this type of annunciation, any claim to union with the deity is an unforgivable sin. The prophet of the ethical God is not an ecstatic mystic, but a sober messenger' (Lindholm 1998, p. 210) bringing God's words and promises of salvation to the world.

This conception of Sufism as the 'home of charisma' aligns with Weber's view of charismatic authority which rests on the 'devotion to the exceptional sanctity, heroism or exemplary character of an individual person, and of the normative patterns or order revealed or ordained by him' (Weber 1968, p. 215). This idea however, that charisma was located in one single personality who had both political and religious authority, was challenged by Peter Worsley (Worsley 1970). Although the cargo cults he studied were led by prophets, there was no central or single system of leadership.

© The Author(s) 2018
T. Cone, *Cultivating Charismatic Power*,
https://doi.org/10.1007/978-3-319-74763-7_2

It was instead made up of several ecstatic leaders who were paired with political leaders. Feuchtwang has noted that charisma in this case was not so much a 'personality as a message which had been recognised because it resonated with and gave authority to religious adherents' expectations and assumptions [...] The *story* of a charismatic leader, rather than his personality, was the authorising symbol' (Feuchtwang and Wang 2001, p. 16). As such, the charismatic leader did not need to be alive. In fact, their charisma was actually 'amplified and enhanced by the absence or death of the prophet' (Feuchtwang and Wang 2001, p. 16). Similar to Worsley, Geertz (1968) and Michael Gilsenan (1982) believed that saintly charisma 'inhered in the complex of myths, legends, and anecdotes about the *shaykh*. Mythical tales invariably concerned feats of extraordinary power that set the *shaykh* apart from mere mortals' (Lizzio 2007, p. 6). For Geertz, these stories constituted a 'discourse of legitimation' that followed an 'established processual narrative: (1) initiation through an ordeal; (2) achievement of and access to esoteric knowledge; and (3) triumph over temporal authority.' The stories became 'persuasive by virtue of the *shaykh's* socially powerful position' (Lizzio 2007, p. 6).[1]

An exemplary character generated through mythical tales and stories has also been explored by Borge Bakken in his study on models, modelling, and the exemplary in Chinese society. Bakken has suggested that China is an 'imitative-repetitive' society, in which modelling has been an important technique in 'upholding social order' (Bakken 2000, p. 135). He suggests that the exemplary model can be viewed as a 'narrative' or 'myth', one that serves both social memory and social cohesion. 'Such models', he argues,

like the Homeric epics or the Nordic sagas, not only represent the social memory, but also provide the moral background for the present. The Chinese narrative of the exemplary person is a modern variant, with themes we have already noted in the debate on moral education. Harmony, stability,

---

[1] In the South Asian Muslim context, stories of Sufi and Muslim saints were known as *tazkiras*. In *Indo-Persian Tazkiras as Memorative Communications*, Hermansen and Lawrence discuss the *tazkiras* or biographical compendium of South Asian Muslims. They discuss how the heroes may have been selected and how their extraordinary lives relate to the everyday (Hermansen and Lawrence 2000, p. 149). Rather than viewing the *tazkiras* as 'mnemonic repetitions', they see them as 'conscious remembrances, and therefore [both] cultural artifacts and cultural reconstructions' (Hermansen and Lawrence 2000, p. 150). See also Hermansen 1997.

cohesion, constancy, sacrifice, control of self, and attachment to the group are story-lines again and again in the narrative (Bakken 2000, p. 136).

Vincent Cornell, in *In the Realm of the Saint*, carries out an analysis of 300 saints' biographies from the Almohad period in Moroccan Sufism (Cornell 1998). He develops a typology for the 'qualified' or 'exemplary' saint: urban, educated, and independent. He also identifies the key feature of sainthood as personal piety linked to asceticism and withdrawal from the world. The saint was also expected to perform 'miracles' and 'paranormal phenomena' and provide patronage and protection of the local community in worldly affairs (Cornell 1998, pp. 118–120). These features resonate with similar characteristics that were found in the Qadiriyya Sufi sources.

Qi Jingyi has long been understood as the founder, the exemplary saint, of Qadiriyya Sufism in Northwest China. Throughout my time at Guo Gongbei, many stories were recounted to me by practitioners about miraculous events in his life—stories that demonstrated particular capabilities and qualities of character. This chapter seeks to explore the nature of the exemplary saint in Guo Gongbei through reflecting on shared memories, biographical details, stories about the saints, and naming practices within the genealogy (Ch. *daotong*, Ar. *silsila*). Specifically, I want to consider the capabilities, habits, and personal qualities promoted within these sources. I argue that these are important to acknowledge because they are foundational to the charismatic habitus in question here. The capabilities, habits, and personal qualities in these stories resonate with contemporary disciples and inspire their emulation in daily charisma-generating practice. Similarly, the naming system that connects each generation to the next implies that each disciple embody the quality implicit in their name and thus develops further a particular idea of what being charismatic—in this context—means.

I refer to two local texts that were referenced frequently by individuals in the *gongbei*, in helping them to understand the practices of their own tradition and in their own context of China. First, *Origins of Islam* (*Qingzhen Genyuan*) is a compiled collection of written stories, religious instructions, and philosophical summaries by Chinese Qadiriyya teachers. It is known to hold the 'truth of the Qadiriyya'. According to the text it was reprinted in 1982 and contains the 'last sermon' by Qi Jingyi (no date), an entry by the leader Qi Daohe (no date), and two entries dating from 1925 by Qadiriyya disciples 'Lama' Yonggui and Ma Fengyue. The second is a local history of Guo Gongbei which was compiled in 1997 by the current *dangjiaren* of Guo Gongbei, Ma Yufang.

NARRATIVES OF THE SAINTS

There are 35 *gongbei* sites within the Qadiriyya network in China: 6 in Sichuan, 13 in Shaanxi, and 16 in the prefecture of Linxia, Gansu. Guo Gongbei is part of this network, all of whom share an historical genealogy that traces their 'origin' to the teacher buried at Da Gongbei, Qi Jingyi. During conversations at Guo Gongbei with current disciples about daily life and practice, reference to historical lineage came up quite often. 'The original saint', 'the grand-master', the 'previous master' (*daozu, baba, dangjiaren, halifa, laorenjia* and *taiye*) were all terms that came up in reference to current and past Sufi teachers, with *dangjiaren* being the most common. The current master (*dangjiaren*) of Guo Gongbei is Ma Yufang. I take him as a starting point in tracing this sense of genealogical connection that came through in daily conversations. The following are Ma Yufang's words on how he came to be at Guo Gongbei:

When I was young, I remember walking down the road to my home one day. I remember looking at the rocks and trees and animals, and wondering what it all meant. It was a moment of deep questioning. At that time, we lived in the rural area and had no money. When I went to high school, it was far from my home and took about an hour to get there. It was different from now—in the old times we had to walk to school but nowadays we have cars to pick up the students. But I studied very hard and one day, my master (Ma Shiming) came to our place and saw all my awards; he said to my father that I was a hardworking student, so my father let me go with the master, and from then we became master and disciple. To live and not fight for the truth is so meaningless [...]. At that time for me the biggest truth was to know myself and to know Islam.

So I started here after junior high school. At that time in the temple, I studied in the daytime and cut wheat in the evenings. In the 1980s, policies encouraged people to do more work in order to gain more, so we gradually got more food and a better place to live. But we did not have too much cash in hand, so we could not afford the text books and notebooks, even if they were only twenty cents. We just used two notebooks that were already used by our uncles.

In making a decision to further pursue religious study, I read a lot of books, especially the Islamic texts which enlighten me to this day. In terms of human beings, people should know the creator through spreading Islam. In the Qur'an, it says eyes are for observing, ears are for listening and heart is for thinking. So we see what the creator has done by our eyes, we use our ears to listen and we use our hearts to contemplate everything in this world. The ultimate goal of people living in this world is not to eat when one gets hungry or drink when one gets thirsty, and getting old all the while—this is the natural rule—the goal should be that we do something during our life, from young to old. The Qur'an says the creator created people to 'teach them to know me (Allah)' and to teach them to pray—for Islam has its own ways of praying.

Before choosing to join the Qadiriyya sect, I compared all of the existing *menhuan* in this region. In terms of morality and achievement, Qadiriyya has a high level (*chunzheng yixie*), and follows the succession of Muhammad through to the saint Ali, the successor of the Prophet.

As discussed earlier, for the Qadiriyya, Ali is revered as their founding teacher, the first shaykh (*jiaozhu*), and is believed to have inherited the saintly power of *baraka* from the Prophet. In a section of the *Origins of Islam* titled A Brief History of Ancestral Sages (written by the sixth-generation leader Qi Daohe), Ali is described as being the 'most confidential among the secrets of Allah and the most mysterious among the mysteries of Allah', praised by the sages 'for his integrity and knowledge' (Qi 1982, p. 22). His sayings were often studied in self-study or group study sessions at the *gongbei*. The book used was known as 'The Path of Eloquence' (Ch. *Ali Renfeiye*, Ar. *Nahj al-Balāghah*) and was a record of Ali's merits and achievements.[2]

'Abd al-Qādir al-Jīlānī

According to Guo Gongbei accounts, 'After Ali developed and taught the Qadiriyya teachings, sages carried it on from generation to generation, and formed the orthodoxy' (Ma 1997, p. 5). After the Prophet Muhammad had been deceased for 400 years, the 13th generation of the Prophet's descendant, who once was the principal of Baghdad College and a famous

---

[2] In the tenth century, a prominent scholar of Shi'ism, Sayyid Sharif al-Radi collated 'many of Ali's sermons, letters, and short sayings dealing with various subjects in the *Nahj al-Balāghah* (The Path of Eloquence). [...] The book continues to be a source of both religious and literary inspiration for both Shi'ites and Sunnis'. Afsaruddin and Nasr (2018) at https://www.britannica.com/biography/Ali-Muslim-caliph.

Persian in Baghdad, 'Abd al-Qādir al-Jīlānī, 'revived the Islamic doctrine, and also lay the foundation and basic content of the Qadiriyya order, creating a new phase in the history of Islam' (Ma 1997, p. 5). Abd al-Qadir was born in 1077 CE in a family who had direct ties to Muhammad through two of Ali's sons—through his father to Hasan and through his mother to Husayn. Accounts of his miracles appear in Sufi diaries, biographies, and dictionaries, which credit him with taming animals and healing illness. Sufis believed that all creatures praise God in their own voice and that Abd al-Qadir's purified soul directly spoke to the animals and communicated with them on some level of consciousness. Other miracles attributed to Abd al-Qadir included curing illnesses by reciting religious scripture. For example, he reportedly 'whispered into a deaf girl's ear so that she could hear, touched the stomach of an infertile woman to enable her to bear children, and alleviated the pain of an infant through prayer' (Jestice 2004, p. 430). Prescience was now accompanied by the capabilities of miraculous healing and understanding the language of animals—skills that I was told the saint Qi Jingyi also possessed.

Khoja Āfāq and Khoja 'Abd Allāh

After Abd al-Qadir, Qadiriyya Sufism was introduced and established in China by two Central Asian Sufi teachers, Khoja Āfāq (1626–1694) and Khoja 'Abd Allāh (1574–1689) (Qi 1982, p. 12). Khoja ('master') Afaq was a Naqshbandi Sufi leader who propagated a version of Naqshbandi Sufism throughout the Tarim Basin and Northwest China in the seventeenth century (Waite 2006, 5; Thum 2012, 295; Lipman 1996, 59). From 1671 to 1672, Khoja Afaq preached in Gansu, visiting Xining (in today's Qinghai Province), Lintao, and Linxia, where he was said to convert some Hui and Salars to Naqshbandi Sufism (Gladney 1999, p. 120). When Khoja Afaq was in Xining in 1672 he was said to have given his blessing to Qi Jingyi (later also known as Hilāl al-Dīn, or Qi Daozu), who then formally introduced Qadiriyya teachings in China (Gladney 1996, p. 44). Today, the mausoleum of Khoja Afaq can be found on the outskirts of Kashgar city (Waite 2006, p. 6). While it was originally built in 1640 to accommodate Khoja Afaq's father, Muhammad Yusuf, after Afaq's death and burial in the tomb in 1694, the mausoleum took on his name (Waite 2006, p. 6). Edmund Waite notes that Khoja Afaq based his religious authority on descent from the Prophet Muhammad and on 'religious charisma: in particular the performance of miracles' (Waite 2006, p. 9).

Fig. 2.1 Khoja Afaq's Mausoleum on the outskirts of Kashgar, Xinjiang

Drawing on an eighteenth-century hagiography, Waite has noted that he was known for healing the sick and 'restoring the dead' (Waite 2006, p. 9) (Fig. 2.1).

Khoja Abd Allah was a 29th-generation descendant of Muhammad, who entered China in 1674 and 'preached in Guangdong, Guangxi, Yunnan, Guizhou and Linxia, Gansu, before his eventual death in Guizhou in 1689' (Gladney 1996, p. 44). He is said to have come from Mecca and to have introduced the doctrine of the Qadiriyya to China (Wang 2001, p. 34). Gladney notes that 'While Abd al-Qadir al-Jilani is the reputed founder of the Qadiri tariqa, it is not surprising to find that Abd Allah perhaps studied in Medina under the renowned Kurdish mystic, Ibrahim b. Hasan al-Kurani (1616–1690), who was initiated into both the Naqshbandi and Qadiri tariqas, as well as several other Sufi orders' (Gladney 1999, p. 118). On a visit to Linxia, he was described as being 'over 100 years old', but at the time of encounter looked 'healthy' and 'like a god'. The description in *A Brief History of Guo Gongbei* goes on to say that 'he knows all about the sect, but never shows off. He spends his time only with the wise men. He is good at horse riding and archery, and especially good at poetry' (Ma 1997, p. 6). These words of Ma Yufang (the current leader) thus characterise him as a man of humility and high literacy.

Khoja Abd Allah supposedly recruited many disciples along his journey, but it was in Hezhou [Linxia] that he taught the 'person in his eye'—that is, the early 'saint' who founded the first Qadiriyya shrine, Da Gongbei—the 'original ancestor' Qi Jingyi.[3] The saint of Guo Gongbei—Chen Yiming— was also one of his disciples (Ma 1997, pp. 10–12).[4] Khoja Abd Allah was also remembered as having miraculous skills, and one *chujiaren* recounted to me his abilities to bend heavy and dense materials such as iron. The written record in the *Origins of Islam* described this capability as follows:

> In the twenty-fifth year of Emperor Kangxi, the governor received a pro-motion to serve in Chuanbei County, Sichuan. He invited the grand-teacher (Khoja Abd Allah) to go with him to Chuanbei County. The grand-teacher was happy and said: "It is not convenient for me to live in the governor house. I want to live in Iron-tower Temple (*tieta si*), it will be convenient for people coming in and going out of the temple." Therefore, the governor ordered soldiers to arrange a clean house in Iron-tower Temple, and the grand-teacher lived there. Qi Jingyi received Ma Ruhuan as a follower, (whose tomb is the Hezhou Dataiye Gongbei). Qi sent him in front of the grand-teacher for orders. As expected the grand-teacher was very glad to see him and said: "This child is destined to belong to our Qadiriyya sect!" At that time, the child was only three years old, he cried all day and night. The grand-teacher held him and rambled in the garden, and said: "Do not cry, do not cry." The grand-teacher patted the iron-tower, the iron-tower hence inclined, and even later reconstructions of the tower could not make it vertical (Qi 1982, p. 15).

[3] Other disciples were Ma Shangren (Hankou), Ma Shangren (Changsha), Lin(Ma) Shangren (Yunnan) and Xining Xianshangren (Qinghai), Ma Chunyi, Ma Xunyi, Ran Jingyi, Ha Huiyi (Uyghur nationality, from Kashgar, Xinjiang), Ma Shenyi, Mu Youlin, Ma Ziyun, and other early saints (Ma 1997, p. 6).

[4] Jianping Wang has noted that before Qi Jingyi was accepted by Khoja Abd Allah, he was 'under the guidance of two Persian Sufis, Baba Gui and Baba Yu, both of whom were Shi'a and came from Iran' (Wang 2014, p. 78). His two other spiritual disciples, Ma Laichi and Ma Mingxin, went to study in Central Asia and the Middle East and upon return to China founded the Khafiyya and the Jahriyya Sufi orders.

Here as well as demonstrating tremendous physical strength, Khoja Abd Allah was also prescient in his knowledge of Qi Jingyi and his future—even as a child. Another capability that appeared in several stories about Khoja Abd Allah was the ability to practise 'exteriorisation', that is, the ability to be present in different places at the same time (Schimmel 2011, p. 205).[5]

> Three years later, on the tenth day in the third month of the twenty-eighth year of Emperor Kangxi, the grand-teacher (Khoja Abd Allah) knew that he would die soon, so he asked the governor to find a site for his tomb. The governor took soldiers and accompanied the grand-teacher to see several places, but the grand-teacher disliked most areas. Then they came to Mt. Panlong, where there were nine wells surrounding a pool. The grand-teacher liked it. The place belonged to the Wang Family. The grand-teacher bought it, then gave instructions to even it out with soil. Unexpectedly, the grand-teacher died on the twenty-fifth day of the third month. Hui people in Baoning addressed the grand-teacher as the Great-Grand Saint. Han people addressed the grand-teacher as the Papa Great-Grand Teacher. Governor Ma felt extremely sad. The governor himself put the grand-teacher down into the tomb and unintentionally his jade thumb ring fell into the tomb. Then in the first ten days of the fourth month, a soldier named Ma Deliang went back home and requested to see the governor. He brought the jade thumb ring and said: "I came across an old man on the road on the twenty-fifth day of the third month (the day of his death). The old man had white hair and a childlike complexion. He asked me to send this to you for appreciation and respects." On hearing this, tears trickled down the governor's cheeks. Since then, the governor prayed in front of the grand-teacher's tomb everyday in the morning and in the evening (Qi 1982, p. 12).

In this story, the 'grand-teacher' Khoja Abd Allah, on the day of his death, was simultaneously placed in a grave at Mt. Panlong but was also found sitting on the side of the road in order to return the jade ring.

---

[5] This is resonant of the qualities described of the *zhenren* in Daoism. As Miura Kunio notes: 'The term *zhenren* denotes one of the highest states in the Taoist spiritual hierarchy [...] While the *Zhuangzi* does not describe a person with supernormal powers as a *zhenren*, it is easy to see how the idea could be adopted into the search for eternal youth and immortality.' He quotes from the speech of Lu Sheng when he was trying to influence Qin Shi Huang (221–210 BCE), who was fascinated by the idea of immortality: 'The *zhenren* enters water but does not get wet, enters fire but does not get burned, flies among the clouds, and has a length of life equal to that of Heaven and Earth' (Pregadio 2013, p. 1265).

This miraculous capability of exteriorisation can also be found in the hagiographical works of other Sufis. Annemarie Schimmel has noted the capability of the Sufi saint to come to the rescue of his disciples wherever they were through the faculty of *tayy al-makan*—that is, of being beyond spatial restriction. In dangerous situations a saint 'might appear in the middle of a robbery to drive them away, or take the shape of the ruler in order to protect a disciple who called for help. In Turkey the master might appear, in spiritualised form, at a sick person's bed in order to cure him or at least relieve him temporarily from his pain' (Schimmel 2011, p. 205).

This story also illustrates the mutual respect accorded to the Sufi saint by local Muslim governors. Based on the story, it would seem Khoja Abd Allah performed this act of generosity out of some sense of allegiance to the local governor. The emotion expressed by the governor, in turn, indicates a deep sense of emotional attachment and profound respect for the Sufi saint. Nile Green has noted a similar phenomenon in encounters between Sufi saints and Muslim rulers in Muslim South Asia. He has argued that in this context Sufis were to be regarded as 'men of power. It was this power—particularly the power to foretell and even shape future events, though also the power of "legitimisation" more familiar to the historian—that charted some of the parameters of such Sufi and royal exchanges' (Green 2004, p. 420). This profound respect for the Sufi saints and their miraculous capabilities by local governors (both Muslim and non-Muslim) is a thematic thread throughout all of the stories that follow.

In 1678 CE, Khoja Abd Allah departed from Gansu through Shaanxi to Sichuan, wandering in the region doing missionary work. He died on March 25th, 1689 CE in Huaxia and was buried in a town called Baoning (now called Langzhong city), located on Panlong Mountain in Sichuan Province. The mosque and *gongbei* that was built in his honour is in the present day known by various names, including Baba Mosque, Jiuzhao Pavilion, the Baoning Mosque, and the Panlong Mountain Qubbah. Ma Yufang described Khoja Abd Allah as a man of great determination, commitment, and courage, remembered for 'spreading the Qadiriyya dogma in our country, regardless of the danger of mountains and rivers, summer and winter, coming over thousands and thousands of miles, from the young age of 16 years, finally to his death [...] He is the foundation stone of our nation's Qadiriyya—the originator' (Ma 1997, p. 7).

Qi Jingyi

Qi Jingyi (1656–1719 CE) was from Xiaoxiguan of Bafang in Linxia. As a boy he was 'eccentric and unsociable', an only child raised by his grandmother. At seven he entered the mosque school, and at 12 he began to study the Islamic canon in the madrasa. Records describe that 'he surpassed all others in intelligence, and his teachers could not stump him' (Lipman 2000, p. 550). With regard to God's commandments and the Prophet's Hadith, he was very obedient, taking 'to brighten the innate virtue (in order to) reveal the mind, to cultivate the self (in order to) bring peace to others' (Lipman 2000, p. 550). In these memories of Qi Jingyi, his intelligence and self-sacrifice for the sake of others was emphasised.

In 1672, when Qi supposedly met with Khoja Afaq in Xining, the master was said to have sent the 16-year-old home, saying 'I am not your teacher, my ancient teaching is not to be passed on to you, your teacher has already crossed the Eastern Sea and arrived in the Eastern land. You must therefore return home quickly, and you will become a famous teacher in the land' (Ma 1983, p. 330). In 1674, records state that Khoja Abd Allah came to Hezhou [Linxia] and lodged temporarily in a Muslim home there. When Qi Jingyi heard this news, he went to visit and was accepted as a disciple. This account has led many Qadiriyya religious adherents to believe that Qi Jingyi received the blessing of Khoja Afaq, while the order was formally founded by his second teacher, Khoja Abd Allah. Here the prescient capability of the saint is again illustrated, this time by Khoja Afaq, who claimed to foresee both who his teacher would be and how Qi Jingyi's future would develop.

Several students at the *gongbei* mentioned to me the unique relationship that Qi Jingyi had with animals. Ma Yong said that 'when Qi practiced (*xiuxing*), there were ferocious animals at his side but these animals had no way of being close to him or hurting him. He only revealed these things to some people around him, and then slowly the story started to spread'. Another student Aihemaide relayed to me similar impressions:

> Once when he [Qi Jingyi] was meditating, there were two cheetahs. One was in front of him, one was behind him. This means he had a very good relationship with nature—in one stage of the Qadiriyya, people and the nature have to connect— *tianren heyi*. He is remembered for performing miracles. I also heard that once when he was in Sichuan in a dangerous place, wolves and tigers [that were there], they did not hurt him because he could understand the languages that these animals spoke.

Abilities such as these to understand the language of animals have been attributed to many Sufi mystics throughout the centuries (and indeed to mediaeval Christian saints and numerous Buddhist practitioners). For the Muslim mystic, this close relationship with the animal world is not particularly remarkable, since 'every creature praises God in its own voice and he who has purified his soul understands their praise and can join them' (Schimmel 2011, p. 208). Schimmel has written about the Indian and Persian miniatures that show the saint sleeping or sitting amongst beasts, 'the lions tamed and obedient, the birds at his service, the shy gazelle conversing with him' (Schimmel 2011, p. 208). Idries Shah, in *Timur Agha and the Speech of Animals*, has recounted the story of a Sufi Turk called Timur Agha, who was given the power to understand the speech of animals by a Sufi dervish, Bahaudin. He could then understand the language of an ox and donkey and influence their behaviour (Shah 1967, p. 186).

Another capability highlighted to me was Qi Jingyi's ability to influence the weather. In the *Origins of Islam* a story recalls that:

> When Qi Jingyi was living in Sichuan, the city of Baoning suffered a great drought. There was no food and water and the government was in great distress. An official heard that the Muslim Qi Jingyi was living on Mt. Panlong and he went up the mountain to beg Qi for rain. Buddhists and Daoists had tried to pray for rain but nothing had worked. Qi agreed compassionately. The official asked: "What do we need to prepare?" Qi answered: "Nothing except a well at Jialin River." So the official built a well beside the river, then he himself went up the mountain to invite Qi to pray for rain. Qi went to the well at once. That day was very hot, there were no clouds in the sky. The official said to Qi: "Today there are no clouds in the sky, the sun is so hot, I am going to bring you an umbrella to shield the sunlight." Qi replied: "Don't bother. You do not need to go and bring an umbrella, soon there will be something to shield the sunlight for me." Then suddenly a cloud appeared in the west sky, and it moved above the head of Qi and shielded the sunlight just like an umbrella. Soon the cloud became dark and spread over the whole sky. Immediately the rain fell and kept falling for three days and nights, which saved people in the region from the drought disaster (Qi 1982, p. 13).

Schimmel has noted that Sufi saints are the 'governors of the universe [...] It is through the blessings of the saints that rain falls from heaven; on the places touched by their sacred feet plants spring up, and thanks to their help the Muslims will gain victory over the unbelievers' (Schimmel 2011, p. 203). Accordingly, the ability of Qi to make the rain fall here indicates his spiritual sophistication in addressing 'weak spots' or 'imperfections' in the universe. Another story highlighted the prescient capabilities of Qi Jingyi around the time of his death. On September 11th, 1719 CE (the 58th year of Emperor Kangxi in the Qing Dynasty), Qi Jingyi died in the Jingshi Mosque of Xixiang County, Shaanxi Province at the age of 63. After he was buried in the eastern side of the Jingshi Mosque, a tomb named the 'long-standing pavilion' was constructed to commemorate him. The remains of Qi Jingyi were eventually moved to the current location of Hongyuan Road in present-day Linxia with the establishment of the tomb house and *bagua* (Eight Trigrams) pavilion.[6] In a story, the way in which this site was determined is recounted:

> On the sixteenth day of the first month in the fifty-ninth year of Emperor Kangxi, his coffin (Qi Jingyi's) reached Hezhou [Linxia]. Bafang people (Muslim part of Linxia) gave a reception in honor of him in Sijiazui. During the meal time, Bafang people seized a chance to lift up the coffin and run away. The Yang Family and Tui Family chased after them immediately, then the two sides argued away. At that time an old man came and said: "Grand-teacher once said in Hezhou [Linxia]: 'If I die, please send me to Hongshi River bend out of the west gate, you go and see, there will be a white rabbit and a cock playing at that place, you can send me to that place." On hearing this, people followed the words and went to see the river bend. As expected, there was a white rabbit and a cock playing at that place. People were surprised and followed Qi's last words to move and bury the coffin and build a *gongbei* there. Hui people and Han people call it Da Gongbei. It is a Qadiriyya place of worship, the only way to be remembered after death, surrounded by stars and in a place of high honour (Qi 1982, p. 15).

In this story, Qi had foreseen the place of his burial. This prescient capability, present in the genealogy of saints before him, was also noted by

---

[6] The Eight Trigrams 'constitute a Chinese conceptual diagram of the cosmos, consisting of all possible combinations of three unbroken (yang) and broken (yin) lines [...] An octagonal building would represent the Eight Trigrams in its architecture' (Lipman 2000, p. 565). Discussed further in Chap. 3.

Aihemaide who said to me that 'Qi Jingyi is remembered for long periods of meditation, eating less, less water. In this way he gets closer and closer to God, to being a saint. Qi Jingyi is nearly a god. He can see some things very exactly that happen in the future'.[7] Qi Jingyi had also noted the presence of a white rabbit and a cock playing at that particular place. Interestingly, the rabbit and the rooster (cock) are two of the 12 animals in the Chinese zodiac (Wu 2010). White rabbits, in particular, are a symbol of longevity, and a rooster is associated with reliability and fidelity. It is significant that it was these two creatures that Qi Jingyi saw at his place of burial as longevity in life and fidelity to the Qadiriyya practice were values that Qi Jingyi would undoubtedly have hoped his adherents and disciples embody.

Chen Yiming

Constructed near Da Gongbei, Guo Gongbei is the cemetery of the Qadiriyya saint Chen Yiming (1646–1718 CE). He was also a student of Khoja Abd Allah. Chen was from Chenjia Alley in Bafang, Linxia. He was born on September 25th, 1646 in the third year of the Shunzhi reign period of the Qing dynasty. His father died when he was very young, and he was raised alone by his mother. He attended classes at the Daqi Mosque in Linxia where he studied the Qur'an, Hadith, and other 'classic books of Islam'. He was 'bright and intelligent, studying hard, and with a great talent, he obtained a deep love for and meticulous cultivation from his teachers. He was a master in Arab language and Persian language, and versed in Chinese. He had a large stock of knowledge, and could often cite the classics when he was teaching, convincing others with his plain words and incisive interpreting' (Ma 1997, p. 9). These were recurring qualities throughout the biographies of these Chinese Qadiriyya saints—qualities of commitment, intelligence, and an aptitude for learning.

When the 29th descendant of the Prophet Khoja Abd Allah came to Hezhou [Linxia] in 1674 CE, Chen Yiming enthusiastically went to pay him a visit and listen to his teaching. Khoja Abd Allah 'saw him and knew he was no common-looking man, knew he could bear the hardest burden',

---

[7] Buehler has noted that within 'each Sufi lineage specific methods developed for disciples to draw near to God, some of whom arrived close enough to become power-wielding friends of God themselves' (Buehler 1998, p. 99). This involves a journey through the *latifas*, or subtle bodies. In Chap. 3 I have detailed the navigation of disciples through key stages in their spiritual cultivation but was not able to document the specifics of navigation through the 'subtle bodies' that Buehler describes.

and he recruited him as a disciple. He taught him the 'subtleties of the Qadiriyya mysteries (*aomiao*), pointing out the great meaning of being Muslim, and demonstrated to him ascetic practice' (Ma 1997, p. 10). After this, Chen Yiming decided to be a teacher. He continued to study, and he lived in isolation in a thatched cottage in Paohan city on the outskirts of Linxia. He lived in seclusion there for three years, and with 'few desires and a pure heart he gradually grabbed the subtle knowledge'. Asceticism and isolation were stressed here as the living habits necessary for spiritual advancement. Khoja Abd Allah arrived to see Chen and praised him for his progress. He taught him 'about the subtleties of heaven and human, the humilities of nature and life, the aim of rationalism, and success of practice' (Ma 1997, p. 10). He also encouraged Chen to serve as a link between the past and future of the 'monastic teachings' and to spread Islam (*zhengjiao*) throughout the region.

Ma Yufang described Chen Yiming as a man that carried out 'many charitable deeds. He helped those in distress, aided those in peril and practiced medicine to save people for free. What he did was awaken the deaf people seeking the teaching across thousands of miles in an endless stream [...]' (Ma 1997, p. 12). During this time, Chen also guarded the Emperor Kangxi of the Qing dynasty (who reigned from 1661 to 1722) on several occasions. He 'cured his dangerous illnesses' and obtained respect and praise from the Emperor. Here again is an illustration of the attribution of power given to Sufi saints by royalty (in this case by a non-Muslim ruler), as the following passage confirms:

> Once when the Emperor was travelling incognito, he was robbed on the road of a suburb in the capital. Chen Yiming met them by chance, and he protected the Emperor from danger. Another time, Emperor Kangxi was visiting the regions south of the Yangtze River. Suddenly, while the Emperor was crossing the river, winds and waves became fast and high. Right before the boat was about to sink, Chen Yiming operated the rudder to get the boat onto shore in safety. A third time, the Emperor Kangxi was seriously ill. The imperial physicians were all very concerned, but after Chen treated him, he effected a miraculous cure and brought the dying back to life. Thus in several dangerous situations, Emperor Kangxi encountered Chen and reflecting on this, he thought it very significant. When he thought about the protection of Chen, and his medical skills, the Emperor gave him the name of Baoguo, meaning to guard the country for the people (Ma 1997, p. 12).

Similarities can be seen between this narrative of Chen Yiming rescuing a sinking ship and stories of other Sufi saints who were 'the patrons of sea travellers' (Green 2008, p. 6). Green has explored the 'miraculous migrations of holy men from across the sea' in the Western Indian Ocean and the ways in which the Sufis offered the seafarers a kind of 'supernatural insurance' (Green 2008, p. 6).

On September 4th, 1718 CE, Chen Yiming died in his former residence at 73 years old. He was buried in the west suburb of Linxia City (which is nowadays Guo Gongbei). On receiving the news of his death, Emperor Kangxi ordered the local officials to build a tomb for him in 1719. The Emperor Kangxi also issued an imperial edict and a yellow satin letter to protect the *gongbei*—a gold plaque with four characters *Bao Guo Wei Min* meaning 'To serve the country and protect the people'. Emperor Kangxi also hung a royal plaque in the Daqi Mosque where the early saint had spent his childhood. The royal inscription read: '*Hong Yang Zheng Jiao*' meaning 'spread the orthodoxy of the sect' to indicate his support in cultivating future disciples. Since then, the early saint Chen Yiming's tomb was called Guo Gongbei (Figs. 2.2 and 2.3).

The genealogy from Chen Yiming to the present day is as follows:

- Muhammad Mahamudi (b. Baghdad, Iraq, 1665 CE, d. 1752 CE at the age of 87).
- Ma Yunfeng (Yagubai) from Guyuan County in Ningxia Hui Autonomous Region (b. March 1, 1709 CE, d. January 21, 1788 CE at the age of 79).
- Ma Nengyun (Zi Longzhai) from Linxia City, Gansu Province (b. January 11, 1767, d. in 1845 CE at the age of 78). Ma Nengyun was one of the disciples of Han Yingfeng who was a disciple of Ma Tenyi, who was a disciple of Qi Jingyi. Ma Nengyun 'had a large stock of information, and superb medical skills' (Ma 1997, p. 27).[8]

---

[8] Ma Nengyun was sent by Da Gongbei to preside over Guo Gongbei teaching affairs for many years. He then went to Haoxi Guanghui Gongbei in Qingchuan County, Sichuan, to be the master. This was the tomb of the saint Ma Chunyi. An earthquake hit during that time resulting in two of the saints' tombs collapsing. Ma Nengyun assisted with donations to make repairs. He wrote many books but most of them were ruined in the earthquake. The only preserved one was a handwritten copy of the Qur'an. Ma Nengyun then went to Baoning and Songpan in Sichuan, Hanzhong and Xixiang in Shaanxi, Haigu in Ningxia, Gongchang in Gansu and other 'early saint holy lands and famous mountains' to cultivate his moral character.

Fig. 2.2 The inscription *Bao Guo Wei Min*—'To serve the country and protect the people'

- Chen Yuexiang (Chen Shanren) from Qisi Street, Bafang, Linxia City, Gansu (b. 1784 CE, d. 1879 CE at the age of 85).
- Ma Daocheng (Yonusu) from Longxi County, Gansu Province (b. 1826 CE, d. 1907 CE at the age of 81 years).
- Zhang Zhengzhuan (Dawood) from Dongxiang County, Gansu Province (b. August 22, 1883 CE, d. 1947 CE February 18 at the age of 61).
- Ma Shiming, b. February 15, 1910 CE in Linxia City, d. 1997.

In his childhood, Ma Shiming was sent by his parents to study with the master of Da Gongbei, Wang Yongrui. At that time, Wang was ordered

He 'presided over teaching affairs and obtained reputation and fame far and near'. After that he was summoned back to Hezhou [Linxia], and he was ordered to Dongxiang Yihachi for final meditation. He was buried there, and the disciples built a tomb pavilion for him named 'Yihachi Gongbei' (Ma 1997, p. 27).

Fig. 2.3 Looking up at one side of the main tomb

to preside over the Sichuan Baba Mosque. Shiming was too young to go with him to Sichuan, so he stayed with his parents. After he grew up a little, he went to the Hanjiaji Mochuan Mosque to study. Then with the support of Wang Yongrui, he formally acknowledged the Guo Gongbei master, Zhang Zhengchuan, as his teacher. At that time, he was 14 years old. Zhang Zhengchuan sent him to Da Gongbei to study with other youth disciples under the Da Gongbei master Wang Yongzhen. These disciples were Yang Shirun, Zhou Shiqing, Ma Shian, Ma Tengfang, Ma Junfang, Zhou Qifang, and 'Bazhou'. At the age of 20, Ma Shiming was elected as the leader of Guo Gongbei, and he remained in that position for 68 years (1929–1997). Ma Yufang wrote that he devoted much attention to cultivating his disciples: 'In his time he overcame many difficulties, covered tuition fees, and worked hard in trying to cultivate qualified successors' (Ma 1997, pp. 32–33).

During one afternoon conversation, I asked Ma Yufang if he believed in the existence of miracles, he replied, 'Yes, I do. Miracles do exist'. I asked, 'Have you seen them with your own eyes?' 'Yes', he replied, 'the last *dangjiaren* [Ma Shiming] performed them. He could precisely foresee events in the coming years, and he could make judgements about whether things will be successful or not. People came to visit him in order to be guided by his special power, and he was willing to help them. He also talked to them about their aims in life because he knew what they were looking for'. Schimmel has noted that one of the main traits in Sufi hagiographical works is the 'cardiognosia' (soul-reading) abilities of a master. Many stories are told about a '*shaykh's* insight into his disciple's heart; he was able to tell his secret wishes, hopes, and dislikes, to understand signs of spiritual pride or hypocrisy the very moment the adept entered his presence' (Schimmel 2011, p. 205). Just as his spiritual ancestors had demonstrated, this was a capability, according to Ma Yufang, that Ma Shiming also embodied.

In 1995, when he was 85 years old, Ma Shiming accompanied his disciple Ma Yufang to undertake the *hajj* pilgrimage to Mecca. As mentioned earlier, he is now the current *dangjiaren* of Guo Gongbei. His name, birthplace, education history, and time of becoming a *chujiaren* are detailed below, along with other *chujiaren* in his generation at Guo Gongbei (Ma 1997, p. 34):

- Ma Yufang; Islamic name: Ibullaheymai; Nationality: Dongxiang; Native Place: Jingouxiang, Linxia County; Birth: 1968; *chujiaren*: 1979 (11 years old); Educational background: College; Current practising school: Iran Khomeini University, Tehran
- Tuoallah Heymai; Islamic name: Ibullaheymai; Nationality: Hui; Native Place: Huangniwanxiang, Linxia County; Birth: 1966; *chujiaren*: 1982 (16 years old); Educational background: Middle School; Current practising school: N/A
- Ma Weilin; Islamic name: Remaizanel; Nationality: Hui; Native Place: Bafang, Linxia City; Birth: 1970; *chujiaren*: 1983 (13 years old); Educational background: Primary school; Current practising school: N/A
- Mu Xinfang; Islamic name: Wumaiqin; Nationality: Hui; Native Place: Zhangzigouxian, Linxia County; Birth: 1970; *chujiaren*: 1979 (12 years old); Educational background: College; Current practising school: Lanzhou Islamic Classics College

- Bai Mansu; Islamic name: Mansu; Nationality: Hui; Native Place: Baijiazhuang, Linxia City; Birth: 1976; *chujiaren*: 1991 (15 years old); Educational background: College; Current practising school: Lanzhou Islamic Classics College
- Tuo Xinfang; Islamic name: Yousufu; Nationality: Hui; Native Place: Yangtuojia, Linxia City; Birth: 1968; *chujiaren*: 1984 (16 years old); Educational background: High school; Current practising school: N/A
- Ma Kelima; Islamic name: Kelimu; Nationality: Dongxiang; Native Place: Hongyakou, Hezheng County; Birth: 1977; *chujiaren*: 1993 (16 years old); Educational background: Middle School; Current practising school: Lanzhou Saonilai Muslim temple

GENERATIONAL NAMES

In order to avoid disconnection between these generations of masters and disciples, Qi Jingyi developed a naming system for the first ten generations of Qadiriyya disciples. These names indicated membership in a generation, but also sought to promote particular personal qualities that were embodied in the meaning of the name itself. It is important therefore to discuss both the individual meanings of the characters themselves and the poetic imagery evoked when they are combined. Qi Jingyi chose the following ten Chinese characters for the first ten generations:

一 清 风 云 月, 道 传 永 世 芳
yī qīng fēng yún yuè dào chuán yǒng shì fāng

The One is a clear breeze and flowing moonlight; The Way passes on eternally with fragrance

Qi Daohe, a *chujiaren* during the Tongzhi Period of the Qing Dynasty, added another ten words to name the next ten generations following 'Fang'. These were:

敬 诚 先 哲 远, 克 念 悟 真 常
jìng chéng xiān zhé yuǎn kè niàn wù zhēn cháng

With reverence and sincerity, think of past sages; Overcoming selfish desires, awaken to truth and permanence.

Currently, the lineage has reached the tenth generation of 'Fang' (芳). Names (*ming*) are very powerful in China. Chad Hansen has even argued that names 'rather than sentences are central to all Chinese philosophy—and that this fact distinguishes the Chinese approach to reality, which is more important than a theory of truth' (Blum 1997, p. 364). In Imperial China, Blum has noted that 'a single ruler could have several different reign periods, changing the names of the periods to change the fortunes of the empire. Emperors' personal names were powerful, tabooed both during life and after death. If their names contained ordinary syllables, like *guang* "glorious", that word had to be replaced in all written texts' (Blum 1997, pp. 358–359). In the domestic spaces of contemporary Chinese society too, the giving of names also carries its own special significance. When an infant's name is selected, it should 'harmonise with the time, and often the place, of the child's birth' and can only 'be changed if, through illness or misfortune, a diagnosis of mismatch with the name is made' (Blum 1997, p. 364).

Similarly, in the Chinese Sufi context, names have played a very important role. Zhao Yufang, a *chujiaren* who had lived at Da Gongbei since the age of 12 (and was a well-known Arabic-Chinese calligrapher in the region), explained that when you join the *gongbei* as a *chujiaren*, the master gives you this name, 'it's a name that only *chujiaren* can have, others can't have this name'. He continued, 'Our names are given in accordance with the given generation (*an beifen suan*). Normally, children are sent at quite a young age by their parents to the *gongbei* to become a *chujiaren*. At our school we teach them to wait until they are 18, and to then make a decision on their own terms about whether they want to become a *chujiaren* or not. If they are willing to continue with the choice that their parents made to send them to the *gongbei*, and to become a *chujiaren*, then at that point we give them a name according to the present generation, such as my name which is *fang* (芳), meaning "fragrant" [literally, or "virtuous"]. If they later on decide to leave and get married, they cannot use this name again, which indicates respect to the *gongbei*. But there are some people who after leaving the *gongbei* continue to use this name—this is mainly to commemorate their own time in the *gongbei*'.

The diagram included (see Fig. 2.4) illustrates the generational naming system in Da Gongbei and Guo Gongbei. It is interesting to note here that sometimes the generation name is the third character of the name. This is different to other Chinese contexts in which it would traditionally be the

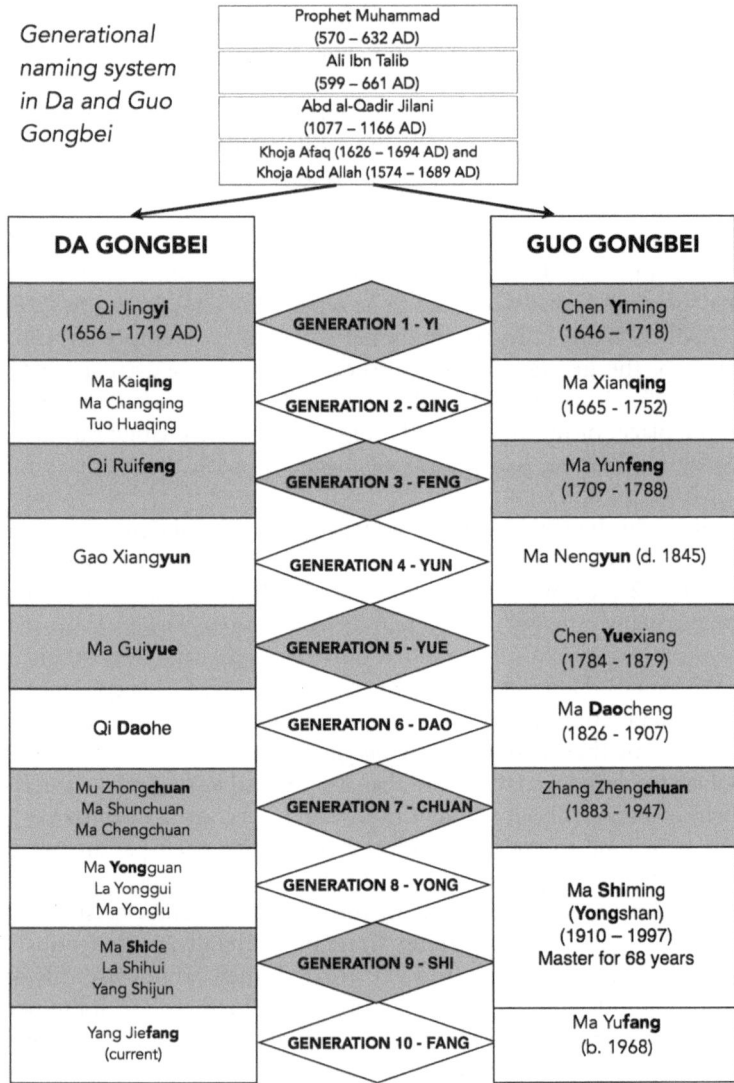

Fig. 2.4 Generational naming diagram depicts the lineage for both Da and Guo Gongbei. The lineage for Da Gongbei is based on the work of Ma Tong and Wang Huizhen (Wang 2009; Lipman 2000) (dates not included). Guo Gongbei lineage is based on an account by the Guo Gongbei internal management committee (Ma 1997)

second character of the name used. In this diagram, I have not included the names of saints that were between the Prophet Muhammad, Ali, and Abd al-Qadir. The purpose here is to demonstrate a very local genealogy that began from within the two *gongbei* of concern here and to illustrate the way this naming system has connected each set of disciples together. The characters in bold are the generational names.

In the first generation, the first character *yi* (一) was used in the name of Qi Jing*yi* in Da Gongbei and Chen *Yi*ming in Guo Gongbei. *Yi* means 'one; whole; all'. This is appropriate as these are the founders, the beginning points of the genealogy in each *gongbei*. In the second generation, the character *qing* (清) was used in the name of Ma Kai*qing*, Ma Chang*qing*, and Tuo Hua*qing* in Da Gongbei and Ma Xian*qing* in Guo Gongbei. *Qing* means 'clear; quiet; pure'. In the third generation, the character *feng* (风) was used for Qi Rui*feng* in Da Gongbei and Ma Yun*feng* in Guo Gongbei. *Feng* means 'wind; air; manner; atmosphere'. In the fourth generation, the character *yun* (云) was used for Gao Xiang*yun* in Da Gongbei and Ma Neng*yun* in Guo Gongbei. *Yun* means 'say; speak; clouds' (the third and fourth characters together (*fengyun*) mean 'weather' or 'unstable situation'. Interestingly Ma Yunfeng of the third generation had both *yun* and *feng* in his name).

In the fifth generation, the character *yue* (月) was used for Ma Gui*yue* in Da Gongbei and Chen *Yue*xiang in Guo Gongbei. *Yue* means 'the moon; month'. In the sixth generation, the character *dao* (道) was used for Qi *Dao*he in Da Gongbei and Ma *Dao*cheng in Guo Gongbei. *Dao* means 'direction; way; road; truth; morality; reason'. It has been translated in the poem as the 'Way' but could also be written as the 'Dao'. In the seventh generation, the character *chuan* (传) was used for Mu Zhong*chuan*, Ma Shun*chuan*, and Ma Cheng*chuan* in Da Gongbei and Zhang Zheng*chuan* in Guo Gongbei. *Chuan* means 'to pass on; to spread; to transmit'. The characters for the eighth and ninth generations, *yong* (永) and *shi* (世), together mean 'eternal/forever'. *Yong* on its own means 'long; perpetual; eternal; forever' and *shi* means 'generation; world; era'. In Da Gongbei, the character *yong* was used to name the eighth-generation masters Ma *Yong*guan, La *Yong*gui, and Ma *Yong*lu, and the character *shi* was used to name the ninth-generation masters Ma *Shi*de, La *Shi*hui, and Yang *Shi*jun. Interestingly, in Guo Gongbei both characters were used to name Ma *Shi*ming (also known as *Yong*shan).

The tenth generation used the character *fang* (芳) for Yang Jie*fang* (the current leader of Da Gongbei) and Ma Yu*fang* (the current leader of Guo Gongbei). *Fang* means 'fragrant; virtuous; beautiful'. It has been translated literally in the poem as 'fragrance'. However, in the context of this poem, it refers to the term *liufang* (流芳), which is a euphemism for admirable or virtuous actions or traits passed on generation after generation. Overall, these chosen characters emphasise the qualities of wholeness, quietness, purity, longevity, reason, transmission, virtuous action, and eternity. The phrasing of these characters can be translated as 'The One is a clear breeze and flowing moonlight; The Way passes on eternally with fragrance'—an aspiration perhaps by Qi Jingyi that disciples, on the path of self-cultivation, emulate the seeming purity, clarity, and integrity of these natural phenomena.

The characters for the next ten generations are not yet in use but are as follows. In the 11th generation, the character *jing* (敬) will be used, which means 'to respect; venerate; to salute'. In the 12th generation, the character *cheng* (诚) will be used, which means 'honest; sincere; true'. The 13th and 14th generation character—*xianzhe* (先哲)—together mean 'distinguished precursor; famous thinker of antiquity'. On their own, *xian* means 'first; former; previous'. *Zhe* means 'wise; sagacious; wise man; sage'. The 15th generation will use the character *yuan* (远), which means 'far; distant; remote'. The 16th generation will use the character *ke* (克), which means 'to be able to; to overcome'. The 17th generation will use the character *nian* (念), which means 'to read; to study'. The 18th generation will use the character *wu* (悟), which means 'to comprehend; to apprehend; to become aware'. The 19th generation will use the character *zhen* (真), which means 'real; true; genuine'. The 20th generation will use the character *chang* (常), which means 'always; often; constant'. Overall, these chosen characters emphasise the qualities of respect, honesty, wisdom, perseverance, learning, awakening, truth, and consistency. The phrasing of these characters can be translated as 'With reverence and sincerity, think of past sages. Overcoming selfish desires, awaken to truth and permanence'. Here Qi Daohe emphasises the importance of looking back to the earlier generations—the early saints—in order to ground contemporary practice.[9]

---

[9] Zhu Yayun, a scholar of classical Chinese at the ANU, translated each term as follows: yi, oneness; qing, purity; feng, breeze; yun, cloud; yue, moon; dao, the Way; chuan, imparting; yong, eternity; shi, generation; fang, fragrance; jing, reverence; cheng, integrity; xian, ancestors; zhe, wise; yuan, far; ke, overcome; nian, remembrance; wu, enlightenment; zhen, truth; chang, permanence (personal correspondence).

It is notable from the diagram that there are more masters in the Da Gongbei genealogy than the Guo Gongbei. This is due to the fact that the election system between the two was different. Since its establishment, the *chujiaren* in Da Gongbei were required to rotate once every three years from the original *gongbei* to another. This rule was created by Qi Jingyi. Now this interval has been narrowed to every two years or in some cases every year. Da Gongbei is responsible for rotating these *chujiaren*. Rotation is advocated primarily as a means to share knowledge and experience amongst the *chujiaren* in different regions and to strengthen the *chujiaren* community as a whole. Currently, Da Gongbei has more than 30 *chujiaren*, and it has a rotation relationship with 11 other Qadiriyya *gongbei* in the region with an approximate total of 90 *chujiaren* across all of the *gongbei* sites.[10] Guo Gongbei did not follow this three-year rotation between various *gongbei* sites as Da Gongbei did. Comparatively, they had fewer masters but each master maintained the position for longer. Ma explained that theirs was a lifelong term which was similar to the situation in Iran where religious leaders 'occupy a lifelong tenure'.[11]

This Chinese Qadiriyya genealogy is a male-oriented patrilineal system which has similarities to the kinship structures of both traditional Chinese family kinship and Chinese Buddhist and Daoist monasticism. The traditional Chinese family (*jia* or *jiating*) has been described as a 'patrilineal, patriarchal, prescriptively virilocal kinship group' (Jordan 2005). That is to say that descent was typically calculated through men. A person descended of course from both a mother and a father, but family membership was inherited from one's father. Jordan notes that 'reverence to ones ancestors (*zuxian*) also prioritised the male line. For a man this referred to his male ancestors and their wives. For a woman it referred to her male ancestors and their wives only a couple of generations up, but was extended also to all of her husband's male ancestors and their wives' (Jordan 2005). After a marriage, a woman was explicitly removed from the family of her birth (her

---

[10] Professor L. noted that this three-year rotation system is not a unique innovation of the Qadiriyya system, but is taken from the *imam/ahong* hiring model in Chinese Mosque education.

[11] While in theory the 'masters' of different *gongbei* enjoy equal status with the 'master' of Da Gongbei, Wang noted that Da Gongbei as the historical centre determines that its master 'enjoys higher status than other masters'. This means that the 'masters of other *gongbei* must be selected from the *chujiaren* of Da Gongbei, and should be appointed by and obey the order of Da Gongbei' (Wang 2009, p. 18).

niangjia) and affiliated to her husband's family (her *pojia*), a transition that can still be seen in local marriage customs.

The Chinese Qadiriyya genealogy takes this patrilineal emphasis a step further in making no mention at all in the record of the matrilineal line (if known) that produced it. This complete removal and separation from the original family line (and the subsequent importance of naming in the process of induction into the Sufi order) is similar to the processes within Chinese Buddhist and Daoist celibate monasticism. Buddhist and Daoist monks were also called *chujiaren* as they are in the Chinese Qadiriyya context. The taking of Buddhist vows removed the individuals from their original families (if they had one) and 'affiliated them in perpetuity to the Buddhist clergy as monks and nuns' (Jordan 2005). A fully ordained monk or nun was given 'the surname *Shi*, the first syllable of the full name of the Shakyamuni Buddha (*Shijiamouni*). He or she was regarded as the disciple of a specific master, made regular offerings of "ancestral" reverence to the master and his/her line of earlier clerics, and was in turn to be reverenced on temple "ancestral" altars by a line of later ones' (Jordan 2005). Similar to the rotation system with the Chinese Qadiriyya order, these 'fully ordained clerics were permitted to change monasteries at will (in theory) and carried their ordination papers with them so that they could be fitted into monastic hierarchies wherever they went' (Jordan 2005). As in the Buddhist clergy, the generational names within the Chinese Qadiriyya context were crucial to building a new form of kinship—one not based on blood ties but on spiritual or charismatic merit.[12]

The capabilities, habits, and personal qualities embedded within the biographical details, shared memories, referenced stories, and given names all have implications for the exemplary model of charisma in this context. The most notable capabilities of the charismatic saint were those of the

[12] In Buddhism and Daoism, merit is known as *gongde*. It is a concept 'whereby merit can be earned or cultivated by performing benevolent Buddhist-related deeds, which will constitute a person's store of benefits in the next life or the lives thereafter. Furthermore, merit can be transferred to another person, living or dead' (Davis 2009, p. 315). Similarly, in Sufism 'merit' or 'charismatic merit' ('baraka') can earned by partaking in specific cultivation practices. However in Sufism this merit is not so much 'transferred' as it is 'recognised' through the granting of 'divine permission' (in Persian *suhbat* or in Chinese *kouchuan xinshou*—phrase meaning 'transmitted orally, received in the heart'). Here, *kouchuan* indicates the transmission of the *baraka*, not the tradition itself. As far as I am aware, in the context of Sufism in China, merit could only be 'passed' to the living, and there was no mention of the 'next life' in which this merit could be used again.

miraculous. Specifically, the ability to see into the future (prescience), to be in two places at once (exteriorise), to read people's souls (cardiognosia), to influence the weather, to heal illnesses, to communicate with animals, and to have tremendous physical strength. Habits that were stressed in the cultivation of charismatic power included living in isolation and quiet, having few desires and practising asceticism, accumulating knowledge, and becoming literate (writing poetry and learning language). The qualities of a person necessary for the cultivation of charismatic power included humility, determination, commitment, courage, intelligence, and an aptitude for learning. The generational names in particular emphasised the qualities of wholeness, quietness, purity, longevity, reason, transmission, eternity, respect, honesty, wisdom, perseverance, learning, awakening, truth, and consistency. As a *chujiaren* of the Qadiriyya, one's very name was not only a link with the patrilineal line of ancestors but also, potentially, a source of emulation. The capabilities, habits, and personal qualities of the exemplary saints, revealed in these written sources, still circulate in daily conversation. They are foundational to the charismatic habitus in this context and continue to underpin contemporary charisma-generating practice in Guo Gongbei.

REFERENCES

Afsaruddin, A. and Nasr, S.H. 2018. *Entry on 'Alī Encyclopedia Britannica'*. Accessed on March 23, 2018 at https://www.britannica.com/biography/Ali-Muslim-caliph.

Bakken, B. 2000. *The Exemplary Society: Human Improvement, Social Control, and the Dangers of Modernity in China*. New York: Oxford University Press.

Blum, S. 1997. Naming Practices and the Power of Words in China. *Language in Society* 26 (03): 357–379.

Buehler, A. 1998. *Sufi Heirs of the Prophet: The Indian Naqshbandiyya and the Rise of the Mediating Sufi Shaykh*. Columbia: University of South Carolina.

Cornell, V.J. 1998. *Realm of the Saint: Power and Authority in Moroccan Sufism*. Austin: University of Texas Press.

Davis, E., ed. *Encyclopedia of Contemporary Chinese Culture*. London: Taylor and Francis.

Feuchtwang, S., and M. Wang. 2001. *Grassroots Charisma: Four Local Leaders in China*. London: Routledge.

Geertz, C. 1968. *Islam Observed: Religious Development in Morocco and Indonesia*. New Haven: Yale University Press.

Gilsenan, M. 1982. *Recognizing Islam: An Anthropologist's Introduction*. London: Croom Helm.

Gladney, D.C. 1996. *Muslim Chinese: Ethnic Nationalism in the People's Republic.* Cambridge: Harvard University Press.

Gladney, D.C. 1999. The Salafiyya Movement in Northwest China: Islamic Fundamentalism Among the Muslim Chinese? In *Muslim Diversity: Local Islam in Global Contexts,* ed. L.O. Manger. Surrey: Nordic Institute of Asian Studies.

Green, N. 2004. Stories of Saints and Sultans: Remembering History at the Sufi Shrines of Aurangabad. *Modern Asian Studies* 38 (02): 419–446.

Green, N. 2008. Saints, Rebels and Booksellers: Sufis in the Cosmopolitan Western Indian Ocean, c. 1850–1920. In *Struggling with History: Islam and Cosmopolitanism in the Western Indian Ocean,* ed. Kresse, K., and Simpson, E. New York: Columbia University Press.

Hermansen, M., and B. Lawrence. 2000. Indo-Persian Tazkiras as Memorative Communication. In *Beyond Turk and Hindu,* ed. D. Gilmartin and B. Lawrence, 149–175. Gainesville: University Press of Florida.

Hermansen, M. 1997. Religious Literature and the Inscription of Identity: The Sufi Tazkira Tradition in Muslim South Asia. *Muslim World* 87: (3–4) 315–329.

Jestice, P.G. 2004. *Holy People of the World: A Cross-cultural Encyclopedia.* Santa Barbara: ABC-CLIO.

Jordan, D. 2005. *The Traditional Chinese Family and Lineage.* http://anthro.ucsd.edu/~dkjordan/chin/hbfamilism-u.html.

Lindholm, C. 1998. Prophets and Pirs. In *Embodying Charisma: Modernity, Locality, and the Performance of Emotion in Sufi Cults,* ed. P. Werbner and H. Basu. London: Routledge.

Lipman, J. 1996. Hyphenated Chinese: Sino-Muslim Identity in Modern China. In *Remapping China: Fissures in Historical Terrain,* ed. G. Hershatter, E. Honig, J. Lipman, and R. Stross. Stanford: Stanford University Press.

Lipman, J. 2000. MA TONG, A Brief History of the Qadiriyya in China (translated from the Chinese and introduced by Jonathan LIPMAN). *Journal of the History of Sufism* 1–2: 547–576 [Zarcone, T. and Buehler, A., editors. Simurg Press].

Lizzio, K. 2007. Ritual and Charisma in Naqshbandi Sufi Mysticism. *Anpere E-Journal for the Anthropological Study of Religion,* 1–37. http://www.anpere.net/2007/3.pdf.

Ma, T. 1983. *Zhongguo Yisilan Jiaopai yu Menhuan Zhidu Shilue (A History of Muslim Factions and the Menhuan System in China).* Yinchuan: Ningxia People's Publishing Society.

Ma, Y. 1997. *Linxia Guo Gongbei Jianshi (A Brief History of Guo Gongbei).* Guo Gongbei Committee.

Pregadio, F. 2013. *The Encyclopedia of Taoism: 2-Volume Set.* London: Routledge.

Qi, D. 1982. *Qingzhen Genyuan (Origins of Islam).* Unknown.

Schimmel, A. 2011. *Mystical Dimensions of Islam.* Chapel Hill: University of North Carolina Press.

Shah, I. 1967. *Tales of the Dervishes: Teaching Stories of the Sufi Masters Over the Past Thousand Years.* London: Octagon Press Ltd.

Thum, R. 2012. Beyond Resistance and Nationalism: Local History and the Case of Afaq Khoja. *Central Asian Survey* 31 (3): 293–310.

Waite, E. 2006. From Holy Man to National Villain: Popular Historical Narratives About Apaq Khoja Amongst Uyghurs in Contemporary Xinjiang. *Inner Asia* 8 (1): 5–28.

Wang, J. 2001. *Glossary of Chinese Islamic terms.* Richmond: Curzon Press.

Wang, H. 2009. *Linxia Da Gongbei Menhuan xingcheng yu zuzhi yunxing moshi yanjiu (Organization and Formation of Da Gongbei Menhuan in Linxia).* Masters, Northwest Minorities University. http://www.cnki.net/KCMS/detail/detail.aspx?QueryID=0&CurRec=19&recid=&filename=LXSK198806009&dbname=CJFD7993&dbcode=CJFQ.

Wang, J. 2014. The Opposition of a Leading Akhund to Shi'a and Sufi Shaykhs in Mid-Nineteenth Century China. *Cross-Currents: East Asian History and Culture Review* 12: 72.

Weber, M. 1968. *Economy and Society; An Outline of Interpretive Sociology.* New York: Bedminster Press.

Werbner, P. 2003. *Pilgrims of Love: The Anthropology of a Global Sufi Cult.* Bloomington: Indiana University Press.

Worsley, P. 1970. *The Trumpet Shall Sound: A Study of "Cargo" Cults in Melanesia.* London: Paladin.

Wu, Z. 2010. *The 12 Chinese Animals: Create Harmony in Your Daily Life Through Ancient Chinese Wisdom.* Singing Dragon.

CHAPTER 3

Charisma and the Disciplined Body

When I asked Ma Yufang if he would be able to perform miracles (*shenji*) similar to the saints who had gone before, he told me that it was a 'natural thing, if you study harder, it will be possible; if you don't put the effort in, you won't be successful. I am aiming for these capabilities'. I asked him: 'What causes miracles? What do you need to do?' He explained that the miracles of the past *dangjiaren* are caused by *gongxiu*: 'If there is no *gongxiu*, there won't be any miracles.' *Gongxiu* translates literally to 'meritorious actions of cultivation' and can also be translated as 'self-cultivation' or 'self-discipline'. In this context, they referred to a graduated system of advancement known as the *sancheng*, or three vehicles.[1] Ma Yufang explained that the most 'foundational instruction of the order is *sancheng* (three vehicles), which is a progression through three stages of learning (from easy to difficult)'. He described that the rate of progression through these stages depends on the individual:

> Everyone has different abilities. If you have strong thoughts, you will improve very fast; if some people speak one way and think another way, then

---

[1] The Sino-Muslim scholar Liu Zhi's use of cheng (vehicle) in this translation from Arabic into Chinese points directly to a 'connection he recognised between Buddhist and Islamic religious ideas. The conventional Chinese translation of Mahayana, one of the central schools of Buddhism, is *Dacheng*, Great Vehicle. This paragraph explains Liu Zhi's rendering of the conventional Sufi path—*sharia, tariqa, haqiqa*—into comprehensible Neo-Confucian Chinese' (Lipman 2000, p. 562).

© The Author(s) 2018
T. Cone, *Cultivating Charismatic Power*,
https://doi.org/10.1007/978-3-319-74763-7_3

they won't improve. *Sancheng* is the cultivation of one's moral character and behaviour. It is the integration of man and nature, and an ongoing permanent practice that cannot be achieved separately or alone (*jue bushi fenkai er dandu qu gan de*). There is a saying: If you do not cultivate your moral character, you will not understand your mind, if you do not understand your mind, your nature will not show, if your nature does not show, your self will be hidden from view (*shen bu xiu buneng ming xin, xin buming buneng xianxing, xing bu xian ze yi si suo zhe*).

The overall goal of this process of cultivation through following the *sancheng* was 'to "purify the heart" (*qing xin xian xing*) sufficiently so as to "recognise oneself to return to Allah (*ren ji guizhen*)," and to achieve "the unity of man and nature" (*tianren hun hua*)'.[2]

Baraka AND THE BODY

This 'unity of man and nature' was the embodiment of charismatic power. Building on the work of Werbner and Lizzio, I argue in this chapter that this charismatic power (*baraka* or *zhanguang* as it was known in the Chinese context) was primarily rooted in the physical body and cultivated through daily disciplined practice. In discussing the generation of this charismatic habitus through the practices of the body (the operation of bodily hexis), I specifically draw on the work of the Arab scholar Farid al-Zahi and the religious studies scholar Scott Kugle. Building upon Farid al-Zahi's notion that there are four basic dimensions of bodily experience that are all integrated into a singular body, Kugle suggests that these can be 'imagined as concentric circles, with the physical body in the centre like a core, with progressively more expansive and diffuse circles surrounding it, connecting the physical body to the wider world and defining, in turn, the body that is their core' (Kugle 2012, p. 16). Al-Zahi designates each circle from the centre outwards as corps or 'body matter', corporal or 'bodily movement', corporeal or 'biological dynamic', and corporeality or

---

[2] It is important to note here the different use of the phrase '*tianren*' in this Chinese Muslim context as compared to its use in Chinese cosmology more broadly. In the Muslim context, Allah is the creator of *tian* (nature), *ren* (man), and *di* (earth), whereas in Daoist and popular cosmology, the universe of *tian is* the world. As Ames and Hall note, 'the God of the Bible, sometimes referred to metonymically as "Heaven", *created* the world, but *tian* in classical Chinese *is* the world. That is, *tian* is both *what* our world is and *how* it is' (Ames and Hall 2003, p. 65).

'interpretation of body's meaning' (Kugle 2012, p. 18). Kugle supplements and refines al-Zahi's scheme by outlining four dimensions of consciousness that affect each layer of the circle and determines the relation between the ego and the body (Kugle 2012, pp. 22–26):

1. Restraint—'being against the body': ascetic control (fasting) but also more moderate restraint exercised in any ritual activity, like prayer or recitation, that focuses awareness away from sensuality of the body;
2. Engagement—'being through the body': instrumental use of the body to create things, to cook, to clean;
3. Rapture—'being with the body': consciousness experiencing intimacy with the body, such as in ecstatic experiences of possession, in which the ego is so intimately suffused with the body that it temporarily loses self-consciousness and is understood to have become united with divinity, possessed by a spirit or divine being;
4. Release—'being in the body': state of slumber, or daydream.

I shall draw on three of Kugle's conceptions here in understanding the generation and embodiment of charismatic power—specifically, that of restraint or 'being against the body', engagement or 'being through the body', and rapture or 'being with the body'. Through a description and analysis of the practices involved within each 'stage' of the *sancheng*, I seek to illustrate these varying relations between the ego and body in the generation of charismatic power.

The descriptions are based on observations and insights from a number of *chujiaren* at the *gongbei* (under 20 and over 40).[3] There were 17 *chujiaren* affiliated with Guo Gongbei. Seven of them were studying in Islamic colleges in China or Iran or running schools in the region. There

---

[3] The Chinese researcher Ma Yuxiu has described 'three classes' of *chujiaren* in Da Gongbei (Ma 2008, p. 5), but aside from *dangjiaren* these were not specific terms I heard used in Guo Gongbei. Yuxiu describes that the first 'class' are *chujiaren* who have gone through a long time of roaming, begging, cultivation, and meditation in the mountains. The second class are 'fakir' or ascetic *chujiaren* (also known as *qinglian ren* or honest person), *qin lian ren* (practiced person), and *ji jiao ren* (person that teaches remembrance), 'who don't need to roam or cultivate in mountains but can settle down in the *gongbei* and obey the three disciplines and five commandments'. The three disciplines are: giving up sexual desire, giving up the desire for wealth, and giving up selfish interests. The five principles are to 'study diligently, beg for food, practise diligently, offer incense in the morning, and take a bath frequently'. The third class is the 'master' or 'host' of the Qubbah (*dangjiaren, zhuchiren*) (Ma 2008).

were five *chujiaren* aged over 40 living in residence at the *gongbei* during my time there, and then there were several *chujiaren* who were under the age of 20 who were also either studying abroad in Iran or at the Islamic Studies College in Lanzhou. Ma explained that there are now eight more *chujiaren* since 1997, but they were not all currently on site: 'Some of them run schools outside the *gongbei* and some of them are inside the *gongbei* still. They left to serve other people, and I would leave if necessary, but I would send someone to cover my position. I would only leave for a short period and I would still take charge of things here. The 7 that are away will still come back, but at the moment they are just moving from place to place every year, depending on need. They are my assistants so they are like working staff. They are all *chujiaren* and they'll always be *chujiaren*, they have committed.' There was one orphaned eight-year-old boy who was also living at the *gongbei* and identified as a *chujiaren*. He was also attending primary school outside of the *gongbei* as well as participating in daily activities inside the *gongbei*. Ma Yufang told me that most of these *chujiaren* have siblings and family who supported them to come to the *gongbei* and that most of them chose to study at the *gongbei* after graduating from junior high school. He explained that 'people all have their different ambitions, and everything is subjective and voluntary [...] The young [orphan] boy may change his mind in the future, now he is too young to really know what he might like to do'.

SACRED SPACE AND THE BODY

The enactment of the *gongbei* as a sacred space (Holloway 2003, p. 1963) was crucial to the project of charismatic cultivation, and while this primarily occurred through bodily practice, it also relied upon architectural, material, and textual elements. The structuring of the physical space of the *gongbei*, to follow Bourdieu, functioned 'at the same time as a principle of vision and division, as a category of perception and appreciation—in short, as a mental structure' (Bourdieu 1996, p. 14). For Bourdieu, there is no space in a hierarchical society

> which is not hierarchised and which does not express social hierarchies and distances in a more or less distorted or euphemised fashion, especially through the effect of naturalisation attendant on the durable inscription of social realities onto and in the physical world: differences produced by social logic can then seem to arise out of the nature of things (Bourdieu 1996, p. 11).

Keith Basso has described this as 'sensing places'—that is, the process in which places are actively sensed, when 'the physical landscape becomes wedded to the landscape of the mind' (Basso 1996, p. 55). While I do discuss here architectural, material, and textual elements in this process of 'sensing place', I follow Julian Holloway in emphasising the primary role of the body and bodily practices in this process of enactment—what he calls the 'corporeal poetics of sacred spatiality' (Holloway 2003, p. 1963).

The material space of the *gongbei*, both within and outside, was structured and decorated in such a way to reflect and encourage a certain vision or mental structure—a vision which encompassed a certain set of values: values of purity, stillness, knowledge, and sincerity. Guo Gongbei was divided into two main areas. The main entrance area was known as the residence yard. This area contained a collection of two-storey buildings, a large courtyard, parking space, and a small garden. Meeting rooms, a kitchen, toilets, the *dangjiaren's* office and private quarters, and the official management headquarters for the *gongbei* were located on the ground floor. Dorm rooms were located on the second floor, where students and *chujiaren* were accommodated in (for the most part depending on numbers) shared rooms. A large room located on the second floor was being used as a classroom for students. An ornately decorated wall provided a boundary between this area and the highly sacralised area of the tomb site itself. This area was named *Jingjing yard* ('clean and quiet' yard) and contained Chen Yiming's tomb (*bagua*) and a book reading hall and religious service room (*Baoxia*) that was attached to it. It also contained several storerooms, an enclosed area behind the main tomb that housed several other tombs of former disciples, and two large incense urns.

Large amounts of incense were constantly burning within the *Jingjing* yard area of the *gongbei*, generating an always fragrant and sweet smell. Adherents and disciples within the *gongbei* space told me that the tomb sites should always be clean and fragrant as this resembled Qur'anic paradise. This is similar to what Saniotis found in a Nizamuddin shrine complex in North India, where 'Scents of roses and incense, for example, are said to "be like the sweet odours of paradise" [...]' (Saniotis 2008, p. 22). The incense was thus an important part of demarcating sacred bodies within the *gongbei* site itself, as an incense urn was always placed, and only placed, outside the area of an entombed saint. The act of burning incense was also a connection between bodies—those of the living and those of the dead. Through offering up incense each time one performed a prayer in front

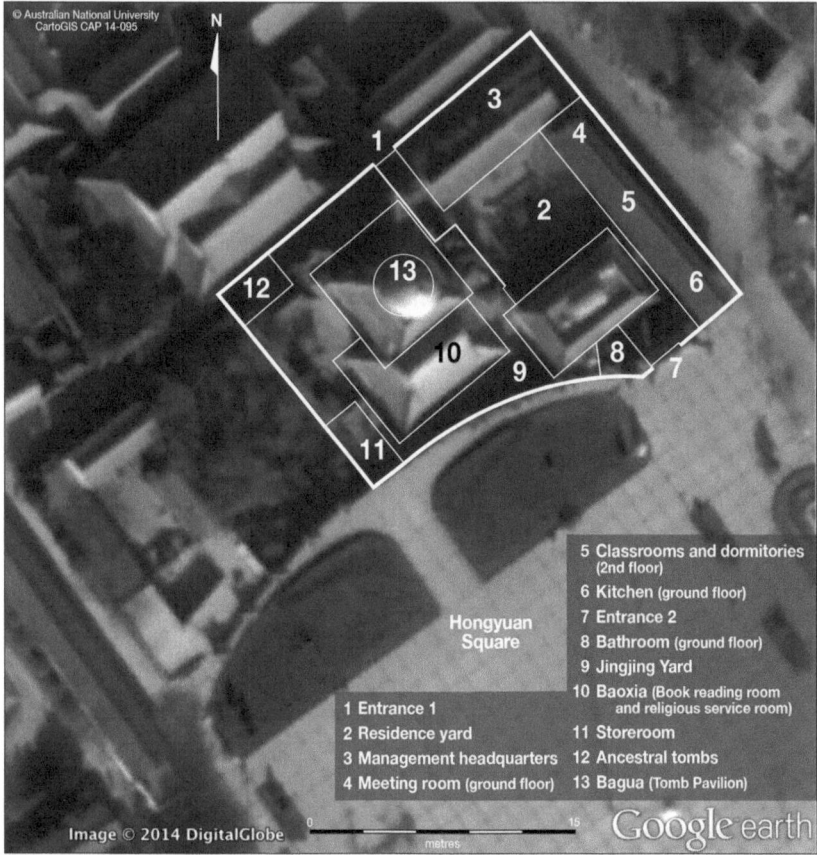

Fig. 3.1   Layout of Guo Gongbei

of the tomb sites, disciples, students, and adherents sought to overcome bodily, spatial, and temporal separation with the saints (Fig. 3.1).

A curved entrance-way provided access between these two areas. It was ornately decorated with carved dragons, lotus flowers, grapes, and picturesque scenes of lofty mountains and trees. From very early times in China, mountains have been viewed as sacred and as the abode of immortals. On either side of the arched gate was a couplet. The first line read: 'To be pure is surely demanding! One who desires for it must be untainted by wordly entanglements' (*Qing qi yi qing, yu qing xu yichenburan*). The second line read: 'To be truthful is indeed difficult! One who wishes for it should be empty of myriad affinities' (*Zhencheng nan zhen, zhen yi wan yuan jie kong*).[4] Here the values of purity, emptiness, and sincerity were emphasised.

The tomb of Chen Yiming was known as the *bagua* or the 'eight trigrams'. The eight trigrams (three-line diagrams) are from the *Yijing* (The Book of Changes) and combine to form the 64 hexagrams (six-line diagrams), believed to represent all possible changes and transformations (based on yin-yang interaction) in the cosmos. It is a correlative and holistic system used to understand and bring the ceaseless spiritual, emotional, and bodily changes of the individual into alignment with the ceaseless changes in the physical environment—that is, to achieve balance and harmony between the body and the cosmos. The eight trigrams are thus related correlatively to the body (Pregadio 2013, p. 1163).[5]

In the context of the Chinese Qadiriyya saints, the *bagua* as an architectural structure was a symbolic representation of the bodily and spiritual sophistication of the individual entombed inside (with eight representing the highest level). Zhao Yufang (a *chujiaren* who used to study at Da Gongbei but was now at Jiezisuma Gongbei outside of Linxia) explained that 'the number of trigrams represents the level of religious practice of a person, the higher the level the more trigrams are represented. The number is determined by the master, and an apprentice cannot have more than the Master. But Qi Jingyi is an exception, his trigrams were more than his master, he has eight trigrams, his master has four. But in his teacher's tomb, there are four sides outside, but inside eight. Qi Jingyi has eight sides because his teacher thought his level was very high, so he should have eight sides'. The tomb of Chen Yiming in Guo Gongbei has four sides, indicating

---

[4] A colleague, Li Geng, has noted the significance of the character for *yuan* here, a concept of Buddhist origin referring to connections, causes, and relationships.

[5] The eight trigrams are still used during diagnostics in Chinese medicine and were used in internal alchemy (*neidan*) in early Daoist alchemy (Komjathy 2007, p. 435). Correlations between cosmos and the human body in early Quanzhen Daoist alchemy: Qian (heaven—head); Kun (earth—feet); Li (fire—heart); Kan (water—kidneys); Dui (lake—lungs); Zhen (thunder—liver); Sun (wind—gall-bladder); Gen (mountain—bladder) (Komjathy 2007, p. 435).

Fig. 3.2 Inside Guo Gongbei—the tall structure is the tomb of Chen Yiming connected to a worship hall

that his spiritual sophistication was not as exceptional as the founder of the Qadiriyya, Qi Jingyi (Fig. 3.2).[6]

The grammar of the body was both determined by and determinant of the nature of these two areas of the *gongbei*. On a daily basis, disciples moved between the area devoted to silence, stillness, prayers, and cleanliness and the other devoted to conversation, eating, rest, and

---

[6] The *bagua* also calls to mind geometric patterns in Islamic architecture which base designs on overlapping circles (the perfect symbol of 'unity'), resulting in tessellations of regular hexagons. Conceptually, these hexagons and eight-fold rosette patterns can continue forever, but 'in practical applications Islamic patterns are generally cropped to form rectangular sections with corners in the centre of key pieces, often stars [...] the perfect visual solution to calling to mind the idea of infinity, and hence the Infinite, without any pretence of being able to truly capture such an enigmatic concept visually' (Sutton 2007, p. 6).

ablutions.[7] While I was able to be in the gongbei during the day and could observe daily comings and goings, I was unable to be in the gongbei overnight. As such, I learnt about activities of prayer during the night from students. I was told that oft-times late in the evening—around 11.30 pm— some of the *chujiaren* undertook brief ablutions in the shared bathroom and then walked with others through the gate and into the *Jingjing* yard. They would enter the main reading room inside the worship hall and for several hours would sit together in silent meditation. Around 3.30 am, they would finish and go to take rest in their rooms in the residence yard. At around 6 am they would wake again and perform morning ablutions. At 6.30 am, in the worship hall connected to the main tomb, the first of the five prayers of the day would be performed—(Ch. *chenli*, Ar. *fajr*)— morning prayer.

Around 8 am, after this morning prayer, I would sometimes join with the students in the kitchen. Here, the students, *chujiaren*, and myself would share bowls of hot Hui mian (Hui beef noodles), sweet Sanpaotai tea, and local breads. Between 9 and 11 am, some *chujiaren* would retire to their rooms for private reading and rest. During this time, the local caretaker and several students often attended to the incense urns and ensured there was sufficient incense burning. At around 1.20 pm, after a meal of dried lamb and bread, students and *chujiaren* gathered for noon prayer (Ch. *shangli*, Ar. *zuhr*). Sometimes, Ma, two students, and one *chujiaren* would leave the *gongbei* for several hours to the home of an adherent. Just after 4 pm, Ma and the others would return to the *gongbei* and prepare for afternoon prayer (Ch. *buli*, Ar. *'asr*)—activity between 3 and 5 pm.

Around 5 pm, with the assistance of a student, the cook would sometimes go outside to the kitchen near the inside of the front gate. Here he performed a ritual slaughter of two chickens that had been sitting in cages since the morning. Before the moment of cutting the neck of the

---

[7] Ablutions were known as greater ablution (*da jing*) and lesser ablution (*xiao jing*). A female follower explained that 'the greater ablution [Ch. *da jing*, Ar. *ghusl*] gives you a state of purity necessary to perform important acts such as prayer. You have to immerse your body in water, or pour water over your body, and before you do that you have to state your intention to Anla [Allah]'. The lesser ablution (Ch. *xiao jing*; Ar. *wudū'*) was a cleansing ritual that I saw performed by women and men, young and old, before entry into mosques or before prayer at home. This was a brief washing of the hands, face, and feet and was performed before daily prayer (provided that the state conferred by the greater ablution had not been lost).

chicken, he repeated the name of God, 'bism allāh'.[8] Each chicken was carried in one by one to the kitchen, and the blood was drained from the neck before they were plucked and cooked in a pot of boiling water on the coal-fired stove. At around 5.45 pm, Ma Yufang would often come back into the kitchen and chat briefly to the disciples and students. After dinner, he would sometimes remind them to attend to their ablutions in preparation for prayer at 6.30 pm. Everyone would then shuffle in the dim evening light to the worship hall for the sunset prayer (Ch. *hunli*, Ar. *maghrib*). Emerging from this prayer, Ma Yufang would sometimes sit with the students in the kitchen area for about half an hour, keeping warm and discussing plans for the following day. Around 7.25 pm he would join the other *chujiaren* and students in the final night prayer (Ch. *xiaoli*, Ar. *'ishā'*). This concluded about 7.40 pm at which point he would return to his room to rest.

In the movement of the disciples and students around the *gongbei*, it was cleanliness of the body that allowed one to pass from one area to another. As with the *qingzhen* (pure and true) practices amongst those outside the *gongbei*, here cleanliness was vital before one could enter the *Jingjing* ('clean and quiet' yard) and undertake prayer. It was also notable that the two most unclean and 'impure' areas of the *gongbei*—the kitchen and the bathroom facilities—were as far from the *Jingjing* yard as possible, near the entrance gate to the residence yard. These daily grammars of the body, along with the architectural shape of the tomb, the use of incense, and the metaphoric images and didactic inscriptions, all worked towards the enacting of the *gongbei* as a sacred space in which charismatic power could be cultivated.

---

[8] Ma Tong has noted that when '(members of) Da Gongbei slaughter animals, they not only repeat the name of God, but they also sever the spinal cord after the animal ceases to move. They believe that living things have two aspects, a spiritual body and a physical body. *Xing* signifies the spiritual body, which returns to God, while *ming* signifies the physical body, which may be eaten'. In the footnote for this text, Lipman notes that the 'Chinese word *xingming*, meaning "living things," consists of two characters, which these Qadiri Sufis hold to refer to the two different aspects of a living being, the soul and the body' (Lipman 2000, p. 560).

THE 'THREE VEHICLES'

The three abstracted 'vehicles' or 'stages' of the *sancheng* that Ma Yufang described were known specifically as *Licheng*, *Daocheng*, and *Zhencheng*. A disciple in the *gongbei* once explained the concepts to me by way of metaphor: '*Licheng* is like a boat, *Daocheng* is like the sea, *Zhencheng* is like the bright pearl; building a boat is for going into the sea, going into the sea is for seeking the pearl.'[9] Another disciple referred me to the work of the Sino-Muslim scholar Liu Zhi in understanding the deeper meaning of these concepts. In *Tianfang xingli*, Liu Zhi explains that human beings have three bodies—the bodily body (*shenti*), the heart body (*xinti*), and the nature body (*xingti*)—and these correspond to the three levels of cultivation available to every human being through their own personal journey of creative transformation. This is 'the true practice of sage endeavour', as summarised by Sachiko Murata et al. as follows (with correlated terms):

> The body is brought into harmony with the Real One (God or ultimate reality) through the *Shariah* (Propriety) [*Jiaocheng / islam / li*], the heart through the *Tariqah* (the Way) [*Daocheng / iman / dao*], and nature through the *Haqiqah* (the Real) [*Zhencheng / ihsan / zhen*] (Murata et al. 2009, p. 79).

Ma Yufang explained that these were 'not only the principles for cultivating oneself, and bringing about the unity of man and nature, but also a way to temper oneself. It is not a single-handed practice but a consistent cultivation'. Here I want to begin a closer exploration of the practices of *sancheng* with regard to the processes of being *through*, *with*, and *against* the body. Some of the key conceptions in the *sancheng* or three vehicles were explained to me in reference to the ideas of Liu Zhi, the Sino-Muslim scholar. Liu Zhi authored many books, including a biography of the Prophet. Two of his important works—*Tianfang xingli* (Islamic Metaphysics) and *Tianfang dianli* (Norms and Rituals of Islam)—were studied by some of the *chujiaren* who were seen to be more 'advanced'. I will thus make some references to Liu Zhi throughout the discussion.

---

[9] The modes of transmission were also explained in *A Brief History of Guo Gongbei*, in the following manner: '*Licheng* is whispering by mouth, *Daocheng* is whispering by mind, *Zhencheng* is whispering by thought' (Ma 1997, pp. 22–23).

Licheng (Ar. Sharī'ah)

Licheng referred to the practices of wugong and wudian. Wugong is the commitment to the five pillars of Islam (Shahada, prayer, fasting, paying alms, and pilgrimage) and wudian is respecting the 'five cardinal relationships'.[10] The primary aim was to cultivate one's moral character through qingzhen (pure and true) practice or engagement of the body.[11]

Wugong

An older chujiaren that I spoke with about the five pillars described the role of each pillar in the following way: 'prayer (li) is about belonging (as an individual, to Allah, and to a community); religious service (nian) helps you to understand the path of returning to Allah; fasting (zhai) makes you yearn for Allah; paying alms (shishe) enables one to sacrifice oneself for another, and pilgrimage (chao) means to restore oneself (to the source). Here not everyone can visit Mecca. So we say that visiting the tomb is equivalent to this.'

This stage also encompassed the development of a knowledge base of the Arabic and Persian languages, of the Qur'an, the Hadith, and the sayings of Ali. Many of the younger chujiaren (from ages 15–25) were studying this foundational knowledge at Islamic colleges either in Iran or elsewhere in the region. But several who were still based at the gongbei were guided in study by older chujiaren in residence there. In my observations, they would lead daily prayer sessions and also take classes on reciting the Qur'an. Ma

[10] In Arabic, the five pillars are known as the Arkān al-Islām. Liu Zhi uses the word gong in the place of pillar. Frankel has noted the numerous connotations of this word in Chinese thought: 'Its conventional meaning is that of "merit, achievement, efficacy or good result" [...] Among the Confucian elite, it was primarily used to describe civil or moral duties, especially those that increased one's rank and honor. In Buddhism, it refers to the acts of karmic merit that lead to higher rebirth, especially in one of Buddhism's Paradises, and ultimately to the attainment of Nirvana' (Frankel 2011, p. 211).

[11] Frankel has noted that Liu Zhi 'couched the discussion of the Five Pillars in Neo-Confucian cosmological terms' (Frankel 2011, p. 112) and described wugong in Chinese terms of cultivation of the Way: 'The Five Meritorious Works of the Sage's Teaching—Recitation, Worship, Fasting, Alms, and Pilgrimage—showed the people how to cultivate the way and return to their primal state' (Liu 1971, p. 41). Liu Zhi syncretised Neo-Confucian ideals about self-cultivation with Sufi notions concerning the 'annihilation of the ego and subsumption into God' (Frankel 2011, p. 112).

Yunhu was an 18-year-old *chujiaren* of Guo Gongbei, but was currently studying at an Islamic college in Lanzhou. I spoke with him while he was on a break from study and back at the *gongbei* helping Ma Yufang prepare for a celebration. He did not have the capability to read Persian or Arabic beyond repeating the sounds of Qur'anic verses. He had two brothers who were both still in school. His parents were both working. He was a child when his family sent him to the *gongbei* to become a *chujiaren*. He explained: 'I understand that being a *chujiaren* involves many responsibilities and obligations, and I plan to do my utmost. In addition to going to school, I help out with *gongbei* life when necessary and help when something happens at home or in the holidays.' At the Islamic college, he was studying the Arabic language and the history and interpretation of the Qur'an.

Bodily exercise was also important. I was told that *chujiaren* in the *gongbei* practised Five Figures Kungfu (*wu zhi gongfu*) and followed Zhao Changjun, a Hui who teaches a particular style of boxing in Shaanxi. In the past Ma Yufang explained that someone used to come from Shaanxi to teach them, but now they go there by bus, 'We usually do that in the afternoons, but we don't do it in winter because it's too cold. In 2007, we went to Sanya and played there for three weeks. We just do it to exercise our bodies, we mean to play it nicely, not to hurt others'.

In this stage of *Licheng*, the *chujiaren* were demonstrating practices of engagement—of being *through* the body—in order to carry out daily tasks in a very specific manner. These included preparing food and eating in the *gongbei* (which required specific preparatory ritual as described earlier), in their *qingzhen* cleaning rituals, in their bodily exercises of Kungfu, and in their studies of Qur'anic scripture and language. During personal and communal prayer, and during the fasting of Ramadan, they demonstrated low-level practices of restraint—of being *against* the body—against the pangs of hunger and against the desire of the body for movement during long prayer cycles. Prayer also demonstrated low-level rapture—of being *with* the body in connecting with the spiritual realm. These specific relations of ego to the body were the groundwork of charismatic embodiment.

Wudian

Another important dimension to the stage of *Licheng* was the development of the individual's morality through their relationships to others. Liu Zhi described this as the five cardinal relationships of the way of man (*renlun wudian*). He interpreted the primordial human relationship between Adam and Eve in the language of Neo-Confucian metaphysics: 'After Heaven and Earth came into existence, the Myriad Creatures were born. After the Male and the Female came into existence, the human race emerged. Thus, the husband and wife are the primary pairing in the Way of Man' (Liu 1971, p. 107).[12] The *chujiaren* at Guo Gongbei also referred to the concept of *wudian* (Liu 1971, p. 12). Their explanation of what it meant was as follows:

> Compliance with God, compliance with the Prophet, compliance with the parents, compliance with the country and compliance with its governor (*shun zhu, shun sheng, shun qin, shun guojia, jiqi zhizhengzhe*) (Ma 1997, p. 25).

Rather than advocating union between male and female as Liu Zhi had written, they advocated celibacy. Amongst the four Sufi orders in China, there are three main types of succession:

• mentor-disciple succession (*shitu xiangji xing*)
• father-son succession (*fuliao shixi xing*)
• family succession (*jiazu shixi xing* which includes other familial relations such as brothers and cousins)

At present, three of the four Sufi schools adopt the father-son hereditary succession and sometimes follow the wider family succession model depending on suitability and willingness of eligible individuals. The Qadiriyya on the other hand follow the mentor-disciple succession mode. Each *gongbei* selects one master (*dangjiaren*) to host and control the religious affairs of the *gongbei*. Generally he serves his whole lifetime, but this title is not hereditary because the master of *gongbei* must be a *chujiaren* and have no family or offspring. In a 2001 volume about the *Anthropology of Celibacy*, Elisa Sobo and Sandra Bell cite Weber, who describes two basic religious positions that favour celibacy as an instrument of salvation:

---

[12] While the idea of the five cardinal relationships 'comes from Confucian philosophy, Liu Zhi syncretised this notion of Chinese culture and society with social mores and customs found in the Islamic world, in order to demonstrate that Islam and Confucianism shared the same ethical ground' (Frankel 2011, p. 113).

The first is "mystical flight from the world," for which celibacy is a "central and indispensable instrument" (Weber and Runciman 1978, p. 603). The other is asceticism, which represents sex as inimical to "rational, ascetic alertness, self control and the planning of life" because it is conceived to be "ultimately and uniquely unsusceptible to rational organisation" (Weber and Runciman 1978, p. 604). In actuality the two perspectives are often combined and, according to Weber, may operate simultaneously to generate hostility toward sexual conduct and related social intermingling, which, as Mary Douglas (Douglas 1966) demonstrates, can be associated with dangerous pollution (Sobo and Bell 2001, p. 11)

Celibacy in the context of Guo Gongbei demonstrated the practice of being *against* the body and combined both of the perspectives raised by Sobo and Bell. It was seen as an instrument that allowed one to achieve more sophisticated levels of spiritual advancement—and ultimately unity with God—a mystical flight from the world. It was also a form of asceticism that saw sex as the loss of self-control and as opening up of oneself to bodily pollution. The practice of celibacy amongst the Qadiriyya in China was first established by Qi Jingyi. The Chinese researcher Ma Yuxiu argues that the Qadiriyya was divided into two schools after being brought into China— one (led by Qi Jingyi) which cut off social ties in favour of strict discipline and silent meditation and the other which embraced marriage and having children as following the 'order of Allah' (Ma 2008, p. 82).

According to Ma Yuxiu, Qi Jingyi refused marriage throughout his whole life, and this determination was established before he learnt of the Qadiriyya theories from Khoja Abd Allah. Ma argues that rather than this religious affirmation being a result of Buddhist or Daoist influence, the Qadiriyya were focused on the transcendent pursuit of Sufi mystics to go 'beyond everything and pursue truth. Looking at the ascetic and disciplined religious cultivation of the Qadiriyya Sufi order even just from inscriptions/writings, we can see that the development of the *chujiaren* system that suppressed sensual desire was an inevitable result' (Ma 2008, p. 83). *Chujiaren* were not able to get married unless they chose to resume secular life. Once they had resumed secular life, they could not then rejoin the *gongbei*.[13] In the Chinese Qadiriyya text, the *Origins of Islam*, women

---

[13] Many Muslim and non-Muslim scholars believe that the *chujiaren* system of the Qadiriyya in China had been affected in this regard by Buddhism and Daoism—a claim of course that the system of *chujiaren* categorically deny. Further discussion of this can be found in Chap. 7.

are described as one of 'four obstacles' that must be overcome in order to find success in the Qadiriyya 'path':

> The human is made of energy, energy is dependent upon the spirit, so the cultivation of energy maintains the spirit. The introduction stage of the Qadiriyya sect is about maintaining vitality, cultivating the spirit, and exercising the body [...] Entering the sect, you will find that the greatest depth is invisible. The wonderful realm of our sect is so deep that you shall jump over the four obstacles in your way, i.e., wine, women, avarice and pride to save your vitality, energy and spirit [...] That is the way to pass the door into the Qadiriyya sect (Qi 1982, p. 45).

Here women are aligned with wine, material greed, and pride in their power to distract a man's energies. The 'Monastic Rules' of Da Gongbei (established by the third-generation master Qi Ruifeng in 1700s and re-instated in the 1940s) also make reference to prohibited behaviour towards women:

- Drinking wine and gathering to gamble, soliciting flowers and seeking willows [prostitutes] (*yinjiu judu, wen hua xun liu*)
- Feeling pulses and taking on patients, but avoiding women (*zhenmai kanbing, bu bi nu xian*)[14]

Lipman has noted that the second half of regulation number one, 'soliciting flowers and seeking willows', refers to illicit sex (Lipman 2000, pp. 557–558). In regulation number two, implicit reference is made to the medical practitioners amongst the Qadiriyya Sufis, 'who might be tempted to take on female patients, a practice often associated with sexual immorality' (Lipman 2000, p. 557).[15]

Ma Yufang emphasised that a *chujiaren* can always give up and marry—both paths are completely voluntary. He was not at all against marriage

---

[14] Ma Tong notes that 'these regulations unquestionably took on a corrective function in such depressed times (during the third generation when they were written). Later, in the 29th year of the Republic (CE 1940), they were (formally) reaffirmed' (Lipman 2000, pp. 556–557). See Ma Tong's work, as translated by Lipman (2000) for a complete list of Monastic Rules.

[15] Ma Yufang mentioned that in the past there were local healing practices and medicines within the Qadiriyya that were used to help cure certain illnesses, but he did not have this knowledge, and it was not currently practised as it once was in Guo Gongbei.

per se (and he saw women as having the same capabilities as a man in terms of religious cultivation), but for him, it was a necessary sacrifice to not do so: 'You need to sacrifice something if you want to get to a certain level. Just like you, far away from your hometown, New Zealand, came to Lanzhou, you devoted much in order to get what you want. It is true that you will be happy when you are with your parents and family, but you will not get what you want if you stay with them. If we want something, we need to give up something, such as marriage, which is not a mandatory thing. It will not be sincere when people have to do something unwillingly. The reason I gave up marriage is because I want to wholeheartedly achieve the unity of God and man (*wo yixin dadao tianrenheyi*).' Several *chujiaren* described to me that celibacy allowed for the individual to wholeheartedly commune with God (*yixinyiyi xiu gong ban dao, xin xiang zhenzhu*). They were of the opinion that in marriage the heart/spirit (*xinling*) and body would be contaminated (*wuran*). As one *chujiaren* said, 'Physical and mental faculties will become dirty (*angzang*), and morality will be destroyed (*daode ye jiang baihuai*). In the end, without a pure body (*chunjie de shenti*) one will not be able to meet with God after this life'.

The commitment to celibacy was the strongest illustration of restraint— of being *against* the body. A 'clean and pure' body here meant an asexual body—a body with only the desire to commune with Allah through ritualised means. It required the exercising of self-control over sexual desire and was a fundamental aspect of charismatic embodiment unique to this Qadiriyya group.

Daocheng (Ar. Ṭarīqah)

The 'second stage', *Daocheng* (also known as *Zhongdao* or *Tuolegeti*; Ar. *Tariqah*) aimed to reveal and mould an individual's 'inherent dispos-itions'. Ma Yufang explained that the meaning of *Dao* here was different from *Dao* in Daoism, 'What we mean here refers to the path that our saint followed (*shengren de daolu*), and the path we must follow in order to become a saint'. It concerned faith or engagement of the heart and mind. As such, the studying of texts (*nianjing*) on one's own and with others and performing silent meditation (*zuojing*) and *dhikr* (recitation) were stressed as the most important activities in this stage. These activities were the focus of what Ma Yufang called *gongxiu*—'the cultivation of the soul (*gongxiu jiushi linghun de jinxiu)*.[16] In Chinese philosophy, self-cultivation (*zixiu*) is a long-standing civilisational practice in the aspiration of becoming a sage or saint (*sheng*) or an immortal (*xian*). Murata has pointed out the association of the term *xiu* with the body in Confucian philosophy and its correlative in Arabic:

> Cultivation (*xiu*) is the process of nurturing and refining oneself, and especially one's activities, by observing Propriety […] The Great Learning associates it with the body, and Zhu Xi made it the fifth of the eight steps that lead to perfection: 'Those who wished to cultivate their bodies would first make their hearts true.' The word suggests as its Arabic equivalent *tazkiyat al-nafs*, 'the cultivation of the soul,' a phrase derived from Koran 91:6–10 and commonly discussed as the means of achieving perfection (Murata et al. 2009, p. 486).

The correlation made here was that a pure and true (*qingzhen*) body would lead to a pure and true (*qingzhen*) heart and mind, and vice versa. Zhao explained this in reference to an inscription written on the entrance to Qi Jingyi's tomb in Da Gongbei: 'In the four Sufi schools we have the concepts of *xing* and *ming*. The relationship of *xing* (nature) and *ming* (life) is similar to the relationship between the soul (*linghun*) and the body (*quti*). If someone has a clear and pure life (*qing ming*) this indicates that their internal heart is clear and transparent with no distractions, then a miracle will appear in this man's body. Real nature (*zhen xing*) and a pure life (*qing ming*) is an approximate meaning, so we can say the greatest saints (*shensheng*) have the cleanest and purest nature and life (*chunjie de xing he ming*).'[17]

The practice of *gongxiu* or the 'cultivation of the soul' was epitomised in what Ma Yufang described as a 'code of conduct' called the 'eight dimensions' or *bawei*: '*Bawei* is a code of conduct to shape our practice. That is, to eat little, drink little, sleep little, speak little, always clean, always memorise (recite), always fast, and always be quiet' (*shao shi, shao yin, shao*

---

[16] Ma Tong referred to this as *jing xiu*, emphasising the quiet nature of this activity.

[17] Lipman, translating from Ma Tong, has noted that Da Gongbei's theory of self-cultivation is "Use *xing* to the utmost and revive *ming*, cultivate the heart-mind and nourish *xing*. They hold that *xing* is the 'root', in the first position and eternal. *Ming* is the shape or form, holding the second position and mortal. Therefore, that which they pursue in leaving the family and silent austerities is *xing*" (Lipman 2000, pp. 561–562).

shui, shao yan, chang jing, chang nian, chang zhai, chang jing). In the practices of meditation and the all-encompassing self-disciplines of *bawei*, the stage of *Daocheng* required a greater degree of restraint—of being *against* the body—than those demonstrated in *Licheng*. The texts studied in this stage included Liu Zhi's *Tianfang xingli* (Islamic Metaphysics) and *Tianfang dianli* (Norms and Rituals of Islam), the *Letters (Maktubat) of Imam Rabbani (Shaykh Ahmad Faruqi al-Sirhindi)*[18], Abu Hamid al-Ghazali's *Revival of Islamic Sciences*, and Abd ar-Rahman Jami's *al-Lama'at* or Divine Flashes (one of the first of Jami's works to be translated into Chinese by Liu Zhi).[19] Ma explained that on an ordinary day, he would read from one of these texts in his spare time (most of which were in Persian or Arabic).[20] This had to be done during a quiet time. The time itself might vary from person to person, but he himself always read before dinner and read silently (*modu*). If he was with a group, he sometimes read aloud (*chusheng*). He explained that one did not have to be in the worship hall of the *gongbei* necessarily—you could also do it in your own room. If they were reading aloud, he would often lead small groups in the reading or ask an *imam* to do it if he was absent. When one reads the texts (*nianjing*), he explained that one does not have certain body positions 'like when you conduct a service. You can sit down on your knees or lie down, however you feel. There are rules for doing service, but when you are doing *gongxiu* by yourself, the Qur'an says that it doesn't matter whether you are sitting down or standing up'.

Zhao Yufang explained one afternoon that one of the distinctive characteristics of Sufis was their practice of commemorating Allah through the heart and through silent *dhikr* and meditation (Ar. *fikr, zuojing*, lit. to sit in silence). As he said, 'other Islamic groups use words to praise Allah, Sufis

[18] This book covers Sufism and the methodologies, beliefs, and practices of Islam.
[19] Jami (August 18, 1414–November 17, 1492) was a famous Sufi scholar, mystic, writer, historian, and poet.
[20] It is interesting to note that these are Naqshbandi sources being used in a Qadiri context. As noted earlier, when the Qadiriyya was established in China, it did so through the teachings of shaykhs Khoja Afaq—a recognised Naqshbandi—and Khoja Abd Allah, who according to Chinese sources was a Qadiri (Wang 2001, p. 34). It has been conjectured that Abd Allah could have studied in Medina under the renowned Kurdish mystic, Ibrahim b. Hasan al-Kurani (1616–1690), who was initiated into both the Naqshbandi and Qadiri tariqas, as well as several other Sufi orders (Gladney 1999, p. 118). It is logical then that historically and still today, sources such as Sirhindi and Jami are used amongst Sufi and non-Sufi factions in China with no apparent conflict—at least as far as the author is aware.

use the heart'. Bakhtiar has argued that in Sufism, meditation (Ar. *fikr*) is the passive counterpart of active invocation (*dhikr* or *zikr*). She explained the process as follows:

> The human form cannot cease to think, but it can transcend thought [...] However, one cannot transcend thought through an act of will; and there is no meditation possible without an invocation, a Name of God, given through a spiritual master who carries the chain of transmission. This brings the Divine Presence into the sound [...] The word *zikr*, invocation, has really three meanings: to mention, to invoke, to remember. When we mention God, we invoke His Name; when we invoke His Name, we remember Him. The symbolism of this is a mystery. God is present in His Names because of His love for us (Bakhtiar 1976, p. 11).

For the Qadiriyya, this invocation was completely silent. Meditation and *dhikr* sometimes occurred around two hours after the last evening prayer (around 11:30 pm) and sometimes in the early morning before the first morning prayer (around 3 am). This night meditation and *dhikr* was not performed every day, and for the most part I was not able to stay in the grounds of the *gongbei* at such hours to see the entire activity from start to finish. My understanding of *dhikr* practice is thus based on limited observations, information from Ma Yufang, my own questions, and an account from Professor L. who had lived in the *gongbei* for a three-day period (and could stay overnight in the compound). 'During this time', Ma explained, 'we read by heart (*xin nian*). This is different from conducting a service (*zuo libai*) such as the weekly Friday *Zhuma* sermon or a particular commemorative event. Generally it does not have a certain time, you just need a quiet time to do it, and generally nights are usually very quiet, usually between 1 and 6 am. We usually sleep in daytime. If you have other work during the day, then you can't conduct it at night. There are some people who manage to work during the daytime, and they also do *gongxiu* at night-time, and they sleep only two hours a day in order to do it'. As well as little sleep, it also required the minimal consumption of food and drink. During a 24-hour period that I witnessed of meditation and prayer, they ate only once in the evening, and it was a rationed amount of food of three dates, a small cup of rice and one to two cups of water. I was told that sometimes during this time they would also sleep while sitting. In general, they performed greater ablutions (Ch. *da jing*, Ar. *ghusl*) at least once a day.

During this silent *dhikr* the *dangjiaren* and *chujiaren* would perform two rak'ahs, speaking quietly to themselves.[21] This was followed by a *dhikr* recitation. This usually lasted two to three hours. After lighting some incense outside, the *dangjiaren* and *chujiaren* would remove their shoes and enter the *Baoxia* (worship hall), closing the door behind them. They would kneel (*guibai*—not cross-legged or in the lotus position) and sit upright with their hands on their knees. Their eyes would then close. They would perform an inner recitation of the *dhikr* in complete silence and stillness and 'perceive through meditation' (*canwu*).[22] When I asked several of the *chujiaren* at a later point what they recited in silence, I was told 'we mainly repeat the Shahada (Ch. *qingzhenyan*) in Arabic (Ar. *Lā ilāha illā Allāh, Muhammadun rasūlu 'Llāh*; Ch. *qingzhenyan: Liang yilaha yinliang anla, Muhanmode laisulinliang*; Eng. There is no God but Allah and Muhammad is his Prophet)'. This would be followed by three prayers as below in Arabic:

- *zan zhu qingjing*/赞主清净—*Subḥān Allāh*—Glorious is God/Glory be to Allah
- *wan zan gui zhu*/ 万 赞 归 主—*Al-ḥamdu lillāh*—Praise be to God/Allah
- *zhenzhu zhi da*/真主至大—*Allahu akbar*—God/Allah is the Greatest.

As with all language, these invocations, these words, whether silent or voiced, were rooted in the body. Saniotis has elegantly described that 'words move within and outside the body in sacred speech, touching and penetrating both the body's fleshy recesses and the "sentient landscape". Words are always imprinted in sound, which are themselves rooted in the body's inner domain. Even in the practice of *fikr*, the sound of silent words is dependent on and attuned to the rhythmic resonances of breathing and

---

[21] A *rak'ah* is literally 'a bowing', from the verb *raka'a* meaning 'to bow'. It refers to one complete cycle of sacred words and gestures during the ritual prayer (*salah*) and includes standing, bowing, prostration, and sitting. Each prayer is made up of several such cycles.

[22] Professor L. told me that he once participated in a *dhikr* ceremony at a different Qadiriyya site in Guanghe county (within the wider Linxia region), where there was a lot of quick movement which he found hard to keep up with: 'When they read "no god" they turned their heads right, and when they read "only Allah" they turned their heads left, and the louder they became, the faster the sound, and the faster the head action. I tried to follow them, but pretty soon I felt dizzy and had to give up.'

the diastolic and systolic pulsations' (Saniotis 2008, p. 23). Zhao explained that while repeating phrases in the mind, the breathing time between inhalation and exhalation had to be long and slow, coming from the diaphragm. In the recitation of the Shahada, they inhaled when reciting the syllable *hai* and exhaled on the *hu*. They would recite each phrase several hundred times. During inhalation, focus was placed on slow and deep breathing from the diaphragm (*dantian*)—the point two inches below the navel where one's *qi* (vital energy) resides. The purpose of this long and slow exhalation and inhalation was to allow enough time and space between invocations so that one could breathe the 'breath of God'. As Liu Zhi explained, 'in a breath that leaves and enters the one who is annihilated, everything from the first to the last of the cosmos is unveiled to him' (Murata et al. 2009, p. 150).[23]

The Prophet Muhammad has been recorded as saying: 'There is in the body a lump of flesh. When it is wholesome, the whole body is wholesome, and when it is corrupt, the whole body is corrupt. Indeed, it is the heart' (Murata and Chittick 2000, p. 38). The purpose of *dhikr* ritual is to make the heart 'wholesome' (*salih*). The heart is 'where people grow intellectually and spiritually, and the Koran says that the human predicament arises because of the heart's illness (*marad*) and rust (*rayn*)' (Murata et al. 2009, pp. 56–57). The image of the rusty heart is a universal image in the Sufi tradition and is well known in China, as Murata notes: 'mirrors used to be made of iron. The original substance of the human heart is like a shiny mirror, reflecting the light and wisdom of God. In the ordinary human state, however, it is rusty with ignorance and forgetfulness, and it needs to be polished. In Islamic terms, polishing the heart is accomplished by remembering (*dhikr*) God' (Murata et al. 2009, pp. 56–57). The Chinese Daoist philosopher Zhuangzi also once said that 'the heart of the Utmost Human functions like a mirror, going after nothing, responding to nothing' (Murata et al. 2009, pp. 56–57). For both the Islamic and Chinese tradition then, the 'heart' is the spiritual organ that is 'specific to the highest possibilities of human nature, especially

---

[23] Liu Zhi's use of the term *xi* (breath) is, according to Murata, a 'literal translation of the Arabic Nafs (breath), which also means moment or instant. [...] The one breath in which the gnostic's vision opens up to the Real is nothing other than the Breath of the All-merciful' (Murata et al. 2009, p. 562).

the understanding of things as they truly are' (Murata and Chittick 2000, p. 38).[24]

The practices during *daocheng* required to varying degrees both restraint and rapture—of being *against* the body in order to experience a state of being *in* the body. Restraint was required in order to commit to the conducts of *bawei* and during intense meditation sessions. These practices in turn led to a state of rapture during meditation, in which a focus on breathing and the heart sought to bring the individual into closer union and communion with God. This use of the entire human body, mind, heart, and navel as an embodied unity in meditation is similar to other traditions. Michael Saso has described that in the meditative process of Daoist and Tantric Buddhist practice, the mind meditates on the

'sacred image, the mouth is used to chant sacred phrases that make the image one with the meditator, and the body is used to seal the union through physical dance steps or hand dance [...] These three locations in the Daoist and the Tantric Buddhist body are focus points for a kind of prayer that visualises the human body and the outer cosmos to be related, that is, to be analogously one in their meditative and orderly physical cycle of activity (Saso 2000, p. 231).

Zhencheng (Ar. Ḥaqīqah)

The highest levels of rapture however, of being *with* the body—in which the ego is 'so intimately suffused with the body that it temporarily loses self-consciousness'—occurred in what they called or the reality, God Himself.

---

[24] I did not note this in my own time in Guo Gongbei, nor was it mentioned to me, but in Da Gongbei, Wang (2009) noted that sometimes during gongxiu, the disciples there would chant 'wordless real classics' (*wu zi zhenjing*) which were the tablets and songs of generations of ancestors. These included the 'Song of Scriptures' (*zhenjing ge*), the 'Song of Cultivation' (*xiudao ge*), the 'Moon Song at the Five Watches of Night' (*wugeng yue ge*), the 'Song of the Bottomless Boat' (*wudi ban ge*), the 'Song of Samadhi Fire' (*san mei zhen huo ge*), and the 'Song of the Rootless Tree' (*wu gen shu ge*). Wang Huizhen explained that the thinking behind this was that 'though each of the three religions and nine schools of thought has a great number of scriptures of their own, none of them is truth, for all of them are written words in paper, they are oral chanting (*kou nian she zan*) so their accuracy cannot be vouched for. Only the No-word Scriptures, which cannot be written down in words, can win the favour of Allah' (Wang 2009, p. 24). According to Ma Tong, these scriptures were not introduced by Qi Jingyi, but by the sixth-generation teacher Ma Daojin and the seventh-generation teacher Qi Daohe (see Wan 2007, pp. 595–597).

Ma Yufang explained that this stage was 'invisible', that is, it could not be easily measured and was very individual. To reach this stage he explained that 'you begin by following steps, the first of which you can find in a book (*wugong* as described in Qur'an and Hadith). First thing is that you finish all of the five requirements, and reach a state of quietness and forget everything. At that time you won't feel anything—no sadness nor joy, just peace'. I asked him what happened then in times of emotional stress, such as the passing away of parents—did he feel nothing? Ma Yufang replied:

> No, that is not possible. It does not mean that your relationships with parents or relatives will be cut off after achieving the state. Just like if you study English for a long time, you will not get used to Chinese then. You can see an example in the story of Abraham, which was largely documented in the Qur'an. He was a saint and the King wouldn't let him go, but he insisted in his thoughts. Then the King sent his people to throw Abraham into the fire. People expected that he would be burnt to death in the fire, but Abraham, while in the fire, viewed himself in a lively garden. Normal people could achieve this level, but generally do not have this sort of strength.

Ma Yufang was referring here to an extreme state of being *with* the body, to the point where physical sensations were no longer felt. Schimmel has written of similar events in the history of religions, and particularly in Sufism, in which 'the pious ones become so transported in his prayers or meditation that he feels no pain when one of his limbs is amputated, or he is so out of himself that he is oblivious to the bites of scorpions or serpents' (Schimmel 2011, p. 209). I asked him how this strength was measured, and he explained that it could not be described by language. I continued, asking 'then how do you know if a person has a high or low level [of cultivation]?' He replied that it depended on one's thinking and asked me 'why should we measure it? Can you deny the existence of what you see? Can you know what you were doing while you were still unborn?'[25] This stage of *Zhencheng* was the highest orthodoxy on the Sufi path, what Murata and William Chittick have described as 'perfection, or transformation of the soul and reintegration into the One' (Murata

---

[25] Abu'l Adyan in the tenth century claimed that he could 'walk through a fire without being hurt, since fire has the capacity to burn only by God's permission. [...] In the same way, the Aissawiyya dervishes in North Africa dance with burning coals in their hands without feeling any pain' (Schimmel 2011, p. 209).

et al. 2009, p. 9). Outside of these formalised three stages, was *Chaocheng* (Ar. *Ma'rifah*), a term which referred to the 'annihilation of the ego,' where man and nature reached a state of complete integration. It has also been described as 'harnessing the beyond', which is to watch over or take care of one's spiritual heart, to acquire knowledge about it, and to finally become attuned to the Divine Presence.

MIRACLES AS PROOF OF THE EMBODIMENT OF CHARISMA

These three stages encompassed varying degrees of *engagement, restraint,* and *rapture* in regard to the relation between the ego and the body, and each were integral to the embodiment of charismatic power. The formal recognition of progression through these stages had to be given by the *dangjiaren* and was understood as 'divine permission' *kouchuan xinshou* in Chinese or *suhbat* in Persian). In the context of a Naqshbandi genealogy in India, Arthur Buehler describes *suhbat* as 'an intimate spiritual communication between human hearts. From a Naqshbandi point of view at least, the heart is the proper receptacle or medium for religious knowledge. Only when it is linked with the companionship (*suhbat*) of a spiritual mentor can this knowledge be transformed into a religious wisdom inherited from the prophets' (Buehler 1998, p. 85).

Zhao explained to me that 'the disciples explain in their hearts, which is the reason it is called *kouchuan xinshou* ("transmitted orally, received in the heart"). The master teaches the disciple and they accept by heart, and no others can know about it. Other religions are different because they do it by giving classes. If you are clever enough and the master said that you could take it, then you could. There are many secrets in language and you can understand it if you have a good comprehension. The actions of breathing—of inhalation and exhalation—are very important in this process too. Ordinary *menhuan* (Sufi orders) don't explain it and can't explain it, because in the Qur'an it is not explained. Ordinary people can't understand it because it requires a certain education level'. Ma Yufang explained that this knowledge of the heart can only be passed on to a 'student if you believe he will understand it. In talking face to face and keeping this confidential, if the other side is not willing to do it, you will be in danger after you have told him. It can only be passed to those who are ready'. There was a great deal of secrecy around the details of this recognition process, even amongst students who interacted with the *dangjiaren* on a daily basis. Several younger students at the *gongbei* thought that this happened during the night meditation (between 1 and 6 am), and they would describe it to me as the time when the master 'passed on secret information' to a disciple.

The level of embodied knowledge required for this form of recognition was not perceived to be attainable by every *chujiaren*. This is similar to what Cornell found in Moroccan Sufism. For Moroccan saints, 'although paranormal knowledge was a gift from God, making the most of it depended on an advanced spiritual training that was available only to a limited number of adepts' (Cornell 1998, p. 119). Zhao Yufang explained that while there were many practicing *chujiaren* (*xiudao de ren*—people cultivating the 'Dao' or in this context the path of the Saint as Ma Yufang explained earlier), there were very few people who had achieved '*chujiarenhood*' (*dedao de ren*). As he said, 'There are many *chujiaren*, but not many of them become saints (*chengsheng de ren*)'. The way in which most people *knew* that someone had become a saint was due to the performance of miracles. 'When *chujiaren* pass away', Zhao explained, 'they are buried in the same place as the saints, but you know someone is a saint because they have special skills and capabilities (*teyi gongneng*) in performing miracles.'

The performance of miracles was the most explicit indication that saints embodied *baraka*, divinely conferred charisma, or *zhanguang*. While bodily discipline has been emphasised in the cultivation of this charisma, two views existed about the nature of this power and how it could be transferred. Zhao Yufang described *baraka* (*bailaketi*) as an 'auspicious atmosphere (*jiqing* or *qifen*)' that could be 'passed through contact. After reaching a certain religious status and performing worship, people will feel that this person has *baraka* (*you bailaketi*). Normally, people with *baraka* will not reveal it, it only shows up as a last resort, when absolutely essential'. He also stressed the secrecy involved in the management of this power: 'After you reach this level, it's unlikely that you will tell anyone, so others will not be able to know.' Ma Yufang understood that many people tended to think of *baraka* as something that could be passed on through touch (in this context often referred to as *jixiang* meaning lucky or auspicious). He initially joked that sometimes religious adherents had asked if they could buy his car, because they thought that it possessed *baraka* and through ownership they too could 'possess it'. But for him, *baraka* was not something that could be transferred in such a way.

Ma: *Baraka* indicates a high level of intellectual and emotional knowledge. Me: Is this like the wisdom of the *chujiaren*, people feel that there is some holy spirit (*hua lingqi*) around him and that it can be passed to you if you make contact with them? Ma: Yes, but we call this spirit (*lingqi*)—*zhanguang* or *jixiang*. It was from Allah and passed from the saint. It's not an object, but a concept (*gainian de dongxi*). Me: For example, masters in Mosques or *dangjiaren* of *gongbei*—will other people find that good things will happen to them if they make contact with these people? Ma: Yes, they have a saying like that. But I would say that [that process] is more a way to show a certain intimacy with someone (*huxiang qinjin de baoxian*). I don't think you can pass this on by simply touching people or coming into contact with people. Perhaps if someone spent a significant amount of time trying to understand they may come to know, but most people will never meet with it (*bujian de*).

For him, *baraka* was a quality that was the result of embodied knowledge and constant cultivation and not an object that could be passed around merely through touch.

POTENTIAL CHARISMA AND FORMAL RECOGNITION

In order for a new *dangjiaren* to be 'certified' as a 'wali' (a 'saint'), he must demonstrate that he has followed the 'three doctrines' (given up sexual desire, given up desire for wealth, and given up selfish interests) and that he has followed the 'five principles' (study diligently, beg for food, practise diligently, offer incense in the morning, and take a bath frequently) (Ma 2008, p. 19). He must also have been confirmed by public selection and the giving of 'divine permission' (*gei kouhuan*, Ar. *idhn*) of the former 'master' (Wang 2009, p. 24). In becoming the *dangjiaren* of Guo Gongbei, Ma Yufang had been given formal recognition ('divine permission') from the former *dangjiaren* Ma Shiming, within which he had received the 'knowledge of the heart' (*kouchuan xinshou*). In other Sufi contexts this divine permission would in itself indicate the passing on of a blessing, of *baraka*, and—in turn—miraculous powers. But here *baraka* was not something that could be 'passed on'—it was a power cultivated over time within an individual, through the *gongxiu* practices that demanded bodily *engagement*, *restraint*, and *rapture*. Thus, at the time of election, the *dangjiaren* did not necessarily require evidence of miraculous capabilities, rather he required the perceived potential for them, as Ma Yuxiu identified, he must be 'capable of miracles' (Ma 2008, p. 19).

He must also continue to practise cultivation himself (Ma 2008, p. 19).[26] Ma Yufang was perceived to have a certain potential for, and had received the knowledge necessary for, the cultivation of *zhanguang*— and now he was learning, through practice and gradual embodiment, to become someone who was able to provide people with real benefit, blessing, and luck. He sought to do this genuinely—unlike a number of *ahong* or *imam* who, as Zhao Yufang commented, were 'believed to have *baraka*, but do not have a high enough level, it's just the opinion of certain people'. For Ma Yufang and others within the tradition, miracles would be the most explicit proof of his power, but it would be up to him as to whether or not he would share it with others.

Ma Yufang became the *dangjiaren* of Guo Gongbei in 1998 after the passing of Ma Shiming in late 1997. While the giving of divine permission (*kouchuan xinshou*) was a private event, the formal election of a new leader or *dangjiaren* was public. Ma Yufang explained that when he became the *dangjiaren*, there was a formal public ceremony called a *chuanyi*, meaning 'ordination' or sometimes called 'donning the cloak': 'During the ceremony, all of the congregations came here, and we had a traditional ceremony in which I was acknowledged by the public to become the leader of the *gongbei*.' I was told that activities during the dressing ceremony were basically the same as other dressing ceremonies of *imams* in other sects— there were no special classics or artefacts. The ceremony was held on a Friday (*libaiwu*), as is common for Chinese Muslim religious activities. The newly elected *dangjiaren* would wear a new head scarf and long white robes. The ceremony would begin with an announcement by a *chujiaren* from within the *gongbei* that they have chosen to elect a certain *chujiaren* to be the representative for that generation of the family (*di dai dangjiaren*). Then words of worship are spoken (*zan zu zan sheng*), followed by 'Ermaili' (Ar. *'amala*). In this case, it was a donation made to the founder or chief of the order. After this, there would be a reading of a chapter from the Qur'an, then the *dangjiaren*, *chujiaren*, *ahong*, and *manla* (students) would all participate in a reading of the Qur'an. This would be followed by prepared snacks and tea, and the ceremony would finish.

---

[26] Professor L. mentioned that in some areas *gongbei* religious adherents were not allowed to participate in the election, only a *chujiaren* had the right to vote and to stand for election.

In the Chinese Sufi context of Guo Gongbei, charismatic power was translated most commonly as *zhanguang* (to bask in the light or to benefit from association with somebody or something) and sometimes as *jixiang* (lucky and auspicious). While there were adherents and *chujiaren* who spoke of it as being a quality that could be procured simply by 'touching' objects or people thought to possess it, Ma Yufang stressed that this was not the case; it was a quality that must be cultivated, and therefore, not many people would ever really 'meet with it'. In order to cultivate this power, Ma Yufang emphasised development of the individual along a three stage path (*sancheng*), each necessary for the development of the next. Within this was a foundational set of bodily practices that were seen as being *qingzhen*. These included adherence to the five pillars of Islam, physical cleanliness, the correct preparation of food, and sexual abstinence. An important part of this stage was also developing a sound knowledge of the Qur'an and Hadith and learning the languages of Islam (Arabic and in this context Persian as well). In the second stage they emphasised eight codes of conduct (*bawei*) and *gongxiu* (which included the study of texts, silent *dhikr*, and meditation). Achieving mastery over these practices enabled one to be given 'permission' to attain a certain religious stature— *gei kouhuan*—('to exchange/give by way of mouth/speech') and to be let in on the 'secret' and 'protected' knowledge passed only through word of mouth and only to be received by those who were deemed 'ready'— *kouchuan xinshou*—('receive oral tradition through/by way of the heart').

The practices associated with each 'stage' were of course intermingled with what at first glance seemed like the rather 'mundane' activities of daily life—cooking, cleaning, shopping, repairing, making arrangements, decorating. But these activities were of course also implicated in the overall goals being played out, and the body was the primary site of it all. To prepare food, and wash one's clothes, to participate in the daily maintenance of the tomb site itself, was to be *through* the body in maintaining an established environment and modes of practice in the realms of food and cleanliness that set the foundations for charismatic cultivation. More rigorous modes of cultivation (such as celibacy, fasting, committing to the 'eight dimensions' (*bawei*) and to the silence and stillness involved in meditation) required the exercise of restraint *against* the sensuality of the body. In meditation, the desired outcome was an 'overcoming' of the body's limited perceptions, an overcoming of the individual ego, the achievement of really being *with* the body—what Kugle would have described as a kind of rapture. These modes of being *through, against*, and *in* the body were fundamental to the procurement of the spiritual gift of *baraka*, or *zhanguang*—the most powerful evidence of which was miracle-making, the kind that the Chinese Qadiriyya saints had demonstrated in the past. This was a possibility for all those who genuinely chose this path, but not a guarantee or probable eventuality for most. Charismatic power was thus rooted in the body. It was a bodily capability, a physical manifestation of the 'spiritually realised' person (Lizzio 2007, p. 33)—most evidenced in the performance of miracles. It was acknowledged by others in the form of their expectations—they may not have necessarily 'seen' evidence of this charismatic power, but they nonetheless had 'expectations' of it from that particular individual or, to borrow from Feuchtwang and Wang Mingming, 'expectations of the extraordinary', a theme that will be explored more in the following chapter.

REFERENCES

Ames, R., and D. Hall. 2003. *Dao De Jing: A Philosophical Translation*. New York: The Ballantine Publishing Group.

Bakhtiar, L. 1976. *Sufi: Expressions of the Mystic Quest*. London: Thames and Hudson.

Basso, K. 1996. *Wisdom Sits in Places: Landscape and Language Among the Western Apache*. Albuquerque: UNM Press.

Bourdieu, P. 1996. *Physical Space, Social Space and Habitus*. http://www.sv. uio.no/iss/forskning/aktuelt/arrangementer/aubert/tidligere/dokumenter/ aubert1995.pdf.

Buehler, A. 1998. *Sufi Heirs of the Prophet: The Indian Naqshbandiyya and the Rise of the Mediating Sufi Shaykh*. Columbia: University of South Carolina.

Cornell, V.J. 1998. *Realm of the Saint: Power and Authority in Moroccan Sufism*. Austin: University of Texas Press.

Douglas, M. 1966. *Purity and Danger: An Analysis of the Concepts of Pollution and Taboo*. London: Routledge.

Frankel, J.D. 2011. *Rectifying God's Name: Liu Zhi's Confucian Translation of Monotheism and Islamic Law*. Honolulu: University of Hawai'i Press.

Gladney, D.C. 1999. The Salafiyya Movement in Northwest China: Islamic Fundamentalism Among the Muslim Chinese? In *Muslim Diversity: Local Islam in Global Contexts*, ed. L.O. Manger. Surrey: Nordic Institute of Asian Studies.

Holloway, J. 2003. Make-Believe: Spiritual Practice, Embodiment, and Sacred Space. *Environment and Planning A* 35 (11): 1961–1974.

Komjathy, L. 2007. *Cultivating Perfection: Mysticism and Self-transformation in Early Quanzhen Daoism*. Leiden: Brill.

Kugle, S. 2012. *Sufis and Saints Mysticism, Corporeality, and Sacred Power in Islam*. Chapel Hill: University of North Carolina Press.

Lipman, J. 2000. MA TONG, A Brief History of the Qadiriyya in China (translated from the Chinese and introduced by Jonathan LIPMAN). *Journal of the History of Sufism* 1–2: 547–576 [Zarcone, T. and Buehler, A., editors. Simurg Press]

Liu, Z. 1971. *Tianfang Dianli (Norms and Rituals of Islam).* Reprint, Hong Kong: Hong Kong Muslim Propagation Society.

Lizzio, K. 2007. Ritual and Charisma in Naqshbandi Sufi Mysticism. *Anpere E-Journal for the Anthropological Study of Religion,* 1–37 http://www.anpere. net/2007/3.pdf.

Ma, Y. 1997. *Linxia Guo Gongbei Jianshi (A Brief History of Guo Gongbei).* Guo Gongbei Committee.

Ma, Y. 2008. Gadelinye Menhuan Chujiaren Zhidu Tanxi (A Discussion of the Monk System of the Qadiriyya Menhuan). *Journal of the Second Northwest University for Nationalities, Department of Philosophy and Religious Studies, Central University for Nationalities, Beijing, China,* 1.

Murata, S., and W.C. Chittick. 2000. *Chinese Gleams of Sufi Light: Wang Tai-yu's Great Learning of the Pure and Real and Liu Chih's Displaying the Concealment of the Real Realm.* Albany: State University of New York Press.

Murata, S., W.C. Chittick, and W. Tu. 2009. *The Sage Learning of Liu Zhi: Islamic Thought in Confucian Terms.* Cambridge: Harvard University Asia Center for the Harvard-Yenching Institute.

Pregadio, F. 2013. *The Encyclopedia of Taoism: 2-Volume Set.* London: Routledge.

Qi, D. 1982. *Qingzhen Genyuan (Origins of Islam).* Unknown.

Saniotis, A. 2008. Enchanted Landscapes: Sensuous Awareness as Mystical Practice Among Sufis in North India. *Australian Journal of Anthropology* 19 (1): 17–26.

Saso, M. 2000. The Taoist Body and Cosmic Prayer. In *Religion and the Body,* ed. S. Coakley. Cambridge: Cambridge University Press.

Schimmel, A. 2011. *Mystical Dimensions of Islam.* Chapel Hill: University of North Carolina Press.

Sobo, E.J., and S. Bell. 2001. *Celibacy, Culture, and Society: The Anthropology of Sexual Abstinence.* Madison: University of Wisconsin Press.

Sutton, D. 2007. *Islamic Design: A Genius for Geometry.* New York: Walker and Company.

Wan, Y. 2007. *Chinese Encyclopedia of Islam.* Chengdu: Sichuan Publishers.

Wang, J. 2001. *Glossary of Chinese Islamic Terms.* Richmond: Curzon Press.

Wang, H. 2009. *Linxia Da Gongbei Menhuan xingcheng yu zuzhi yunxing moshi yanjiu (Organization and Formation of Da Gongbei Menhuan in Linxia).* Masters, Northwest Minorities University. http://www.cnki. net/KCMS/detail/detail.aspx?QueryID=0&CurRec=19&recid=&filename= LXSK198806009&dbname=CJFD7993&dbcode=CJFQ.

Weber, M., and W. Runciman. 1978. *Max Weber: Selections in Translation.* Cambridge: Cambridge University Press.

CHAPTER 4

Charisma and Emulation

Shan Xiaohui was a native of Linxia and a religious adherent (*jiaomin*) of Guo Gongbei. Since he had been a little boy, his parents had taken him to the *gongbei* site to pray every Friday. He was now 23 and worked for a phone company in downtown Linxia. He was very committed to going to the *gongbei* any time he could manage it and would often relay to me his sheer admiration for the *chujiaren* in the *gongbei*: 'They (the *chujiaren*), have the highest spiritual grade (*shengren de pinji*), compared to other Sufi networks in this region. They know Persian and Arabic, which most people do not know. They are so committed to Islam and their knowledge is very profound (*shenhou*).' One afternoon I was walking with Shan in Hongyuan Square in front of Guo Gongbei. He pointed out a sign displayed near one of the entrance-ways. It displayed the expected code of conduct in the area surrounding the *gongbei*: 'In front of the entrance to the shrine, it is strictly prohibited to smoke, consume alcohol, play chess, play card games, go to the toilet, or make a loud disturbance. The shrine is a place to cultivate purity and cleanliness of the body, please keep away from this area, thank you for your co-operation.' This was a most explicit reinforcement of the exemplary model of charisma that Shan Xiaohui so often described.

Vincent Goossaert has noted that in their study of charisma in the Chinese context, Feuchtwang and Wang Mingming define charisma as an 'expectation of the extraordinary' and stress that charisma is a 'relationship mutually constructed by leaders and religious adherents rather than an innate set of powers possessed by an awe-inspiring leader' (Goossaert

© The Author(s) 2018
T. Cone, *Cultivating Charismatic Power*,
https://doi.org/10.1007/978-3-319-74763-7_4

2008, p. 5). Here, Goossaert observes, 'Achievement of charisma—the embodiment of the qualities of leadership, the attraction of religious adherents, the representation of their interests and dreams in real or utopian projects—requires constant attention to the shifting terrain of real and symbolic domains of political and moral authority' (Goossaert 2008, p. 5). This shifting terrain between real and symbolic domains echoes an important observation made by Bakken in his study on models, modelling, and the exemplary in Chinese society (mentioned in Chap. 2)—that the stories, or texts of the exemplary, 'vacillate between myth and biography' (Bakken 2000, p. 136). They are mixtures of historical imaginary and historical 'fact'—the exemplary is a 'recounted person' (Bakken 2000, p. 136). One could say the same of the living exemplar, that is, he exists as a model through reputation, a reputation that results from a mix of 'imagined' qualities and 'real' facts.

In this chapter, I focus on this relational element of charismatic power—arguing that charisma is further strengthened and reinforced through the emulation of various practices of the charismatic exemplar by his students and religious adherents. The identification of individuals with a teacher or master and the desire to emulate him/her, calls to mind Bourdieu and Passeron's notion of 'implicit pedagogy' (Bourdieu and Passeron 1990). This refers to a 'mode of inculcation producing a habitus by the unconscious inculcation of principles which manifest themselves only in their practical state, within the practice that is imposed' (Bourdieu and Passeron 1990, p. 47). It is a process that occurs 'without explicit pedagogical intervention' and 'unfolds in people's own daily social practices (in the family, at school, etc.) over a long span of time, being so persistent (repeated) that people come to accept it as natural [...]' (Vicini 2013, p. 391). While Bourdieu has been criticised for emphasising the unconscious over the conscious in this process, Vicini has suggested that we think of these terms as 'two ideal moments, never fully realised but continuously alternating within the learning process' (Vicini 2013, p. 393). For the students, this learning process was embodied in the daily disciplines within the *gongbei* itself—in close proximity with the leader and disciples. For the religious adherents, it was embodied in daily disciplines within the family home, in interactions with *gongbei* leaders, and in visits to the *gongbei* sites.

Notably, these daily practices of emulation, for both students and religious adherents (male and female), were often inspired by ideas of a miraculous past and expectations of a miraculous future. As I stressed earlier, charisma in Sufism is always dependent on some sense of routine and institutionalisation. Although the students and adherents here were not seeking to achieve the same level of spiritual sophistication as the leader or *chujiaren* (and thus to have the capability to perform miracles), they understood that the daily routines and disciplines encouraged by the disciples were the 'groundwork' for the development of their own religious cultivation and/or authority (Feuchtwang and Wang 2001, p. 17).[1] In this chapter I will explore the daily disciplines being emulated by students and adherents, with reference throughout to the inspirations for participating in these disciplines.

DAILY DISCIPLINES AND INSPIRATIONS FOR STUDENTS

There were 17 *chujiaren* at the *gongbei*, some of whom lived in residence there and others who were studying and living outside. As well as the *chujiaren*, there were a number of students who had previously studied at the *gongbei* who were now studying at the Islamic College in Lanzhou or overseas. About two years ago, two of these former students had been asked by Ma Yufang to return to the *gongbei* to help teach a class of students who were now in residence there.

This class of students included 15 boys and three girls between the ages of 18 and 25. Seventeen of these students were of Hui ethnicity, and one was of Dongxiang ethnicity (another Muslim minority in the region). The students and their two teachers initially lived in a building rented out by the *gongbei*. This was located directly opposite to the *gongbei*, on the other side of the town square. During fieldwork, this building was torn down to make way for new developments, and subsequently the students were housed and taught at the *gongbei* in a small classroom space. Students were paying 2000 CNY per year to live and study at the *gongbei*. This covered classes, food, and accommodation. Their classes focused mainly on Persian language, but also included Qur'anic recitation in Arabic.

---

[1] Buehler noted in the context of a Naqshbandi Sufi lineage in India that 'since there are varying degrees of connected-ness to the Prophet, even non-Sufis can receive some divine energy (*fayd*), but without a shaykh there is seldom enough divine grace to make spiritual progress' (Buehler 1998, p. 83).

A standard week for students in the *gongbei* involved six days of classes. These days were interspersed with prayer, meals, and free time. The older *chujiaren* who were living at the *gongbei* did not participate in the language classes and tended to spend much more time in private study and worship. A student of the *gongbei*, Ma Xiaolong, observed:

> The *chujiaren* sleep a very short time, in the evenings they do *gongxiu* (further acts of cultivation such as textual study, meditation and night prayer) and sometimes they will sleep during the day, standing. They rarely speak with outsiders, because they want to maintain their own image, and protect their purity. They study different texts to us, but the master does not teach us, so we don't know. The *chujiaren* are very diligent. Most of their time is devoted to worship. Apart to day-to-day affairs, they are performing *gongxiu*. Usually they will also go to the home of religious adherents for recitation, usually they are very busy.

Students and several of the younger *chujiaren* in the *gongbei* began every morning at around 6 am. At this time, they would wake to perform morning ablutions in the shared bathroom near the front gate. This involved a brief washing of the hands, face, and feet and served to prepare them ritually for the morning prayer. At around 6.30 am they would make their way to the worship hall connected to the main tomb (the *baoxia*). Removing their shoes at the door, they would enter and kneel down on the carpeted floor. Following the lead of an older *chujiaren*, they would perform the morning prayer (*chenli*). After this they would gather in the main meeting room to warm up around the coal fired stove and to share noodles, tea, and breads.

At 8 am the students would meet with their other classmates in the upstairs classroom, preparing their texts ready for the first class. From 8 am until 10 am, a teacher would lead the first Persian language class of the day. They worked from a Persian language textbook, repeating phrases and words back to the teacher who also checked their reading comprehension. From 10 am until 11 am they had a Persian conversation class. From 11 am until 12 pm, the second teacher would arrive and lead them for an hour in recitation of the Qur'an in Arabic. At 12 pm they paused for lunch and washed their dishes ready to be served a meal of dried lamb and bread. Around 1.20 pm, most of the students would again perform smaller ablutions and then join together in the worship hall for midday prayer (*shangli*).

Within the *gongbei*, daily activities were noted on a blackboard near the front entrance. It read:

* 22nd—Request for ten people to attend a prayer service for a man who has died (*tuo jia*)
* First day of the month—10 am—hosting Manager Su
* 21st—9 am—six people to go to Zhoujiazhuang (small village)
* 22nd—11 am—eight people to go to Jinsui Garden Community

Usually after the midday prayer, the *dangjiaren* would make these visits out in the community (often at the invite of a family to commemorate the deceased or read and explain scripture). During such time he would often take *chujiaren* and some students with him if he needed any assistance. If guests arrived at the *gongbei*, one or two students would usually be asked to assist Ma Yufang in preparing cups of tea and dishes for them, and they would often stand quietly in his meeting room while they chatted. Some students also assisted in preparing the meals and running errands during the day to collect food and drink.

Afternoon classes continued from 3 pm until 4 pm with an hour of Persian language drills. Sometimes the *dangjiaren* would come into the class near the start or the end to make announcements about upcoming tests or just to observe students in their work. Between 4 and 4.30 pm, they broke for afternoon prayer (*buli*). The day's classes finished with a discussion from 4.30 pm until 5 pm, concerning a variety of questions often related to religion and ethics. At 5 pm the students would chat with younger *chujiaren* in the meeting room, or together in their classroom, before taking a short break in their dorms.

Around 5.45 pm, the *dangjiaren* would usually come into the kitchen and chat briefly with any students or *chujiaren* present. After sharing dinner together, he would remind the students to attend to their ablutions in preparation for prayer at 6.30 pm. Everyone would then attend the early evening prayer (*hunli*) in the worship hall. Emerging from this prayer, some of the students would sit together in the meeting room for about half an hour, keeping warm and discussing plans for the following day. At 7.25 pm they would return to the worship hall to perform the final night prayer (*xiaoli*). This would conclude about 7.40 pm, and the students would usually return to their dorms to rest.

While students were not seeking charismatic power in the same sense as the *dangjiaren* and *chujiaren* of the *gongbei*, they were partaking in their own pathways of charismatic distinction. Students were very explicit to me in their desire for self-cultivation and the ways in which the *dangjiaren* inspired them. They also recalled to me stories of miracles performed by deceased saints. Ma Yong was a 23-year-old student who had family connections with the *gongbei* and had studied there for several years. With the support of the current *dangjiaren*, he was now studying at the Lanzhou Islamic College. After he had finished college, he wanted to study again in the *gongbei* and then overseas if possible—but knew that this 'wasn't guaranteed or easy to do'.[2] His daily routine was very similar to those of the students at the *gongbei*, but his classes focused mainly on Arabic language, not Persian: 'Here (at the Islamic college), every morning I get up and do the morning prayer, but sometimes I get to sleep quite late, so I don't get up early every morning. At noon-time I eat in the cafeteria, and then return to the dorm to pray, after that I go to class, and that finishes about 4 pm. I usually go to play basketball after that. Our course content is mainly about the Arabic language, we don't study the Qur'an and Sunnah. In the evenings we don't do *gongxiu*, because (unlike those in the *gongbei*), we have not reached the same level.' Ma Yong spoke about his family background and the inspiration of the 'masters' in the gongbei who inspired and motivated him to become a 'better Muslim':

> My family, beginning from the generation of my grandfather, have all belonged to the Qadiriyya *menhuan*. My mother has now passed away, and my father has retired. They never studied Arabic, they had only a primary school education, and my father was a soldier. My oldest brother is married, and has children. He is a civil servant. My second eldest brother also married last year, but he doesn't have children yet. This brother is a taxi driver in Linxia at the moment.
> I have not decided to become a disciple. I read [texts] for a few years in Guo Gongbei, and I usually go to help there during holidays. I received quite a heavy influence from my family about religion. When I was small, my parents would often take me to the *gongbei*. I really liked the environment there, the atmosphere and the people inside. At that time I thought the people inside the *gongbei* were like masters, they were not the same as us. I really

---

[2] Ma Yong is now studying Arabic at a Language Institute in Egypt and plans to continue on to university after that.

worshipped them, and hoped that one day I also can do as well as them. So later I came to the *gongbei* to study. In our family, the most pious is my father. He also used to smoke, and drink, but when he later joined the *menhuan*, he was very pious, hoping to make up for the mistakes he'd made. My oldest brother doesn't pray very often, he's not very devout, I'm a bit better than my brother (in this regard), but still not enough, now I'm working hard, and trying to make an effort to be a hard-working Muslim.

Ma Yong also explained his own experiences in seeing or hearing about the performance of miracles. He explained that these inspired him in his own practice. Here as well as foreseeing the future was the capability of embodying 'glowing light', calling to mind the meaning of the word for *baraka* in this context—*zhanguang*—to touch a light:

Miracles are passed on orally, but these things are all real. We have seen ourselves these things. For example, there was a teacher who went on the *Hajj*, and the head and soles of his feet were glowing. Ma Yufang took a photo, and everybody has seen this, or has seen the photo. Many years after his death, there are people who still follow him. A teacher (*laorenjia*) at Taizi Gongbei also had a miracle revealed. Once he went out to see an old grandmother, he touched her hand, and then said that the old lady would die by two o'clock that day. By two o'clock, the old lady really was dead.

Yang Shuijie (21) was a Hui student living and studying at the *gongbei*. He was a native of Linxia and came from a large family with three brothers and two sisters who were all in high school. He explained that they were all hoping to continue on to university. During holiday breaks from his studies at the *gongbei*, he would often go home to visit his family. His parents had not studied Arabic in the past, but last year his mother had started to study the Qur'an. He frequently lamented the lack of Qur'anic knowledge amongst Muslim youth, and his admiration for the *dangjiaren* whose knowledge was 'so deep':

Before, we Hui children from a young age studied Arabic, basically we were able to recite the Qur'an, and recite for prayer, but following society, for economic reasons, many people now finish their studies and go to find part time work, so many people have no knowledge of Arabic. I can recite the Qur'an now, but I don't yet understand it. The Qur'an is a miraculous scripture, people of different levels will be able to comprehend different knowledge. The *dangjiaren* of Guo Gongbei is very knowledgeable. He understands (the meaning of the Arabic), he is like a scholar.

Yang Shuijie emphasised the influence of the current *dangjiaren* on the educational opportunities in the *gongbei* as compared to others. The *dangjiaren* 'was also a foreign student. This is why in Guo Gongbei you have a relatively big language school, but in other *gongbei* there is not. In the past Da Gongbei ran a school, but only *chujiaren* could go inside the *gongbei* to do study; the other students (who were not *chujiaren*) would have to study at a mosque'. He explained that he'd like to continue studying and perhaps even pursue a PhD: 'In Islam we really promote learning and my dream is to wander to a far away place to do so.' In conversations with Yang Shuijie, he frequently emphasised the importance of Islamic education and the depth of knowledge in the tradition: 'Islamic literature is very deep. The realms of thought are very high. Many poets succeed as Muslim scholars also. They are people with an advanced understanding of God. We Muslims have outside cultivation and inner cultivation. On the outside we purify our bodies, on the inside, we purify our spirits. Inner cultivation enhances outer cultivation, we embody our innate character.' He thought that studying overseas would be really beneficial, particularly in a 'centre of Islamic learning' such as Qum, in Iran. After finishing his studies at the *gongbei*, he hoped to study there, and he and his classmates often expressed concern that current political tensions between the USA and Iran might impact this possibility.

Yang Shuijie's friend and classmate, Aihemaide, was 22 years old and had been at the *gongbei* for almost a year. He had no previous affiliation with the Qadiriyya network and did not claim to belong to any particular *menhuan*. He was the youngest in a family of three children and had grown up in Linxia. He had two sisters, both of whom had children and had married men from Linxia around the age of 20. They now lived and worked in Nanjing. One sister had graduated from junior high school, the other from a School of Commerce in Beijing. Ai's parents were farmers and still lived in a small village outside of Linxia City. He explained that they don't work anymore, but 'performing their prayers everyday is like their only work or occupation'. They had never studied Arabic or Persian, but had studied the Qur'an and *Shariah* law (*jiaofa*). During the holidays he would go home to see his parents and help them with daily life activities.

Aihemaide had graduated from junior high school. At the time of graduation, he did not want to continue on to senior high school because he 'would not be able to continue to study Islamic knowledge there', and, thus, 'high schools were not as good as mosques'. After junior high school he had studied for several years at a mosque in Hezuo (in the Gannan Tibetan Autonomous Region). He then decided to study at the *gongbei* instead, because 'even though he could study Persian at the mosque, at the *gongbei* it was a particular speciality. The current teachers' major is Persian'. In his opinion, education and knowledge were prioritised in the *gongbei*, because the *dangjiaren* 'had such a high degree of knowledge, especially of Persian, Arabic and Chinese. He also takes lessons on philosophy and belief, and usually uses Arabic texts to do so'. After he finished at the *gongbei*, he wanted to continue to study Persian and go to Iran to study. Like his fellow classmates, he was unsure if this would be possible and reiterated that 'everything is determined by God (*yiqie dou shi zhenzhu de qianding*)'. His parents had always encouraged him to keep developing his Islamic knowledge, and he saw great value in studying Persian, because 'Persia is an ancient country with a long-established civilisation, that's why I want to study Persian. Also, many important texts in Islam are written in Persian'. In the future he explained that he would be happy if he could contribute to Islam by becoming a teacher or *imam*.

Ma Zhengjun (22) was another student at the *gongbei*. He was originally from Xiahe, also in Gannan Autonomous Prefecture. He had one older sister and one older brother. His sister was not married yet and was still based in Xiahe, and his brother had moved to Hangzhou to open a restaurant. He had graduated from junior high school and hadn't been studying at the *gongbei* very long. Prior to coming to the *gongbei*, he had already spent three years in a mosque studying Arabic. He explained that he studied at the *gongbei* in order to study Sufism and Sufi materials in Persian, as 'Sufi ideas complement Islamic law (*Shariah*), and other schools don't always teach this material'. Unlike Ai, his parents belonged to the Qadiriyya sect, and from a young age he had visited the *gongbei* on a weekly basis. He had chosen himself to study at the *gongbei*, both as it was familiar to him and because, in his opinion, 'other *gongbei* don't have such a strong focus on studying, [...] and I was able to study Persian here'.

For Ma Zhengjun, the most important goal in Sufism was to perfect yourself through the remembrance of Allah. He explained that if you reach a certain level, then 'in your [own] eyes there is no other besides Allah— but few people can reach this limit'. When I asked him if anyone in the *gongbei* had reached this level, he replied, 'Actually, some people keep things hidden deeply, so this I also do not know! This means that they have some kind of knowledge or expertise, but it will not show up in front of people. Such people are generally very modest'. Ma Zhengjun was more familiar with the Khafiyya Sufi order than the Qadiriyya, but he knew of miracle stories associated with both. He relayed to me a story he knew about a Sufi saint Ma Laichi (who was the founder of the Khafiyya order, known as Huasi Menhuan in Linxia). 'He is our greatest Chinese Sufi', he explained, 'there are many miracles associated with him, I can tell you one of them […] There is a belief in Lhasa among Muslim Tibetans […] He [Ma Laichi] told those Tibetans to use prayer to help them cross the Yellow River. The Tibetans who were true in faith were able to cross and were thus converted to believe fully in Islam. If Ma Laichi did not use a miracle, then it would have been difficult to give any influence. This is a fact, if you go to Lhasa, you listen to Tibetan Muslims, they will speak Tibetan, they wear Tibetan clothes, but they follow the Islamic faith'.

DAILY DISCIPLINES AND INSPIRATIONS AMONGST RELIGIOUS ADHERENTS

Outside of the *gongbei*, practices of emulation amongst adherents differed in terms of consistency and end-goals. Men and women also tended to have different ways of engaging with the charismatic habitus.

Ma Shimi was a 60-year-old Muslim man who worked for a local *qingzhen* food company. He lived up the road from the central square of Linxia where the *gongbei* were located and was married with four children. He had three girls (two of whom were married with one child each and one who had just graduated high school) and one boy (who had been out of high school for a few years working). All of his children worked for his company in varying capacities. Unlike other religious adherents who were 'born into' families whose parents and grandparents had affiliated themselves with the Qadiriyya, Ma Shimi explained that he had chosen to join the Qadiriyya as a young adult: 'I was born into a Muslim family, and we would often go to the mosque and the *gongbei*, to pray and recite (*zuo libai he nianjing*). When I became an adherent of the Qadiriyya, you had to understand the other *menhuan* of Khafiyya and Jahriyya, then you could understand the good aspects of Qadiriyya, and why you'd choose this *menhuan*. The Qadiriyya's practice is a gradual process, slowly slowly you understand the secret (*qizhong de shenmiao*), this is not the same as other *menhuan*, only if you arrive at this knowledge can you be regarded as a Qadiriyya.'

Ma Shimi was clearly not emulating the celibate life of the *chujiaren,* but he sought to model aspects of his own religious practice after theirs by emulating their meditation techniques in his daily practice. I asked him what the 'Qadiriyya method' for religious adherents involved, and he demonstrated in his answer a relatively sophisticated knowledge of the Qadiriyya techniques of cultivation. He explained that they used to go to quiet places for prayer and recitation, 'where there were no people, such as mountains'. But now 'society is not the same, so we have to practice in daily life. During the day-time we have work, so we usually practice from 2 to 3 pm, because this time is relatively quiet. We usually don't go past 4 pm. Our work is relatively busy, some people eat dinner relatively early, and then from 9 pm we begin again and go through until the morning of the next day. We try to practice what we preach, not only use your mouth to read, it is also important to allow thought to come (*yinian ye yaodao*). Our Qadiriyya practice is a little like Daoist practice. Recitations (*nianjing*) focus on different parts of the body'.[3] Ma Shimi explained that in the body there are 28 acupuncture points that correspond with the 28 heavenly celestial constellations (*xingxiu*). These 28 constellations correspond to the 28 primary meridians in the human body in Chinese Daoist thought and were used as focal points for channelling energy during meditation.[4] He explained that prayer and recitation are not the same. Prayer usually involves using the voice, speaking out loud, whereas recitation does not involve the voice and is meditative (*monian*). He would usually go to mosques to perform prayers, whereas the recitation and meditation could be done at home.

He also emulated the Qadiriyya practice by maintaining a devotional space within his own home—with an incense urn and incense as it was in the *gongbei.* He would light incense here every few days, often before he was

---

[3] This is very reminiscent of the Sufi idea that the spiritual journey is made through different levels of 'being', by way of *latifas,* or subtle faculties, through an ongoing process of unveiling (*tajilli*). These *latifas* have a physical and a corresponding spiritual presence. Their physical location in the chest is: *qalb* (*xin,* heart), left side, and *rūh* (soul/spirit, *xing*), right side both in the lower part of the chest. *Sirr* (*xing,* spirit) and *khafi* (secret) are located in the upper left and right side of the chest, respectively. *Akhfa* (most secret and mysterious) is located in the centre of the chest. *Nafs* (*ziwo,* ego) is located by some in the navel and by others in the centre of the forehead (Lizzio 2007, pp. 12–13).

[4] In Sufism, it also connects to the 28 Divine Names and the 28 stations of the moon, each of which corresponds to a letter of the Arabic alphabet (Bakhtiar 1976, p. 7).

about to begin a meditation. He also had a large collection of religious texts in Chinese and Arabic and a framed text of a Sufi poem that he especially treasured. The poem was by Chinese Muslim scholar Liu Zhi and titled *wugeng yue* or 'The Poem of the Five Sessions of the Moon'. In the poem Liu Zhi uses the cycle of the moon as a metaphor for personal development through its various phases.[5] Liu Zhi was studied by the *chujiaren* in the Qadiriyya and would have been familiar with this piece of work. Ma Shimi was obviously aware of this and proud of the fact that he had a copy.

Ma Shimi felt that in the history of Qadiriyya, there had been many *chujiaren*, but their levels of cultivation had not been the same. Qi Jingyi had 'an incredibly high level of cultivation', but he was also very busy and 'he had no time to marry'. He explained that 'if you have a family, family members may affect an individual's practice, so many people of high cultivation levels chose not to marry'. The process in his opinion was very long and very hard and not something he himself could thus emulate entirely. From the beginning 'you must reduce eating, and sleeping, and later their level becomes very high, and they eat even less and finally almost have no sleep'. People of the 'highest level', he explained, will 'have some special capabilities and there will be some special phenomena, you can say a sort of supernatural power (*teyigongneng*)'. However despite the fact he could not commit to celibacy and the rigorous schedule of the *chujiaren*, he indicated that some Qadiriyya religious adherents, such as himself, could still develop a certain degree of skill and intuition in foreseeing the future as the saints could do. Around the time of the Sichuan earthquake in 2008, he explained that 'we Qadiriyya religious adherents also felt and sensed what was going to happen. After the earthquake, we read scriptures for ten days, because the earthquake killed so many children, and we had to come together to chant prayers for all of those who died'. Particular 'miraculous' capabilities here too were also emulated.

Male adherents such as Ma Shimi tended to seek a deeper level of esoteric knowledge of the Sufi teachings. Female adherents on the other hand, while not completely disregarding the importance of religious scriptural 'knowledge', tended to emphasise the emotional comfort found in connecting to the saint and site of the saint. This is similar to what Ozorak found in her study of women's empowerment through religion in

---

[5] See David Lee's English translation of this poem in full with an associated commentary (Lee 2015, Appendix 1).

America, where male and female adherents sought different benefits from church association and involvement. While men often sought economic reward, institutional office, and social capital, women were more likely to seek out personal and emotional benefits from the supportive relationships developed through the church (Ozorak 1996).

Ma Yuhong, known to me as 'Aunty', was 56 years old and had been an adherent of the Qadiriyya since she was a little girl. She came from a large family with a total of seven children (three boys, four girls), but now only her and her sister remained. She explained that her mother gave birth to eleven children, but only seven survived. I had met Aunty in the market place outside the *gongbei*, where she sold trinkets every morning to passers-by. Her husband was deceased, but she had two adult children, a boy (20) and girl (23), who were both now married with their own children. She lived on the outskirts of Linxia City in a typical courtyard style house (*Linxia siheyuan*). She had a very good knowledge of the history of the Qadiriyya in China and undertook regular attendance to both Da and Guo Gongbei for worship and learning.

Like Ma Shimi, in her own home Aunty had a devotional space in the corner of her kitchen (Fig. 4.1). She did not always carry out prayer five times a day, because as she said, 'I can't always be working in the markets and then come home to shower and change my clothes, in order to pray, it's not always possible'. When she had time to prepare however, she would often light incense and perform prayer at home. This was her way of emulating the daily prayer of the *chujiaren* and 'connect to Allah, and also confess my sins'. Unlike Ma Shimi, she was not familiar with the works of Liu Zhi and had never attempted meditation.

She stressed the notion of purity (*chunjie*), in her descriptions of the *chujiaren*: 'They have very little contact with women, so their heart (*xinling*) and spirit (*linghun*) remains pure.' As the students and Ma Shimi had done, she too spoke of an idealised past of miracle-making.

He (Ma Yufang) cannot at the moment, but in the future there will be the possibility. Our ancestor Qi Jingyi was able to perform those, he possessed a special power (*zhangguang*), and our current master must also be able to eventually do the same. Society now, however, is not the same as it was in the past. Now the disciples face many temptations, although they can commit to their beliefs, they are not as pure as the disciples before. This is a test for them, to be a *chujiaren*, to be a *dangjiaren*, you have to set yourself some standards, people's eyes are sharp, they look at you, judge whether you do well or not, we can all see.

Fig. 4.1   In Ma Yuhong's home, she displays pictures of Qadiriyya *gongbei* sites throughout the region. A clock, teacups, incense, and an incense burner sit in front. A photo of the former leader of Da Gongbei sits to the right

In terms of her interaction with the religious authority at the *gongbei* and what she learnt from them, she explained that sometimes the *dangjiaren* would come to the homes of sick family members to read scripture, or 'if you have a problem or if something happens you can go to the *gongbei* and ask him to come and recite for you'. Sometimes the *dangjiaren* would also teach people how to chant (recite), but 'most of the time the students and *imam* (*jiaochang*) would give the classes, and give us some of the basic Islamic rules'. Aunty explained that she did not have a high level of Islamic knowledge and could not read Arabic. But she had participated in some of these classes at the *gongbei* in the past, in an effort to 'improve her religious knowledge'. Her daughter, Ma Xueling (22), had a young family and was under pressure like her mother to sustain an income. She shared that 'the foundation of my knowledge is still only a little. While I was born into a

Muslim family, most of the learning is done on my own, because I have to work, and I don't have that much time to go to the *gongbei*. So now I have not mastered many aspects of Islam. But I will continue to work hard and try to improve'.

Similarly, Ma Huiyan had a young family and restricted time to study. She was a 28-year-old mother of two who lived in Linxia City. Her parents and grandparents were religious adherents of the Qadiriyya *menhuan*, and she had been taken to the *gongbei* since she was a young girl. She now lived with her parents-in-law and her two young children on the outskirts of Linxia. She had a younger brother who still lived at home with their parents in central Linxia City. Her husband was away for lengthy periods throughout the year working in Qinghai, and she relied heavily on her in-laws and especially her sister-in-law to help out with the children. She lived next door to her sister-in-law, and on a daily basis they shared cooking and child-care duties.

Inside their home, Ma Huiyan's parents-in-law had turned an area of an upstairs room into a devotional space. Similar to other homes, this included a commemorative poster of an event at Da Gongbei and an incense urn. For the most part, the parents-in-law used it most frequently. They would light incense every morning and perform prayers in Chinese for Allah to bless their family's health and prosperity. Ma Huiyan did not have the time to go to the *gongbei* on a weekly basis but explained to me that she felt she needed to bring some element of the practice within the *gongbei* into her daily life. Thus when Ma Huiyan was not busy with the children or shopping, she would also spend a few moments, most commonly in the evening, to light an incense stick and make a 'small wish to Allah'.

While she knew the *dangjiaren* of various Qadiriyya *gongbei* quite well, she told me she did not know much about Sufism *per se* or about the differences between the different Sufi *menhuan* in the region. She mentioned that some of the *dangjiaren* and *chujiaren* would come out to the homes of religious adherents to visit and offer advice, though 'some are more conservative than others in doing this'. She made particular mention of Ma Yufang, whom she did not see very often but greatly respected. She explained that he had a very good reputation in the community due to his overseas experience and language knowledge. In comparison with other leaders, he was also seen to be comparatively open-minded, 'not like the leaders at the other *gongbei* who are relatively old-fashioned (*shoujiu*) in their thinking'. During August, she had undertaken a trip with her sister-in-law and other family members to visit a remote *gongbei* called *Yangjuangou* in Xunhua County. It required a boat to access and then a steep climb up a rocky hill. She explained that as well as attending *gongbei* ceremonies within Linxia City, they tried to make a special trip every year to this more remote *gongbei* as a kind of religious pilgrimage. While there are an increasing number of religious adherents undertaking pilgrimage to Mecca nowadays in China, for many following the pilgrimage paths of the early Qadiriyya saints such as Chen Yiming to *gongbei* sites throughout Gansu and further field in Sichuan and Shaanxi was more practical and possible. In these trips, Ma Huiyan and her family were seeking to emulate the practice of pilgrimage performed by saints in the *gongbei*.

The examples of the young mothers provide a stark contrast to the lives of the students (of whom the female students were a minority). Though they could see how important religious study was—and they greatly respected those who demonstrated this knowledge—they had to attend to all of the responsibilities of domestic life. Their husbands were often working in another province for months at a time, and as women, they were shouldered with taking care not only of their children but of both their ailing parents-in-law and their own parents. They could not necessarily commit to daily prayer and the study of languages or text, and so for them emulation meant acknowledgement through lighting incense at home, through the occasional visit to the *gongbei* for a commemoration, and through annual family pilgrimages.

More rigorous practices of emulation were exemplified by an adherent of the Qadiriyya, Ma Xiefang. She was a 74-year-old Muslim lady who, unlike the others, lived in Lanzhou. I met her during a visit to a commemoration at Lingmingtang (a Qadiriyya *gongbei* on the outskirts of Lanzhou). Her parents and grandparents were all religious adherents of the Qadiriyya. She used to be a primary school teacher and came from a large family of three sisters and two brothers. She had four boys of her own, who were all married with one child each (three boys and one girl). She explained that they had all graduated from senior high school (*gaozhong*) and had then all started their working lives.

In several of our conversations, she often stressed the problems amongst young Muslims who didn't adhere to the rules of Islam and how hard it was to be a good 'genuine' Muslim. She herself prayed five times daily and was very strict about praying only in *laojiao* sites ('old religion') rather than *xinjiao* sites ('new religion'). For Ma Xiefang, *xinjiao* referred to Yihewani or Salafiyya communities. *Laojiao* on the other hand referred to the Sufi menhuan or Gedimu communities. She explained that she would go to all of the major Qadiriyya *gongbei* in the Gansu region at least once a year—including Da Gongbei and Guo Gongbei in Linxia. Similarly to Ma Huiyan, Ma Xiefang had never undertaken the *hajj*, and this was an alternate spiritual pilgrimage that was realistic for her to undertake. When in Lanzhou she would most often pray at home during the week, but would join her husband for Friday prayer service at a Qadiriyya *gongbei* called Qinglongshan. Inside the office headquarters of Qinglongshan *gongbei*, photos of Guo Gongbei and other Qadiriyya *gongbei* in the network were displayed on a shelf, surrounded by incense.[6]

Ma Xiefang explained that in the smaller Qadiriyya *gongbei* such as Qinglongshan, the majority of the 'residents' are more like 'custodians' rather than *chujiaren* as they are at Da Gongbei—thus people there do get married. 'The centre of the Qadiriyya is in Linxia, where the greatest teacher is (Qi Jingyi at Da Gongbei)', she explained, 'Other *dangjiaren* in other *gongbei* also have high spiritual levels, but not as high as Qi. The master of Guo Gongbei, for example, he is very well respected. Some say he may reach the same level as Qi, but we can't be sure of this yet'. Ma Xiefang had not studied the esoteric work of Liu Zhi and did not perform meditation, but she was extremely consistent in her personal prayer and thought very highly of the *dangjiaren* of the Qadiriyya.

In this chapter I have explored the ways in which charisma was further strengthened through the emulation of exemplary practice, by students and by religious adherents in the wider community. Through processes of emulation, the living exemplar of the *dangjiaren* and other *chujiaren* at Guo Gongbei were constantly created and re-created through a mix of 'imagined' qualities and 'real' facts. The *dangjiaren* was a living exemplar of self-mastery and religious knowledge. Students within the *gongbei* lived and studied alongside him and other *chujiaren*—in close proximity. Here, processes of 'implicit pedagogy', of unconscious inculcation, were at their strongest. The students watched their mentors on a daily basis perform the five daily prayers, perform regular and strict cleaning practices, and undertake lengthy recitations. Through emulation of these practices, they took on elements of the charismatic habitus. Religious adherents, too,

---

[6] One *chujiaren* that I met explained that he had come from Taitai Gongbei in Linxia (a Qadiriyya *gongbei* that commemorates a female Sufi saint). He had been instructed to come to this *gongbei* by the *dangjiaren* at Da Gongbei and to visit the *imam* there to discuss issues related to the management and upkeep of the site.

sought to emulate the exemplary model of the *dangjiaren* in various ways. They emulated his quest for knowledge in going to the *gongbei* to speak with him about religious teachings or by taking classes at the *gongbei* held for members of the community. In their homes, some religious adherents (like the *chujiaren*) tried to meditate during the night, and some went out of their way to perform an annual pilgrimage to key Qadiriyya *gongbei* sites in the region. Some simply emulated his character by being deeply committed to daily prayer and weekly attendance at Qadiriyya *gongbei* sites. Students and religious adherents grounded these practices of charismatic emulation, explicitly and implicitly, in the reality of a miraculous past. Stories of the miraculous capabilities of past Sufi saints played an important part in the deference paid to the current leader, for many students and adherents knew how committed the *dangjiaren* was to his own project of miracle-making and that his belief in the possibility of them was real. While no one had seen miracles performed by the current *dangjiaren*, most students and religious adherents had expectations that the 'extraordinary' could happen again (Feuchtwang and Wang 2008).

REFERENCES

Bakhtiar, L. 1976. *Sufi: Expressions of the Mystic Quest*. London: Thames and Hudson.
Bakken, B. 2000. *The Exemplary Society: Human Improvement, Social Control, and the Dangers of Modernity in China*. Oxford: Oxford University Press.
Bourdieu, P., and J.C. Passeron. 1990. *Reproduction in Education, Society, and Culture*. Theory, Culture & Society. London: Sage.
Buehler, A. 1998. *Sufi Heirs of the Prophet: The Indian Naqshbandiyya and the Rise of the Mediating Sufi Shaykh*. Columbia: University of South Carolina.
Feuchtwang, S., and M. Wang. 2001. *Grassroots Charisma: Four Local Leaders in China*. London: Routledge
Feuchtwang, S., and M. Wang. 2008. Suggestions for a Redefinition of Charisma. *Nova Religio: The Journal of Alternative and Emergent Religions* 12 (2): 90–105.
Goossaert, V. 2008. Mapping Charisma in Chinese Religion. *Nova Religio: The Journal of Alternative and Emergent Religions* 12 (2): 12–28 (Special Edition).
Lee, D. 2015. *Contextualization of Sufi Spirituality in Seventeenth and Eighteenth-Century China: The Role of Liu Zhi*. Eugene: Pickwick.
Lizzio, K. 2007. Ritual and Charisma in Naqshbandi Sufi Mysticism. *Anpere E-Journal for the Anthropological Study of Religion* 32–33: 1–37.

Ozorak, E. 1996. The Power, but Not the Glory: How Women Empower Themselves Through Religion. *Journal for the Scientific Study of Religion* 35 (1): 17–29.

Vicini, F. 2013. Pedagogies of Affection: The Role of Exemplariness and Emulation in Learning Processes: Extracurricular Islamic Education in the Fethullah Gulen Community in Istanbul. *Anthropology and Education Quarterly* 44 (4): 381–398.

CHAPTER 5

Charisma and Ritual: Social Distance and Proximity

Ma Yuhong, Ma Huiyan, Ma Shimi, Shan Xiaohui, and Ma Xiefang were all religious adherents of Guo Gongbei. They all went individually or with family members to the *gongbei* when they sought blessing or solace for happenings in their own lives. They described charismatic power as both a blessing (*jixiang*) and a source of light (*zhanguang*). Some felt they could gain from this power by venerating the saints whose bodies rested inside the tombs, by offering prayers up to Allah through the saints as intermediaries, or by coming into contact with the *dangjiaren*. They thus often attended events organised by the *gongbei* such as commemorations and weekly prayer services. Like mosques in the region, Guo Gongbei hosted Friday prayer service (Ch. *zhuma*, Ar. *Jum'a*) every week. This formal service (led by the *imam* of the *gongbei*) began around 12 pm. The other two *gongbei* in the vicinity (Da and Taizi) each held their own service at the same time, and calls to prayer echoed simultaneously from loudspeakers from within each *gongbei*.

Typically people would start to arrive at the *gongbei* around 11.30 am, and before the sermon they would follow a circuit around the site placing incense in front of every tomb. After purchasing a bundle of incense sticks from the stalls near the entrance-way, they would enter Da Gongbei, saying '*As-salāmu 'alaykum*' as they greeted *chujiaren* who were making preparations inside. They would pause outside every collection of tombs and stand or crouch with their hands in open supplication while saying a

© The Author(s) 2018
T. Cone, *Cultivating Charismatic Power*,
https://doi.org/10.1007/978-3-319-74763-7_5

quiet prayer (*duwayi*) under his or her breath.[1] They would then move towards the urn, bringing the incense sticks to their mouth briefly before placing them in the urn. Though she did not frequent the *gongbei* that often any more, an older lady Mu Jie described the *gongbei* as a specific place to seek 'blessing' (*jixiang*) and consolation. On one Friday she shared with me her personal prayer:

> My parents, my mother-in-law, my father-in-law, have all left this world; I hope in the world beyond that their sins have been forgiven; finally, I hope work is smooth and successful for my husband, I wish my son and daughter-in-law safety, I hope that they will be able to become pregnant, and that the mother and baby will be safe and sound.

In some cases during the prayer, people would kiss the urn itself. Others would crawl in and around the tombs touching and kissing them lightly. Often there were tears. When it was time to prepare for the sermon, men typically would remove their shoes and enter the worship hall, kneeling on the carpeted floor, while women set up rugs outside the worship hall. During the prayer service of *Zhuma*, unlike individual prayer at the tomb urns, men and women would perform prostrations (Ch. *saliangte*, Ar. *salat*), bringing their head to the ground.

This chapter explores the role of public rituals (such as the one just described) in the strengthening and maintenance of charisma. Here by public ritual I include any act of individual worship or large-scale worship, celebration, or commemoration performed in a public space. In particular, the discussion focuses on the role of social proximity and distance in public ritual and how these alternate with notions of sacred and profane bodies and practices. I argue that these practices contribute to the perception and/ or generation of feeling (affect) towards the leader (both those deceased and those living) and, in turn, to the strengthening of his charismatic potency and power.

---

[1] *du'a'* (*duwayi*) is an individual prayer, which can be spontaneous, with personal requests. It is different from the ritual prayer (*salah*) which is a non-individual prayer performed five times a day. The *du'a'*,'whether in a group or alone, is performed with the palms of the hand open to heaven; at the end, the words *'Al-ḥamdu lillāh'* ('praise to God') are said and the palms are drawn over the face and down, crossing over the shoulders, as if one were anointing oneself with a Divine blessing' (Glassé 1989, p. 104).

Weber saw charisma as an attribution given to an outstanding leader by his followers. In an article on charismatic leadership and organisational hierarchy, Dana Yagil follows up this observation in relation to a number of theorists from the 1980s who argued that charisma should be defined in relation to people's perceptions of and responses to a leader (Yagil 1998). Specifically, that 'it is not what the leader is but what people see the leader as that counts in generating the charismatic relationship' (Willner 1985, p. 14). An important element in this cultivation of reputation, and the subsequent attribution of charisma, is the social distance that a leader maintains from his followers (Yagil 1998, p. 162). As Daniel Katz and Robert Kahn found, leaders who are also supervisors are always being evaluated and being 'very human and very fallible [...] their subordinates cannot build an aura of magic about them [...] Day to day intimacy destroys illusions' (Katz and Kahn 1978, p. 546). More recently, Erik Harms has described social distance as a kind of 'conspicuous invisibility'. Building on the work of Erving Goffman in *The Presentation of Self in Everyday Life*, Harms explores the practices of a wealthy 'boss' in Vietnam who controls 'what can and cannot be seen about his life and money' (Harms 2013, p. 1).

A kind of 'conspicuous invisibility' could also be seen in the context of Guo Gongbei, where there was either a notable absence and/or certainly a very limited involvement by the *dangjiaren* in particular public rituals—most notably weddings, Friday prayers, and funeral procedures. Many of the ceremonial duties required at these events tended to be run by the *imam* in the *gongbei*. He was responsible for leading Friday prayer, for assisting with education on scriptures, officiating during wedding and funeral rites, leading religious adherents in worshipping at the tomb site during celebrations, and organising commemoration festivities (*'amala*). Unlike the *chujiaren* or the *dangjiaren*, he did not engage in rigorous textual study or focused meditation.

This delegating of ritual performance and the distancing that it established between religious adherents and the *dangjiaren* was an important component in the 'mystique' that was built up around him. People often mentioned the fact that while he was willing to give advice if requested, attend gatherings, or provide Qur'anic explication, he did not go out of his way to speak to people. As Ma Shimi explained to me, 'we have a head of the *menhuan*, and he usually does not talk to people because it will affect his practice (*xiuxing*)'. The *dangjiaren* himself told me that while he would like to be a better host, and take me out to see sites and share dinner, it was best that he not be seen in public with me (as a female) and so he could not do so. This distance established between himself and his religious adherents maintained an important perception surrounding his bodily purity and, in turn, perceptions of his spiritual capacities and charismatic power.

This is a clear example of the role of the human body in the maintenance of social boundaries. As Anders Hansson has described:

> Ritual is used to separate and create boundaries, and rules about pollution serve to control experience and support the social and cultural structure. To maintain the social order individuals must behave according to the rules for the categories to which they belong. Those who are in transition from one status to another and those who are in a marginal state and have no place in society (such as outcasts) are a source of danger but sometimes also of power (Hansson 1996, p. 12).

Here, the body must be kept whole and complete. It is vulnerable at its margins—as margins are potentially polluting and dangerous. In particular, 'the social pressures of sexual relations are potentially explosive and pollution fears seem to cluster around contradictions that involve sexuality' (Hansson 1996, p. 13). This risk of bodily pollution increases with greater proximity to those persons, objects, practices, or places seen as profane. Profane is a term Emile Durkheim first used in the context of religion to refer to that which is impure and sacrilegious (Law 2010, p. 166), what Mary Douglas would have referred to as 'dirt' (Douglas 1966).[2]

In the context of Guo Gongbei, while the *dangjiaren* and *imam* maintained *distance* from particular practices that could have been seen as 'profane' and thus potentially polluting of their 'bodily purity', religious adherents, on the other hand, sought proximity to that which was deemed 'pure' (*qingzhen*) or 'sacred' during rituals in order to receive blessings and further their own connection to God. The 'sacred' here refers specifically to the saintly *body*—either the living body of the *dangjiaren* or *imam* or the entombed saints. This desire of proximity, of wanting to be near a body

---

[2] For Douglas, the analysis of 'dirt' is a matter of social perception and interpretation, as she says: 'there is no such thing as absolute dirt: it exists in the eye of the beholder' (Douglas 1966, p. 2). Reinhart connects the work of Douglas to the Islamic context, laying out the nuances of purity and what is 'dirty' and 'clean' in the specific contexts and meanings of Islamic practice. See his article *Impurity/No Danger* (Reinhart 1990).

that is for the most part so far away, also has implications for the perception of charismatic power as it often engenders a heightened degree of affect or emotion.

The affect or emotion generated through proximity to charismatic centres has been studied by several scholars eager to understand the locus of charismatic power. In his study of the charismatic relationship between a leader and his/her religious adherents, Lindholm identified two kinds of charisma that emerged—from the states of 'Enlightenment' and 'Sleep' (Lindholm 1990). 'Enlightenment' referred to the collective energy generated through the performance of a play or a piece of music by a group. Sleep on the other hand induced 'an ecstatic loss of self in the collective group, similar to a state of hypnosis or trance' (Feuchtwang and Wang 2008, p. 13). Csordas located charisma in an intensification of the disciplines of self-formation, a process he called 'ritual involution'. Rather than seeing the locus of charisma as being in the personality of the leader, in the relationship between a leader and his followers, in the 'cultural media by means of which it is expressed, in the symbolic resources drawn on for its formulation, or in the relation of its possessors to the centres of social order', Csordas suggested that perhaps the locus of charisma was amongst participants in a religious movement. He thus asked: '[…] could not charisma be a product of the rhetorical apparatus in use of which leader and follower alike convince themselves that the world is constituted in a certain way?' (Csordas 1997, p. 39).

Extending on this, what of the body within this rhetorical apparatus? That is, how do we account for the energies generated by bodily presence? The 'collective sentiments' described by many in relation to the production of charisma could also be described in terms of affect, which, following Lisa Blackman, allows conceptual room to consider the role of energies and bodies in the generation of charisma. For Blackman, 'Affect is never simply something one "catches" but rather a process that one is "caught up" in. Its complexity is revealed through the linkages and connections of the body to other practices, techniques, bodies (human and non-human), energies, judgements, inscriptions and so forth that are relationally embodied' (as cited in Wetherell 2012, p. 140). In this chapter I frame affect and emotion generated in proximity to sacred bodies as 'affective practice', that is, practice that 'focuses on the emotional as it appears in social life and tries to follow what participants do. It finds shifting, flexible and often over-determined figurations rather than simple lines of causation, character types and neat emotion categories […]' (Wetherell 2012, p. 4).

PUBLIC RITUALS

As well as weekly prayer service, Guo Gongbei also held celebrations for Ramadan (Ch. Kaizhaijie, Ar. Īd al-Fiṭr—Fast-breaking at the end of Ramadan), the Feast of Sacrifice ('Īd al-Aḍḥā), and the birthday of the Prophet Muhammad (Ch. *Maolide naibi*, Ar. Maulid al-Nabīy). During Īd al-Fiṭr, many religious adherents of the Qadiriyya went to visit the Sufi tombs, and some of them attended the Salāt al-Īdayn (Prayers for the Festivals).[3] They would then pay visits to the homes of relatives, sharing gifts and food. For the birthday of the Prophet Muhammad, a large-scale commemoration was held in the *gongbei*.

Along with other Qadiriyya sites in the region, Guo Gongbei also celebrated some notably Shi'a traditions. On the tenth day of the first month of the Islamic calendar, they held a festival celebrating Ashula (Ar. *al-'ashura'*), remembering the day on which Ali's second son, Husayn (the Prophet's grandson), was killed at the battle of Karbala. On the 15th day of the sixth month of the Islamic Calendar, they commemorated Fātimah, the daughter of the Prophet Muhammad and wife of Ali. Guo Gongbei also shared several anniversaries and commemorations with other Qadiriyya sites that were specific to their unique development. These were calculated according to the Chinese calendar.

- 正月初一日 (*zhengyuechuyi ri*). New Year's Day in the lunar calendar. This date had dual significance. Firstly, it memorialised when Khoja Abd Allah (the 29th generation of Muhammad) first set out from Mecca to come to China. Secondly, it was the date when the Yang Shuijietuojia people of Hezhou [Linxia] set out from Luling Temple Gongbei, Xixiang County, Shanxi, to move the bones of Qi Jingyi back to Linxia.
- 三月二十五日 (*Sanyue ershi wu ri*). Third month (of the lunar year)— March 25th. It was the death anniversary of Khoja Abd Allah in Langzhong City, Sichuan.

---

[3] Salāt al-Īdayn is offered early in the morning after sunrise, preferably at a place other than the mosque. Some religious adherents such as Ma Yuhong explained that she did not attend these public prayers because it was *xinjiao* ('new religion') to do so. Rather prayers at this time were carried out at the *gongbei* or at home.

- 九月十一日—九月十九日 (*Jiuyue shiyi ri— Jiuyue shijiu ri*). Ninth month (of the lunar year)—September 11th, September 19th. These were the death and birth anniversary dates of Qi Jingyi.

Finally, Guo Gongbei had its own anniversaries on September 4th (九月初四日 - *Jiu yuechu si ri*) and September 25th (九月二十五日 - *Jiuyue ershi wu ri*), marking respectively the death and birth anniversary dates of Chen Yiming. As well as these special commemorative events, Ma Yufang also explained that the *gongbei* officiated weddings and funerals in the wider community. Sometimes they hosted them (usually in the homes of the religious adherents), and other times they attended to give blessings. During these ceremonies, they followed 'common Islamic procedures' in the region. In this chapter I will discuss three events. I begin with a 'typical' Hui wedding and then a Hui funeral ceremony, both occurring outside Guo Gongbei. The wedding involves an *imam*, and the funeral an *imam* and *dangjiaren*. I then discuss a large-scale commemoration event within Guo Gongbei which involves the *dangjiaren* from several *gongbei*, several *imam*, and many *chujiaren* and students.

A Hui Wedding

The wedding is a particular illustration of the distance maintained by the leadership from practices that are deemed profane. It may seem incongruent that an institution such as Guo Gongbei that practised celibacy should also be involved in the commemoration of weddings. However marriage for religious adherents was not problematic. Ma Yufang supported marriage for others as a life choice—for him a meaningful life was either lived in complete union with God or in complete union with another human being. Due to the need to maintain distance from women and protect his own physical and spiritual purity, however, he had to consciously restrict his presence at such events. The complete absence of the *dangjiaren* was a symbolic act maintaining particular social boundaries around his celibate status—boundaries that established clear lines between sacred (asexual) and profane (sexualised) bodies. As such, he delegated ceremonial duties to the *imam*.

I witnessed a marriage ceremony for a young Hui couple in Lintan County, Gansu Province. Though they were not 'religious adherents' of the Qadiriyya, the wedding ceremony was described to me as typical for

Hui couples in the Gansu region. If the *imam* from Guo Gongbei had been involved, he would have performed a similar ceremonial role to the *imam* described here. Many young married women and men in families of Qadiriyya religious adherents explained to me that the *imam* from the *gongbei* had given them advice on the importance of marriage and the Islamic procedure involved. The majority of them had then gone through a matchmaker to get a formal marriage proposal, to write up a marriage licence, and select an auspicious day for the wedding.[4]

After the marriage licence was given to the new couple, the bridegroom's family chose an auspicious day (which was generally a Friday—*Jum'a*) and informed the bride's family for approval. Once the date was agreed, then two or three days prior to the wedding, the bridegroom's family gave steamed bread and whole mutton to the bride's family. This was known as a 'marriage-urging gift' (*cui zhuang li*, literally an 'urge the adornment of the female gift').[5] On the first day of the wedding ceremony, I travelled with some relatives of the bridegroom's family to the home of the bride's family. Large quantities of vegetables, mutton, and steamed bread were served to friends and relatives as they arrived. The bride stayed in her bedroom in the house, surrounded by her female relatives and family. She underwent a thorough cleansing using water known ritually as 'mother-departing water' (*li niang shui*). Fine hairs were also plucked from her face and body (*bo hanmao*).

At a later point the young bridegroom arrived. He was offered a short meal and tea. The *imam* arrived shortly after and arranged a corner of the living room space ready for the formal service. The bridegroom and his male relatives and friends gathered around him. The *imam* then began the marriage (*nikkah*) ceremony. This began with a formal reading from the Qur'an, followed by a short sermon emphasising the freedom of choice in marriage and the importance of faith (full sermon is in the Appendix). After a closing prayer in which all heads were lowered in silence, the *imam* grasped a handful of walnuts and dried fruits from the plate set before him and threw them out to the crowd. There was a mad scramble as people tried to snatch as many as they could. A man beside me explained that this

---

[4] The Chinese researcher Wang Ping says that in the past 'the [Hui] wedding cannot be discussed unless there are three matchmakers and one *imam*. If the persons-in-charge of wedding affairs reach agreement on a wedding date, they will shake hands [to indicate] commitment' (Wang 2005, p. 4).

[5] The character *zhuang* in *jiazhuang* means dowry.

was an auspicious symbol, indicating luck (*jili*) and prosperity, and was the climax of the wedding ceremony. The more walnuts and fruits one collected the more luck one could have. This was the end of what was described as the more formal 'religious' procedures for the day, and the *imam* was no longer required and took his leave.

During the first day and a half of the wedding ceremony, boundaries were constantly maintained between women and men. The male and female were to be completely separated until their union had been formally sanctioned—that is, until their inevitable and assumed sexual union had been sacralised. Women (including the bride) were not even present during the reading of the *nikkah*. Professor L. explained that in some places such as Linxia and Lintan, when the *imam* reads the *nikkah*, only the bridegroom is present and the bride is usually in her bedroom: 'This custom is a religious one, as the wife is not allowed to see people from the outside.' However in some other places, such as Shaanxi, when the *imam* reads the *nikkah*, the bridegroom and bride are both present in the same place, but the bride, in accordance with the *Shariah*, wears a headscarf.

The activities in the afternoon and evening were informal and in a sense 'sacrilegious' as they involved a lot of (albeit good-natured) mockery towards family members of the bridegroom and the bride and bridegroom themselves. In the afternoon at the family home of the bridegroom, the bride was escorted into the 'nuptial' room by her mother and mother-in-law. Meanwhile, the father of the bridegroom was chosen to be the target in a game known as *shua gongpo* or 'playing with the in-laws'. A nephew of the groom explained to me that 'when a Hui man and woman get married, in some places people who attend the wedding play *shua xin lang*—"to play with the groom." Beforehand, we have a pot of black powder and ink, and we rub it on the groom's face, until we have succeeded in covering his face (*heibaogong*) and he is taken to the bridal chamber'. On this occasion, it was not the groom who participated but the mother and father of the groom. When the bride had gone into the bridal chamber, everyone forcibly pulled the husband's parents into the yard. His face was painted using a black powder mixture, and he was tossed around amongst a group of men. They yelled out asking for money from him and if he didn't give in and agree, then they would keep pushing him around but with increased vigour, effectively 'dumping' him on the ground and pulling up his shirt to tickle his stomach. As one participant commented, 'If he gives us money, then we will not hassle him, but if he does not give the money, then the games will become even more cheeky'.[6]

Later on that evening, from approximately 7 pm until 10 pm, there was a round of *nao dong fang* (games in the bridal room). In front of a very crowded, jostling, and noisy room of male and female friends and relatives, the bride and bridegroom stood up the front on their bed, and a friend of the groom stood beside them. Using a can of confetti as a microphone, he asked some questions to the groom and bridegroom about their future plans. Questions included how many children will you have and how long will you wait before having children. Noisy chatter and laughter continued throughout. People also encouraged the couple to link arms and for the groom to put his arm around her while they posed for photographs. Considering the rigorous separation between the bride and bridegroom up until this point, this was an intense contrast, and also a rather intimate interrogation, with conversation venturing into very personal and profane territory. It was clearly quite difficult for the bride who rarely spoke and held her head to the ground most of the time.

The *imam* returned the following morning to the home of the bride-groom's family for the final part of the process—that of the 'presentation' of the bride to family and extended family. This was very formal and subdued compared to the proceedings of the night before. In the morning the *imam* joined with family members and extended family members in a breakfast of buns, vegetables, and noodles. Men sat together in one room and women in another. The women were seated according to age, with older women grouped together at a table near the window. Once everyone was settled, the wife was brought in by her mother who linked her arm and presented her to everyone in formal wedding attire. Later on she came around a second time, but this time with her husband who introduced her by name to people in his family. Most people, except for immediate family, dispersed around 11.30 am.

While the *imam*, himself being married, was involved in the formal (one could say more 'sacralised') aspects of the wedding, he too was noticeably absent from the more informal (what some might have felt were the more 'profane') events that took place throughout. While he, unlike the

---

[6] The nephew also explained to me that sometimes they will 'hang red chilli peppers from their ears, put a broken straw hat on their head, hang a bell around their neck, wear a coat inside out, and sometimes the parents-in-law ride the donkey in a circle'.

dangjiaren, could be present during wedding ceremonies, he maintained boundaries around his status as a religious figure by avoiding particular elements of the ceremony.

A Hui Funeral

The ritual of a funeral is a particular illustration both of the distance maintained by the *dangjiaren* from some aspects of ceremonial performance and also the need of religious adherents to seek proximity to the sacred. During the process of the funeral, the *dangjiaren* was often present during initial blessings and in the commemorations that followed the burial, as a source of good luck and religious authority, but it was often the *imam* who conducted the formal part of the service. While I was in the field, there were no funeral ceremonies for disciples within the *gongbei* itself. However, the process was described to me by a religious adherent. I was also able to witness part of a local funeral ceremony for a well-known *imam*, which gave me further insights into the social roles ascribed to various religious authorities. The following account is based on both of these sources.

I was told that in anticipation of death, the family of the ill patient would call the *dangjiaren*, the *imam*, and three other *chujiaren* to his/her bedside (a male pronoun will be used from now on for ease of explanation). The *dangjiaren* would pray to Allah to forgive any guilt felt by the patient (*tao bai*) and then give him a chance to make any confessions.[7] At this point, several other people would come to give 'greetings' (*seliamu* from the Arabic *salam*) to the patient in order to seek forgiveness for any unresolved conflicts. As he passed away, his closest family would stand around him, as well as the *dangjiaren*, the *imam*, and some *chujiaren* from the *gongbei*. When he had stopped breathing, two relatives and the *imam* would assist in closing the eyes and mouth, settling the legs and feet, and trimming the hair.

The next part of the process was known as 'laying the remains' or *ting mai ti*. The body would be placed on a bed and positioned so that the head pointed towards the north, feet towards the south, and face slightly towards

---

[7] Part of this process also included the checking of the will of the deceased. Contents of the will or testament (*yizhu*) generally included the distribution of properties and the treatment to all his/her debts so that he/she can leave the world honestly; no matter if he/she is old, young, male, or female, his/her families and relatives should recite the Shahada for the purpose that the dead doesn't forget Allah before his/her death.

the west. A clean white sheet was pulled over the body. Later, some of the family members would be sent out to notify relatives and friends of the deceased. Several others were chosen to take charge of making preparations for the funeral ceremony itself. If the man was not buried on the same day as his death, the *imam* from Guo Gongbei was invited to sit and guard him overnight. The *imam* would have to thoroughly clean his own body in preparation and then light incense sticks and candles until daylight came. If there were family members still awake during the night, he might also tell stories of Muhammad and 'persuade people to do good deeds'.

The body of the deceased would then be cleaned (*xing shui*). A male was not allowed to clean the body of a female, and vice versa. Water used for cleaning generally came from the well of a nearby mosque and was boiled and then poured into three flat pots. The cleaning was then undertaken by three people who began the process after completing their own thorough self-cleansing. After his body had been cleaned, he was dressed in graveclothes (*chuan ke fan*). These were white in colour and could be made only of cotton, calico, or bleached cloth but not silk or satin or any other 'high-ranking' fabric. During this process, some spices, camphor, or perfume were added to the graveclothes to prevent corrosion and expel parasites. After the dressing was complete, relatives and friends would make a final farewell to the deceased, and the body was placed in a specially made carrying box (*ta bai ti*).

As with the daily cleansing of the body in preparation for prayer, it is also an important element in the preparation of a body for burial. Islam emphasises the preservation of the dignity of the deceased person at all times and accordingly requires that the body be washed and cleaned thoroughly and in a specific way (Glassé 1989, p. 134). Here the physically clean body, the one free from 'dirt', is the 'pure' body, the body that is most fit and 'ready' to return to Allah. It is this body that is granted proximity to the sacred.[8]

The funeral ceremony itself (*janāza*) was usually held in the home of the deceased. The body was placed facing west (towards Mecca), and the *imam* stood beside the body, while other participants stood in a line

---

[8] A Hadith, attributed to Ahmad, An-Nasa'i, and At-Tirmidhi, speaks of the importance of a clean and sanitary environment at all times during funeral proceedings: 'Let whoever washes a dead person take a bath; and let whoever carries him perform wuḍū' (Abdul-Malik 2013, p. 33).

behind him (the *dangjiaren* and *chujiaren* stood at the front of the line).[9] He quietly recited the first *Surah* of the Qur'an, Al-Fātiḥa, then prayed to God to bestow peace, mercy, and blessings upon the Islamic Prophet Muhammad. Prayers were also made to Allah to forgive all those who were living, deceased, the old, the young, men, and women, 'If they are alive, encourage them to follow the Islamic path, and if they have died let them have died in faith'.

In Linxia most Muslims were buried together in a large graveyard on the hillside. The body of the deceased was usually transported by vehicle to the main gate of the cemetery, and then it was carried on a wooden plank by eight males through the crowd. During the funeral that I witnessed at this site, the majority of the crowd was male, and I was granted special permission to attend as a 'foreign visitor'.[10] The *dangjiaren* and *imam* arrived together with a number of *chujiaren*. A crowd of people gathered as the body was carried towards the grave site, while others chose to watch from the hilltops. At times there was much clamour and noise as people sought to be close to the body. Once the body had reached the burial site, the person inside the plot and those standing above delivered it down slowly. Later, they unfolded the big and small sleeping sheets which had been bundled around the body. After placing the body and before refilling the earth, the mourners held up three handfuls of earth in the direction of the deceased's head and put the earth into the pit, saying in Arabic: 'I create all of you from the earth' while holding the first handful of earth; 'I help you return to the earth' while holding the second; and 'I will bring you back to life from the earth again' while holding the third. Later, more earth was used to fill in the pit.

After the ceremony, several further commemorations were held known as 'amal to commemorate the dead' (*wei jinian wang ren er gan ermaili*).

---

[9] While the majority of the Sufi orders take off their shoes during the service, those in Guo Gongbei did not take off their shoes during this time, explaining that for them, 'janāza' is not for religious service but for prayer. During religious service, one stands, bows, prostrates, and sits in meditation, but there are no such rituals during 'janāza', thus they don't take off their shoes.

[10] Similar to other sites elsewhere in the Islamic world, here women were generally discouraged from participating in the funeral procession. I was told this was because women had a tendency to be overly emotional and 'cry too much'. While not permitted nowadays, in pre-Islamic Arabia, loud 'wailing for the dead' was a common practice for grieving women (Halevi 2004, p. 3).

In these ceremonies, the *dangjiaren* was often invited, along with the *imam* and some of the *chujiaren*, but it was usually the *imam* who carried out any necessary recitation of scriptures. In the family home, a commemoration would last for seven days. During this time, flour cakes and lamb would be prepared, and the *dangjiaren*, the *imam*, and *chujiaren* would be invited to share a meal. As there was a belief that the soul of the dead still lived in the house up until 40 days after the death, sometimes the *imam* or the *dangjiaren* was invited to light incense sticks, and make a prayer at the house, in order to bring blessings upon the deceased and their family. Some religious adherents would also go to the *gongbei* during this time to light incense and make their own prayers to the buried saints. In order to rescue the dead and 'beg Allah to open the door to the heaven', the *imam* would also give *zakat* (a monetary donation) to people coming to the *gongbei* to recite scriptures. On the 40th day, it was believed that the soul of the dead would leave the house and a grander commemoration would be prepared. On that day, the *imam* and *dangjiaren* were invited in the morning to check the gravesite, and after doing so, they, along with relatives, friends, and neighbours, would be invited to the home of the deceased's family to share cakes and breads. On the 100th day, the 1st, 3rd, 10th, and 30th anniversaries, they would also sometimes be invited to assist in the ritual slaughter of lambs and share bread. After the 30th anniversary, no large-scale commemorations took place.

Throughout the entire funeral process, from the initial moment of death through to the commemoration in the family home after the burial ceremony, religious adherents sought proximity to the sacred through the presence and blessing of the *dangjiaren*. While it was the *imam* who conducted the formal part of the ceremony (*janāza*), it was important for the *dangjiaren* to be present. While he was not expected to perform 'routine' religious duties as such, in situations such as these, it was his presence alone that for many embodied what they sought most—divine blessing and protection. This delegation of ritual responsibility and the social distance that resulted both created and strengthened his charismatic appeal.

Birth Commemoration of Chen Yiming

The commemoration of the birth of the saint Chen Yiming provides another illustration of the need of religious adherents to seek proximity to the sacred during ritual in order to receive blessings and to further their sense of connection with the divine. It also provides the strongest illustration of the heightened affect and emotion engendered in proximity to the sacred bodies of the *dangjiaren*, other *chujiaren*, and the entombed saints.

On September 27th, 2011, a ceremony was held at Guo Gongbei that served both to commemorate the birth of Chen Yiming (the founder of Guo Gongbei) and to celebrate the completion of a recent re-building of a section of the *gongbei*. The event was spread over three days. On the first day, guests from other mosques were welcomed into the *gongbei*. Men and women said '*salaam alaykuum*' as they met each other (which meant in Chinese, '*zhu ni pingan, zhu ni jixiang*—wish you safety, wish you blessing'.)[11] They streamed in one after the other and often brought animals with them as sacrificial gifts. Most of them offered one or two sheep, but some brought in a cow.[12] People also made donations of money. In the courtyard of the *gongbei*, the *dangjiaren*, *chujiaren*, students, and helpers were standing at a table that was set up to welcome guests and take their monetary donations. Every time guests entered, they would all recite the Shahada at least three times ('*Lā ilāha illā Allāh, Muhammadun rasūlu 'Llāh*'). During this recitation, many older men sought proximity to Ma Yufang, kissing his hands when greeting him. Many appeared moved by this experience, bowing their heads in deference. After this they would move through to the tomb space and proceed to undertake prayers again.

On the second day, official speeches were made outside the main *gongbei* in the courtyard. Dignitaries, government officials, and local religious leaders were positioned up in front of a large seated crowd, which was mostly male (females stood crowded around the outside of the seated area). Students of the *gongbei* stood near the front of the crowd, holding lit incense. Everyone stood for prayer. The young Persian teacher arrived and gave a reading of the first *Sūrah* (passage) of the Qur'an in Arabic Al-Fatiha. After he had finished, three other young orators came onto the podium and recited another passage from the Qur'an. While this occurred, Ma Yufang was dressed in silk wraps. He then stepped up to

---

[11] According to Islamic custom, it was explained to me that women could not shake the hand of a man, so during greetings women often just nodded in acknowledgement as they entered and walked into the tomb, while men would pause for longer, shaking hands and sharing a longer prayer.

[12] Three camels were also presented on the first day but were not part of the sacrifice.

make a speech in which he thanked other *dangjiaren, imams,* and local government officials for their help and remembered the efforts of Chen Yiming in 'protecting the country'. The next two speakers were two Muslim government representatives (one of these speeches is mentioned in Chap. 6, and the other can be found in the Appendix.)

Later in the afternoon, crowds continued to move through to the tomb courtyard to put incense in the urn outside, and many men, women, and children went into the tomb itself. Here adherents sought physical proximity to the entombed saint. Many placed their hands on the structure, lowered their heads, and lay light kisses on the tomb. As they did so, several of them became emotionally overwhelmed and cried softly. Many who were further away from the tomb and not able to touch it, wiped their faces with their hands, as if to offer a kiss at the same time.

An hour later, a cloth was brought in to the worship hall and men held on to it while a recitation was made. They then carried the cloth to the tomb enclosure and hoisting it up on sticks they placed it over the top of the other cloths that hung over the tomb. An hour later, another cloth was brought in and people spread it amongst themselves. A different group of men and women carried the cloth into the tomb enclosure and hoisted it up on sticks, placing it over the tomb. The placing of the cloth (*shandan*) was explained to me as a way to both demonstrate respect and to offer protection to the saint.

Ma Yufang and a group of *chujiaren* and students then came into the main worship hall. They distributed prayer beads, and each began a silent individual prayer, releasing a bead onto the floor every time they finished a prayer cycle. Prayer books (a collection of *Sūrah* or passages from the Qur'an) were handed out to those who could read Arabic. A *chujiaren* began the reading, while the rest were getting organised with books. More women and men kept streaming in to see the tomb. On his way out, an older man held the hand of a *chujiaren* who was standing near the door and shed some tears. Here an adherent found emotional comfort from proximity to the *chujiaren*—whom he perceived as a living saintly, 'sacred' body.

On the final day, there was a low hum of prayer in the *gongbei* space as it filled up with religious adherents. Women predominantly sat outside the main door on mats that had been rolled out, while men lined the inside of the worship hall. People prayed individually under their breath, some loud, some quiet. Outside Ma Yufang talked with other *chujiaren* and students who were organising microphones and testing sound for the upcoming service. When they determined they were ready, one of the students, Ma Xiaolong, carried a large copy of the Qur'an wrapped in red silk through to the worship hall. Ma Yufang and other *chujiaren* followed behind. They walked to the *gongbei* urn. They gathered there, reciting the first passage from the Qur'an all the while. More religious adherents gathered behind them, and they all finished the recitation together cupping their hands in prayer and wiping their face twice when done. Wiping or rubbing the face indicated that the person was accepting the grace of Allah, as one follower expressed, 'as if Allah had put His grace (Ch. *zhanguang*, Ar. *baraka*) into your hands'. People then scrambled in the crush of the crowd to put their incense sticks in the urn and prepared themselves for a led prayer session.

Inside the *gongbei* again, Ma Yufang, the *chujiaren*, and students sat down on either side of a long table that had been set up down the centre of the worship hall, in line with the tomb. Ma Yufang was fitted with a microphone, prayer beads were distributed, and the large Qur'an was placed on a table in front of him. Following his lead, everyone began a silent prayer, indicated by the closing of eyes and lowering of heads. Ma Yufang, along with other *chujiaren* at the front table, took a bead and raised it to his forehead and lips before placing it on the table. Ma Yufang uncovered the Qur'an from its material wrapping. Prayer books were distributed. Ma Yufang opened the first page of the Qur'an. After he began to recite the first *Surah*, people joined in. The Qur'an is divided into 30 different *ajzā* (or parts), and they were reciting different parts of the Qur'an at the same time as follows:

- First part—from *Āyah 1, Sūrah 1* (Al-Fātiḥa) to *Āyah 141 Sūrah 2* (Al-Baqarah)
- Second part—from *Āyah 142, Sūrah 1* (Al-Baqarah) to *Āyah 252, Sūrah 2* (Al-Baqarah)
- Tenth part—from *Āyah 41, Sūrah 8* (Al-Anfāl) to *Āyah 92, Sūrah 9* (At-Tawbah)

This resulted in a cacophony of voices. When they had finished, the books were collected by one of the young students and placed in a pile near the door. They then began to chant praises in Arabic for the Prophet Muhammad from the beginning of a text known in Chinese as the *Maidayiha*. After this had finished, one *chujiaren* then began speaking in front of a microphone. He was reciting a *takbīr* (Ch. *Da zanci*) in Arabic: *'Allahu akbar'*. As he did this, incense sticks were handed out to everyone in the crowd and everyone stood up. The crowd joined the *chujiaren* in the recitation. After a short while, women began crying outside, and inside a man near the door started to break down. There was a feeling of shared catharsis as this shared recitation continued, and as it went on, it began to sound like singing. Sometimes it was as if the recitation flowed from one person to another, in fluctuating intensity. This shared invocation in close proximity to the sacralised bodies of Chen Yiming and the living *dangjiaren* seemed to generate a most explicit expression of emotion and affective practice. This went on for about six minutes. After it had finished, incense sticks were gathered, and people fell back down to their knees.

Now a shared recitation of the Shahada began—'*Liang yilaha yinliang anla, Muhanmode laisulinliang*'. This lasted for about a minute. People then muttered a final prayer to themselves with their hands cupped together, palms upwards. After this finished, people turned in the direction of the *dangjiaren* from Da Gongbei, who began a sermon (Ar. *khuṭba*). He commenced the sermon in Arabic, offering words in praise of God and prayers of blessing for Prophet Muhammad. He then delivered his sermon in Chinese, focusing on the importance of *īmāni* or faith:

Today is September's first *Zhuma*, in the Islamic calendar it is November. Under the leadership of our *dangjiaren*, with all the support and help of our religious adherents (*jiaomin*), we successfully held the ceremony today to commemorate the completion of the *gongbei* and remember Chen Yiming. It is a gratifying day. These are our great ancestors of Da Gongbei. We have just held our ceremony for the completion of Chen Yiming's *gongbei* [...] Allah says in the Qur'an, your faith is a prerequisite for success, the first row of stations are saints, the second row of stations is disciples, the third row is a Muslim station (*Mumin*), fourth row of station is people who do not believe in Allah. Allah will ask them: 'Am I not your lord?' The people of the second and first station will answer: 'Yes, you are our God.' The third station of Muslim people will follow the first and second rows and answer: 'Yes, you are our only Lord.' The fourth row of people may also speak, but their heart and mouth will be at variance (*xinkoubuyi*). If your heart does not follow your mouth, then it is not really faith. In the third row of Muslim people, there are some whose heart and mouth are also at variance, but the fourth row of people is the majority whose heart and mind are at variance. Here there is no true faith. There are some people who can speak some of the words/language, this small group of people become the new *Mumin* (muslims) […] As our sage Chen Yiming—we speak of his various miracles. He lived in Sichuan for 46 years, and only those most devout (who perform *zikr* to Allah) can recognise his greatness.

At the end of this sermon, people raised their hands in supplication once more, carrying out silent prayers under their breath. In the silence, one could hear people continuing to cry. Finally, the *dangjiaren* of Taizi Gongbei, dressed in grey, stood with his back to the crowd and began a recitation in Arabic from the Qur'an. Gradually, his call became more and more intense. After his call, people stood up, and together they prayed with him. They supplicated three times to their knees and came back up again. He then turned to the crowd, holding a polished branch in his hand, and recited it again, but this time very slow and drawn out in its delivery. As he did so, people sat with their heads down. His call was very beautiful and plaintive. After five minutes, he turned his back to the crowd again and everyone participated in supplication. People placed their hands to their ears. The recitation continued, and people bent to pray. They bent halfway, then they stood, then they knelt and prostrated, touching their heads to the ground. The second time they stayed on the ground longer. After this, the formalities of the ceremony were completed, and people began to stream out of the grounds.

Throughout this commemoration event, shaking or kissing Ma Yufang's hands or Chen Yiming's tomb was visibly moving for many people— a source of potential relief and catharsis to have made a close physical connection. During the series of shared recitations in particular, the physical proximity of the adherents to the *dangjiaren, chujiaren,* and the tomb of Chen Yiming generated a heightened degree of affect or emotion, expressed through the tears of many people who were visibly upset. During these rousing practices, the charismatic bodies drew the adherents together and, to draw from Blackman, 'caught' them up in an affective process that was relationally embodied.

In this chapter I have explored the role of public rituals in the strengthening of charisma through focusing particularly on social proximity and distance and the ways in which these alternate with notions of the sacred and profane. In the first example of the wedding, the 'conspicuous invisibility' of the *dangjiaren* was a symbolic act maintaining particular social boundaries around his celibate status. Here distance was maintained by the leadership from profane practices—that is, from practices there were felt to be potentially polluting of the purity of the body. During the process of the funeral, the *dangjiaren* was often present during initial blessings and in the commemorations that followed the burial, as a source of good luck and religious authority, but it was often the *imam* that conducted the formal part of the service. This was a particular illustration both of the distance maintained by the *dangjiaren* from 'routinised' aspects of ceremonial performance and also the need of religious adherents to seek proximity to the sacred. This distancing added to the charismatic appeal of his presence. The commemoration of the birth of the saint Chen Yiming was another illustration of the need of religious adherents to seek proximity to the sacred during ritual in order to receive blessings and further their connection to God through and with the saints. Here what was most notable was the affective response that occurred amongst adherents through proximity to the charismatic body—either proximity to the *dangjiaren* himself or to the entombed saints. Public rituals were thus an important means of generating and sustaining charismatic power—both through conscious acts of distancing from that which was deemed profane by the leadership and conscious allowances of proximity to that which was deemed sacred by the adherents.

REFERENCES

Abdul-Malik, A.J. 2013. *Janaazah: How to Bury the Muslim*. Rochester: Al-Manhaj 3 Publishing.

Csordas, T.J. 1997. *Language, Charisma, and Creativity: The Ritual Life of a Religious Movement*. Berkeley: University of California Press.

Douglas, M. 1966. *Purity and Danger: An Analysis of the Concepts of Pollution and Taboo*. Abingdon: Routledge.

Feuchtwang, S., and M. Wang. 2008. Suggestions for a Redefinition of Charisma. *Nova Religio: The Journal of Alternative and Emergent Religions* 12 (2): 90–105.

Glassé, C. 1989. *The Concise Encyclopedia of Islam*. London: Stacey International.

Halevi, L. 2004. Wailing for the Dead: The Role of Women in Early Islamic Funerals. *Past and Present* 183 (1): 3–39.

Hansson, A. 1996. *Chinese Outcasts: Discrimination and Emancipation in Late Imperial China*. Leiden: Brill.

Harms, E. 2013. The Boss: Conspicuous Invisibility in Ho Chi Minh City. *City and Society* 25 (2): 195–215.

Katz, D., and R. Kahn. 1978. *The Social Psychology of Organizations*. New York: Wiley.

Law, A. 2010. *Key Concepts in Classical Social Theory*. Los Angeles: Sage Publications.

Lindholm, C. 1990. *Charisma*. Oxford: Blackwell.
Reinhart, K.A. 1990. Impurity/No Danger. *History of Religions* 30 (1): 1–24.
Wang, P. 2005. *Xibei Huizu yanxiqu gailun (Survey of Banquets Amongst Hui in Northwest China)*. Beijing: China Federation of Literary and Art Circles.
Wetherell, M. 2012. *Affect and Emotion: A New Social Science Understanding*. London: Sage Publications.
Willner, A. 1985. *The Spellbinders: Charismatic Political Leadership*. New Haven: Yale University Press.
Yagil, D. 1998. Charismatic Leadership and Organizational Hierarchy: Attribution of Charisma to Close and Distant Leaders. *The Leadership Quarterly* 9 (2): 161–176.

CHAPTER 6

Charisma and Religious Capital: Mobility and Education

In describing the reasons why he was chosen as the *dangjiaren*, Ma Yufang replied, 'there are too many qualities, but I was assigned by my master (Ma Shiming). Life was poor and people did not pay enough attention to learning, but I was willing to study abroad. He felt I had potential to develop my knowledge to a deeper level'. For him, it was not enough to have good morality, a good 'heart', you have to be equipped with some knowledge, such as knowing the language of the classic texts: 'As in all areas, there is a foundation of knowledge. If you don't have any knowledge, you cannot convince and communicate with other people. Religion is a sacred occupation, and you must have a certain level of knowledge.' In his overseas study, performance of the *hajj* and commitment to achieve fluency in Persian and Arabic, Ma Yufang was following on from the example of his own teacher, Ma Shiming, and his spiritual ancestors who had stressed the importance of travel in their religious development and charismatic cultivation.

In this chapter I want to explore the role of education (and the possible mobility that results from education) in the construction of religious authenticity and authority in *Guo Gongbei* and how this strengthens the charismatic reputation. Following Bourdieu, this could also be described as the accumulation of religious capital. For Bourdieu, religious capital has two forms: 'religious symbolic systems (myths and ideologies), on the one hand, and religious competencies (mastery of specific practices and bodies of knowledge), on the other' (Bourdieu and Thompson 1991,

© The Author(s) 2018 141
T. Cone, *Cultivating Charismatic Power*,
https://doi.org/10.1007/978-3-319-74763-7_6

pp. 107–116). Travel for the sake of furthering religious knowledge could be understood as an important part of the religious capital required in the accumulation of charismatic power for the leader and something that his disciples also aspired to. For students and *chujiaren* at the *gongbei*, the accumulation of this religious capital began through an Islamic education. Those students and *chujiaren* who successfully achieved a certain degree of knowledge then had the opportunity to travel for further study.

RELIGIOUS TRAVEL IN THE CULTIVATION OF SUFI SAINTS

A central commandment in Islam has been the undertaking of travel in the pursuit of knowledge. As a famous Hadith states, 'If anyone travels on a road in search of knowledge, God will cause him to travel on one of the roads of Paradise' (Robson 1965, p. 53). Yousef Meri has written that in Islam this travel takes 'on different forms, from travel in the pursuit of knowledge, to performing the pilgrimage to Mecca and visiting holy sites' (Meri 2010, p. 3). However Muslim travel:

> like all travel, […] is principally a journey of the mind. Travel is pre-eminently an act of imagination, […] a literal reading of *hajj* (pilgrimage), *hijra* (emigration), *rihla* (travel for learning and other purposes), *ziyara* (visits to shrines), and even labour migration, is inappropriate. These obviously constitute physical movement from one place to another, but, owing to the power of the religious imagination, they involve spiritual or temporal movement at the same time (Eickelman and Piscatori 1990, p. 2).

For saints in Guo Gongbei, pilgrimage (Ch. *chao hanzhi*, Ar. *hajj*) meant the undertaking of a 'long journey, climbing mountains and wading rivers' in order to 'eradicate avaricious desires and be close to the original source', that is, to 'return to Allah' (Liu 1971, p. 77). It was a physical journey in order to enable a spiritual one—that of a sense of 'return' to an imagined source. An important part of this spiritual journey was also the acquisition of new knowledge and understanding of Islamic sites, figures, and practices.

The way in which Sufism arrived in China (and indeed spread throughout other parts of the world) was inherently reliant on the mobility and movement of various Sufi teachers. Qadiriyya Sufism, as mentioned in Chap. 2, was introduced and established in China by two Central Asian Sufi teachers, Khoja Afaq (1626–1694) and Khoja Abd Allah (1574–1689).

In the 1670s, Khoja Afaq travelled extensively throughout Northwest China making visits to Lanzhou, Didao, Xining, and Linxia, 'having a profound effect on both Muslim and non-Muslim communities' (Lipman 1997, p. 59). Khoja Abd Allah, according to the historical records of Guo Gongbei, set off from Mecca on his journey to China on the first of January (Ma 1997, p. 39). He entered China in 1674 and died in Guizhou in 1689. During this time he preached in Guangdong, Guangxi, Yunnan, Guizhou, and Linxia, Gansu. Lipman has noted that 'Khoja is not an Arabic title, but 'Abd Allah is reported to have studied all over the Muslim world, from Medina to Baghdad and India, so he might have picked it up elsewhere' (Lipman 1997, p. 88). Chen Yiming, the founder of Guo Gongbei, was a student of Khoja Abd Allah. Chen also visited other countries in order to broaden his studies. Specifically, he went to 'Syria, Jerusalem, Iran and Iraq (amongst other places) to visit wise men, to broaden his knowledge and to study for five years. During that time, he also studied Arabian medical science and astronomy' (Ma 1997, p. 11). He also visited a person in Baghdad, Iraq, named Muhammad Mahamudi and recruited him to be his disciple. In 1684 CE, Chen and Muhammad Mahamudi went back to China along the Silk Road.

In performing sacred pilgrimages, as Pnina Werbner has argued, 'pil- grims expect not only to undergo a spiritual renewal but a renewal of personhood through contact with the sacred, and a renewal of community through the bearing of what has been in contact with the sacred home, into the structured mundane world' (Werbner 2003, pp. 101–102). Chen Yiming returned from his pilgrimage to China, 'stronger in mind and purpose', and was determined to 'cultivate his moral character further, eventually reaching the upper level' (Ma 1997, p. 19). To borrow from Werbner, his 'spiritual renewal' led to a renewal of his community. After he returned, 'he moved about the country—including the Hehuang Area, Hexi Corridor, inside and outside the Great Wall, North and South, journeying to and fro for over thousands of miles—trying hard to spread Islamic doctrine and the Qadiriyya purpose' (Ma 1997, p. 19).

There have been seven other leaders between Chen Yiming and the current leader of Guo Gongbei. Aside from Muhammad Mahamudi from Baghdad, all the others were from Linxia City itself or surrounding areas including the Ningxia Hui Autonomous Region and the Dongxiang and Longxi counties. Historical records indicate that not all of them were able to undertake the *hajj* or travel outside of China. But the last two generations have been able to. The former leader of Guo Gongbei, Ma

Shiming, was elected at the age of 20, and he remained in that position for 68 years (1929–1997). Under his teaching instruction, 'the disciples were sent out all over the country to study—from north to south, east to west. Some overseas Chinese Muslims even came thousands of miles to *hajj* and to listen to his teaching' (Ma 1997, pp. 29–30). In 1995, when he was 85 years old, Ma Shiming was accompanied by one of his most promising disciples, Ma Yufang, to undertake the *hajj* pilgrimage to Mecca. Ma Yufang then studied at the Islamic Studies College in Lanzhou and completed studies abroad at Imam Khomeini University in Iran. In his capacity as the current leader of Guo Gongbei, this history of pilgrimage and travel plays an important part in his contemporary emphasis on overseas education for his *chujiaren* and students.

ISLAMIC EDUCATION IN CHINA

The broader situation regarding Islamic education in the region is of direct relevance in understanding activities within the *gongbei*, encouraging local and overseas study. Most Sufi communities in China have a mosque where education is provided to disciples within their *menhuan* or network. Mosque-based education (*jingtang jiaoyu*, 'education in the hall of the classics') is still the most prevalent form of Islamic education and, excluding Xinjiang, can be found throughout all of China (Armijo-Hussein 2006, p. 5). Ma Qicheng (a Hui Muslim scholar from Ningxia) and Gladney argue that mosque education in China has been one of the primary catalysts in preserving and promulgating Hui Muslim identity (Gladney and Ma 1996). Alles noted in 2003 that there are currently estimated to be about 40,000 mosques in China, each of which would in theory have a school: 'While the average number of students can be estimated at twenty per mosque, some of them, which have space, and better facilities, and where the teaching of the *ahong* is renowned, can bring together a hundred students' (Alles et al. 2003, p. 2). Mosque education is made up of three levels: elementary, intermediate (middle school), and advanced (college). The elementary school teaches the alphabet and phonetics of Arabic, primary Qur'anic knowledge, and readings on ritual practices (including prayer, fasting, funerals, and marriages). Middle-level mosque education teaches Arabic grammar, syntax, logic, rhetoric, ethics, and theology (including the *Shariah* and Hadith). The 'college' level is where the students further their knowledge of Arabic or Persian, rhetoric and commentaries on the Qur'an, and the Hadith (Gladney 1999, p. 81). All forms of religious practice were outlawed during the Cultural Revolution, including communal prayer, religious instruction, and religious festivals, and although it ended in 1976, Jacqueline Armijo-Hussein has noted that 'it was not until the early 1980s that most Muslim communities in China were allowed to regain control of their mosques' (Armijo-Hussein 2006, pp. 2–3). During this time the state also established Islamic colleges throughout the country that offered formal training for *imams*. In doing so, the Chinese government was able to 'begin to rebuild that which they had helped destroy, but also have a strong influence on how the study of Islam was reconstituted' (Armijo-Hussein 2006, p. 4). Within state-run Islamic institutions, the government strictly controlled the hiring of teachers, the selection of students, and the content of courses. As a result, there were concerns amongst some in the Muslim community that their schools were not 'sufficiently independent' (Armijo-Hussein 2006, p. 4). In response to doubts about the government-run Islamic colleges, from the late 1980s a number of independent Islamic colleges were established (Armijo-Hussein 2006, p. 4). Today, there are dozens of these independent Islamic colleges throughout China.[1]

For the past 30–40 years, China's Muslim population have been engaged in a 'process of reaffirmation of their religion and identity: construction and renovation of mosques, the dissemination of information on Islam in the world and in the translation of religious texts' (Alles et al. 2003, p. 1). There has also been a steady increase in the number of Muslims making the pilgrimage to Mecca and in undertaking overseas religious education. In 1999, Armijo-Hussein noted that there were an estimated 500–1000 Chinese Muslims presently studying in Egypt, Syria, Pakistan, Iran, Saudi Arabia, Libya, the Sudan, Turkey, Malaysia, and Indonesia (Armijo-Hussein 1999). While students struggled to adapt to life in Egypt, they were very aware of the historical importance of Al-Azhar in Islamic history (Armijo-Hussein 1999). Today, tens of thousands of Chinese Muslim students study the Qur'an and Islamic theology in both public and private schools, and many continue advanced studies abroad.

---

[1] It should be noted that there are no legal independent Islamic colleges in Xinjiang. As such, this is an inconsistency in the implementation of state policy (Tan and Ding 2014, Chapter 3, para. 11).

Most students are sponsored by family and their surrounding community and receive a small stipend at whichever Islamic university they attend. Most recently, Alexander Stewart has described this drive to study abroad amongst Islamic scholars and students in China as part of a wider cultural trend of Chinese people looking for a more 'cosmopolitan and authentic education' (Stewart 2017, Chapter 8, para. 11). For Chinese Muslims, he notes that it is the 'goal of every student to study in Islamic nations like Saudi Arabia, Egypt, Pakistan, or Malaysia' (Stewart 2017, ibid).

There are ongoing concerns however about the uptake of religious education (or education full stop) amongst Muslim youth. In an article published in 2003 titled *Chinese Islam: Unity and Fragmentation*, the authors note that 'the Hui, lay intellectuals and clerics alike, deplore the poor educational provision which is disadvantaging their community' (Alles et al. 2003, p. 22). Alles stresses however that different sections of the community have their own objectives. For the Hui who are not 'practising' Muslims, the main aim is to improve living standards and to participate in the broader processes of modernisation within China itself by educating more 'intellectuals, more cadres and more technicians. For religious activities, better education is seen as a means of improving Chinese society's understanding of and respect of Islam' (Alles et al. 2003, p. 16). The rationale behind this is that 'studying leads to a deeper religious understanding while dispelling superstitions, erroneous beliefs and suchlike signs of backwardness. Properly educated Muslims gain a stronger sense of belonging to the umma (community of the faithful), as they do not have to feel ashamed about deficiencies in their pronunciation of Arabic or their understanding of Islamic ritual' (Alles et al. 2003, p. 22).

Ma Zhiqiang, a Hui masters student in anthropology, was most concerned to improve Muslim attitudes towards education more broadly. I mentioned to him one day what the Han taxi driver had told me, that 'the Hui have no culture/education'. To this he replied, 'What the [Han taxi] driver said is very reasonable. This situation still exists, however it does not comply with Islamic culture. Islam commands that all men and women learn knowledge—this is everyone's fate (*zhuming*). But now Muslims, for example the Hui, do not do well in education, there is a lack of knowledge. For now, it seems that people have a psychological rejection of education. It is not just about Islam, but also [their] general scientific and cultural knowledge is relatively poor. We really do need education'. He went on to explore possible reasons as to why education levels were so low in the Northwest region.

Amongst Muslims in the Northwest, marriage is normally early, especially among women. Generally around 20 years of age they will get married, some at 18 years of age, or earlier. Of course, there are those who marry after 20. It's not a Hui tradition, but a tradition in Chinese rural areas. The reason why it is especially prevalent among women is to do with ideology. Northwest parents in remote areas, they feel that women should get married earlier. Women are also less likely to receive a complete education. In the northwest territories, there has been a lot of female bondage. China used to have some of the feudal ideology, such as the idiom 'a woman's virtue is to have no talent' (*nuzi wucai bianshe de*). And now, the current situation relates to this history. There are many men too, many of whom do not complete junior high school. Among us Hui, many will follow their parents to do business, or to earn money, this is often their reason, but for family economics, it's not a good reason. When the parents' cultural knowledge is not enough, family education will fail. This is one aspect.

According to Ma Zhiqiang, amongst women religious education suffered due to expectations of early marriage and consequently an often incomplete education. Amongst families more broadly it was due to pressures on economic stability and the prioritising of money over education, particularly if the child demonstrated no aptitude for study. The issue, Ma argued, 'is indeed ideas. Minorities have a high birth rate, however the ratio of education to birth rate is very low. In the interior of China (in contrast to the frontiers like Gansu) it is generally two children, in poor or remote areas they allow three. Many parents want their children to follow a good path, but if the child is not good at studying, they are very likely to give up pursuing this path. My two brothers are like this, but my parents would encourage them to acquire knowledge, not to lose their faith and culture. However, I have some relatives and neighbours, they do not want their children to follow any path in religion. They want their children to be able to make money'.[2]

---

[2] Ma Zhiqiang's own family situation: 'My father graduated from *gaozhong*, my mother only attained third year level of primary school, but my mother often uses Chinese characters. Our family does simple mechanical handicraft and produces plastic rope. Eight years ago our family also did farming. Later, due to farming, our land was expropriated. We are not farming now, we are only processing plastic rope. My father is regarded as a small businessman. My mother is responsible for billing at home. Her computing power is very good. I have an older brother and a younger brother, they are both married and each has a child. One brother is two years older than me, another brother two years younger than me.'

In Linxia, for those students (both male and female) who did want a religious education and whose families could afford it, it was compulsory to complete junior high school before they could do so. This relates to an observation by Jaschok that education, as a site of cultural reproduction, is linked to the survival of Islamic faith and Muslim identity in China. But it is also 'a state's most urgent priority to exercise control over this same site. Education thus becomes a field of tension where the vested and competing interests of the state and of patriarchal Islamic institutions intersect, their respective dominance marked by controls over bodies and minds of recipients of education and by the moral and social consequences of society' (Jaschok and Chan 2009, p. 20). As such, the government requires that religious schools teach subjects such as history and politics to ensure nationalistic sentiment amongst Muslims and other religious communities. Despite the fundamental purpose of Arabic language schools in Linxia being for 'religious' teaching, Ma Zhiqiang explained that the government 'will let them teach some other courses, such as politics, Chinese history, and so on. In accordance with policy, a student must complete compulsory education in order to enter an Arabic school. This is required by the government. Our laws say that if you are under 16 years, you are not allowed to enter a religious profession. The government considers Arabic schools as religious schools, (and I think) government regulations are justified, because in China before you learn Arabic, you must have good Chinese language. The government is worried that the Muslim community, or Buddhist, Daoist and other groups, will only accept religious knowledge and ignore national education, and (thus) be more prone to splitting (from the government)'.[3]

---

[3] Even though the law states that you have to be at least 16 years of age to learn in a mosque, I encountered students in schools in Linxia who were sometimes younger. Ma Zhiqiang explained that 'this is rather special. Although the Government has provided [this ruling], it can be more lenient. [...] We often say: Above there are policies, below there are measures [countermeasures for dealing with a situation] (*shangyouzhengce, xiayouduice*). In fact, we already have a lot of intervention. There are some things, though they did not comply with the requirements of the minorities, as long as [there is] no accident, and [it is] within the control of the government, it does not matter. The government will open one eye and close the other (*yi zhi yang bi yi zhi yan di*). Ethnic issues in China, unlike the political and other issues, are very sensitive and [people] are easily hurt. In Linxia, many officials are Muslims. They will act [both] as a Muslim, but also [in order to do] government work. This is the benefit of the government [being involved in] training minority cadres'.

In Islamic education in China, Gladney has argued that two distinct educational worlds have appeared—the public (constituted by state—run colleges) and the private (constituted by independent colleges and mosques). He has postulated that Muslims can learn little of their religious heritage in state Islamic schools, given the Marxist-atheistic critique of religion and the widespread expectation that all religion, with nationality and class, will disappear. This may, he has asserted, be driving more religious Muslims away from state schools into the private schools—exactly counter to the state's intention of integration and secularisation through public schooling. In the end, he posits that 'until state education in China begins to incorporate more Muslim information about Islam, the mosque might become an even more practical source for an alternative education, a source of knowledge that has persisted throughout China's Muslim regions since they first settled in China' (Gladney 1999, p. 94). In an interview with Professor S. in 2012 however, he talked of almost the opposite problem, that is, how do we get the best and brightest students into the mosque schools?

> Education is a very important thing in [the] development of Islamic culture and civilisation in China. Also the challenges of modern education. In modern times, people don't want to send their next generation to the mosque to get an Islamic education. I think this is the biggest challenge. In history, Islam developed very fast through *jingtang jiaoyu* education [mosque education]. So I think *jingtang jiaoyu* is the most important thing in [the] development of China. Nowadays, people are willing to send their children to school, to university, or even to work in society. But [they] do not want to send them to the mosque. So it is a big problem. I think it's one of the challenges.

In a review of Islamic education in China in 2014 by Charlene Tan and Kejia Ding, the authors argued that Islamic schools in China need to 'revise their system, curriculum and pedagogy in order to equip their graduates for survival and success in a knowledge economy' (Tan and Ding 2014, Chapter 3, conclusion). This is in line with what Professor S. also suggested, specifically, that:

> We must add some new textbooks. This is one thing. Another thing is, I feel during my survey in Ningxia, Yunnan, that the situation is going to change, it is already changing now. In previous times, in the past 10 to 20 years, only low quality youth go to the mosque for Islamic education, but nowadays

because of job pressures, university students began to enter the mosque to get an education. I met so many people in Yunnan and also in Ningxia, so I think it is a good phenomena. Maybe in the future, Islamic education may improve to some extent. That's why I call for the improvement of *jingtang jiaoyu*. I'm going to organise another conference in Lanzhou University, talking about *jingtang jiaoyu*. So many people ask me to do that, so I think it is time to do that.

In terms of how the Sufi *gongbei* were contributing to the promotion of education, Professor S. explained that:

There is not much difference between *gongbei* education and *jingtang jiaoyu*. Whether the Islamic education in Mosque or *gongbei* we call it *jingtang jiaoyu*. Maybe the Sufism is more focused in *gongbei*. In the past decades, the *gongbei* have made little contributions to Islamic education. Only in recent years some Masters such as Ma Yufang of Guo Gongbei and Hongyang of Honggangzi in Ningxia have promoted education within the *gongbei*.

EDUCATION IN GUO GONGBEI

Although mosque education was well-developed in Linxia with many mosque-based schools and language schools for girls and boys, the majority of the Qadiriyya *gongbei* sites did not have any schools for Muslim youth to attend. In these sites, 'religious education' as such was only something that was offered to *chujiaren*, as part of their lifelong commitment to a religious life. Da Gongbei, the largest centre of Qadiriyya Sufism in the network, had offered mosque education in the past, beginning in 1944. In that year, the Board of Directors established a Linxia Da Gongbei Primary School. Ma Ziguo (the *dangjiaren* at the time) was the president, and he employed two teachers with a recruitment of about 80 students. Over 20 of the students were disciples of Da Gongbei, and the funds to support them were at the expense of Da Gongbei. Linxia Da Gongbei Primary School offered the elementary curriculum of mosque education. It was an educational platform for Hui Muslim children to receive a basic knowledge in religion. Students learnt to read and spell Arabic letters, chanted the 'Shahada' (*qingzhen yan*), chanted Khatm al-Qur'an (selected readings of the Qur'an), and practised worshipping and fasting. Though the study of scripture is still available as part of the study of disciples, nowadays, this traditional mosque education does not exist anymore in Da Gongbei. Guo

Gongbei, however, is distinctive in that it opened a school several years ago for Muslim youth—both male and female. The promotion and improvement of religious education was a key issue of concern for Ma Yufang:

> We offer poor people in the *gongbei* medication, education as well as economic support. We also help non-Muslims, but Muslim people are more devoted and several groups of our students have gone out (abroad). Those who had difficulties in life, we offered them free education to help them to study in other provinces. Some villages and families also ask us to help them with problems.

Guo Gongbei promoted and supported not only education at the local level but the international education of both Muslim youth and of their own celibate practitioners (*chujiaren*). They maintained a very strong link with educational institutions in Iran and provided support and preparation necessary to send *chujiaren* and students there to study for varying periods of time.[4] As well as providing financial assistance and making logistical arrangements for this select group of students and *chujiaren* to study abroad every year, Ma Yufang was also making further preparations to build a Foreign Languages University in the area, in collaboration with Beijing Language and Culture University. He wanted to improve the educational opportunities for the local Muslim community, with the broader hope that Muslims in China could contribute to the country's growth and development—not just in religious education but also in secular fields such as engineering and medicine. In his opinion, Muslims must help others around them—this is 'God's wish.' These practices were generative of charisma—for both himself and his disciples and students. He drew on 'resources' in his own journey of charismatic cultivation in order to assist others in theirs. He felt very lucky to have been given the chance to perform the *hajj*, and to then study overseas, and he saw great value in an overseas

---

[4] Matthew Erie has also described a Sufi private school in Linxia founded in 1993 by 'members affiliated with the Qadiriyya Ma Wenchuan Sufi order'. Like Guo Gongbei, this school emphasises the study of Persian as a gateway to Islamic knowledge. Interestingly, he notes that 'in contrast to the Yihewani private school's cultivation of ties with business contacts in Saudi Arabia, the Sufi private school builds ties with Iran. The Yihewani and Sufi private schools, anchoring their teaching in opposing authorizing traditions, thus represent in Northwest China the ideological tug-of-war between Saudi Arabia and Iran' (Erie 2016, p. 196).

educational experience for young Muslim students. He hoped that many of the students who returned could become language teachers and work at his school.

The contribution of Guo Gongbei to the promotion and support of overseas education was often recognised at public events. The speech below occurred in 2011 during the commemoration event described in Chap. 5 and was by a provincial member of the China Islamic Association.

> Distinguished leaders, colleagues, church members, friends. Today is Guo Gongbei's completion ceremony. It is gratifying for everyone here who has awaited this moment. I am here on behalf of the Linxia City Committee, to join with the *dangjiaren* of every *gongbei*, with the *imams* of mosques in the region, with the families and construction workers, friends from afar, experts and scholars and all leaders sitting here, who have shared their sincere greetings. We cannot change the past (life and youth cannot be traced back in the passage of time), but the party's national policy for the religious development of our little Mecca—Linxia—provides a strong guarantee that we can now feel legitimate to hold our heads high. The teachings and doctrine of Linxia's Guo Gongbei have always been to promote and set up education as a subject, and to relieve suffering in all walks of life. In recent years, Guo Gongbei's Ma Yufang has cultivated batch after batch of young, knowledgeable, virtuous new *imams*, and transported many students to study abroad for further study. He has made a great contribution to the development of Islam in China. We sincerely hope that he will follow this path unswervingly in order to cultivate more talent within Islam. Sages achieved great wisdom and spared no efforts. Through their dedication, they perfected themselves and are role models for us all. Finally, I encourage Guo Gongbei and his leader Ma Yufang. Under his leadership, may we maintain social stability, and build a harmonious society, and make more contributions to national unity and national economic development. (Wang Yongjun, China Islamic Association Provincial Member, CPPCC Vice Chairman, September 2011)

In speeches such as these given at public events, the Sufi leaders praise the government for their support, and likewise the government representatives praise the contributions of the Sufi leaders to education in the region (see Appendix for the other two speeches that occurred at the commemoration event). While in reality throughout the past century this has not always been the case, the current rhetoric of mutual support between government and the *gongbei* is not without precedent. One must recall here that the founder of Guo Gongbei—Chen Yiming—was a guardian of Emperor Kangxi of the Qing Dynasty, healing his illnesses and rescuing him in stormy seas. Indeed, the very name, Guo Gongbei, was the result of a special edict given by Emperor Kangxi—'*Bao Guo Wei Min*'—to serve the country and protect the people.

MOBILE STUDENTS AND *CHUJIAREN*

Several of the students currently studying at Guo Gongbei did not have any previous family affiliation with the Qadiriyya network. They had gone there because of the leader's educational history, knowledge of Persian and Arabic, and his international connections. In an effort to cultivate their religious selves, on a daily basis they studied the Qur'an and Hadith, and the languages of Persian and Arabic, and participated in practices of prayer, eating, and cleaning that were unique to Islam. In demonstrating such a commitment, they opened up the possibility of being chosen to study overseas. Iran, in particular, was seen by some of these students as the source of Persian Sufism and Persian Sufi texts and literature, and studying at the *gongbei* allowed for a direct connection to this 'sacred' place, where this material and knowledge could be studied further. This geographic mobility was both intellectually and spiritually important. In the acquisition of new Islamic knowledge and experience in a site of historic significance in terms of Islamic learning and pilgrimage, they felt they could become more deeply learned Muslims and develop their 'understanding of God'.

Several other factors related to the personal backgrounds of these individuals were also important in motivating them to study overseas and to contribute in some form to the ongoing development of Islamic learning in China. Most of the students came from relatively large families, in which there were at least three or four children and in which both their siblings and parents had very little religious education and knowledge. Furthermore, there was an inherent dissatisfaction with the options of continued study in the state education system, due to the limited support for religious learning. To combat both of these frustrations, they were all pursuing pathways of distinction, ways to distinguish themselves both as exemplary Muslims within their own families and as successful Hui in a Han majority country.[5] They wanted to be role models for their families, peers, and eventually, for their communities—which is to say they wished to become charismatic. For most, the 'worldly' knowledge, experience, and educational background of the current *gongbei* leader was the primary factor in attracting them to the *gongbei*. Secondary to this was the knowledge that this leader could offer opportunities to study abroad—an experience that could benefit the development of their own religious authenticity and authority as potential leaders and teachers in their home communities.

Many students and *chujiaren* have followed Ma Yufang's example and are now studying overseas, taking advantage of the educational opportunities that the *gongbei* has provided. There are students and *chujiaren* both within and outside the *gongbei* who want to study overseas, those who are now currently doing so and those who are weighing up options for life back in China. They all had common aspirations to study in Iran and to contribute in some form to the ongoing development of Islamic learning in China. In 1999 Armijo-Hussein met with a student who had graduated from an Islamic university in Iran and commented, 'Little is known of the students studying in Iran, for almost all of those who have completed their studies there have chosen to stay. Indeed, this student spoke very highly of the quality of the education and living conditions of the Chinese students in Iran' (Armijo-Hussein 1999). In 2006, she also noted that the (Chinese) students 'who studied in Iran were among the most satisfied, even though their studies and training proved to be more rigorous than that offered anywhere else since they must study Persian as well as Arabic, and the Shi'a school of law in addition to the four classic Sunni schools of law (most Muslims in China follow the Hanafi school of law)' (Armijo-Hussein 2006, p. 7). The teacher who took the Persian class was a former student of the *gongbei* who had been supported and guided by the leader to study in Iran. Several years after studying in Iran, he had been requested to return to Linxia to assist with language teaching at the *gongbei*. He talked a little about his time in Iran and how he was very grateful for the opportunity to go there.

---

[5] In this context, to be exemplary as a Muslim meant to fully embody and seek a deeper understanding of the practices and values of their Islamic faith. To be successful as a Hui meant to be well-educated and able to contribute meaningfully not only to the Chinese Muslim community but also to Chinese society as a whole.

I was 17 when I went to Iran, now I am 24. At that time my parents sent me, and Ma Laoshi (leader) recommended me. I studied Persian in Iran, after one year I started my bachelor's degree, I studied Religious Studies, mainly Shi'ism […] When I was studying language, I didn't think it was very difficult, it was okay. The main aspects of my major were studying *Shariah* law and belief. With regards to language, except for Persian, I also studied Arabic. At the moment, I still have not chosen a teacher/master, because I have not decided to choose Sufism. I have only studied the Islamic laws— such as the rituals of fasting (one of the five pillars).

He has now returned to Iran and is continuing graduate studies there in Islamic philosophy. He is unsure exactly what direction he will take upon completion (either becoming an *imam*, a translator or a businessman in China), but he expressed his gratitude to the leader for the opportunity to study abroad and to be of assistance in the education of other Muslim students back home. Several months after I departed the field, I was in touch with a former student, Yang Shuijie, and he was now studying at a language school in Qum, Iran. He told me that he missed his family in certain moments, but generally he found people in Iran to be very friendly. He was still not accustomed to the food, describing it as 'really different. Here they eat a lot of sweet and sour dishes, we prefer spicy dishes'. At the moment, apart from his own daily living expenses, he was not paying tuition fees. His main tuition fees were covered by the *gongbei*. He was really interested in Persian literature and wanted to continue on to major in it, either in Iran or at home in China. Yang felt that his experience in Iran was enabling him to see what was lacking in his own country in terms of Islamic education, and he spoke of how he wanted to contribute to its improvement:

When I arrived in this foreign country, I discovered that the preservation of Islamic teaching in China is very good, very complete, but in some ways a little behind. In terms of the changes happening in the world all the time, at the core there should be something unchanging and constant, which should go along with the world, because in the Qur'an it says, Islam is a religion that can suit and adapt to any epoch. But there are many aspects of knowledge in which we are behind. Before, in order to maintain religion, Chinese Muslims would study at a young age, and would only study Islamic knowledge. But after studying they were not able to use Chinese to express themselves very well. They could bring about a good understanding of their own heart, but were not able to give others a good understanding.

This caused misunderstandings [of Qur'anic knowledge] to happen [...] the Qur'an emphasises the importance of education and knowledge. Muhammad the Prophet said, the ink of the scholar is more precious than the blood of the martyr [...] Now I want to study well, my hope is to run a school, and all children can attend the school for a period of time and study the academic program of the nation [China], and simultaneously study and understand religious knowledge, because now the economic pressures in society are very large, it's impossible for one person to finish university and run away to a mosque to study religious knowledge. My hope is to allow everyone to understand knowledge of the Muslims, they should understand and have that knowledge.

Yang's astute observations here parallel the concerns also raised by Ma Zhiqiang and Professor S. For someone to finish a university degree and then pursue religious education (if they got that far) was nigh on impossible due to economic pressures. Thus many of the 'best and the brightest' weren't enrolling in mosque education. He also recognised the importance of a sound education in both Chinese and Islamic languages and literature. Without a foundation in both, a Chinese Muslim could not communicate successfully between the two cultural worlds and bring about a deeper mutual understanding. These concerns were driving him to open up his own school in the future—as Ma Yufang had done— and they had also led him to overseas study in Iran. The desire for his own charismatic cultivation had led to this geographic mobility. Yang's friends and classmates, Aihemaide and Zheng, were also both now in Iran, continuing their Persian language studies as they had hoped. After a year and a half there, they were both hoping to return to China to see their families. Zheng mentioned that he was also not accustomed to the food yet, but was enjoying his study there so far.[6]

Zhang Yufang (from the Dongxiang minority) was one of three female students who were in the same class with Yang and his friends. She was 17 at the time and had been at the *gongbei* for four months. She had graduated from senior high school (*gaozhong*) and was staying with her

---

[6] Armijo-Hussein has noted that some students expressed disillusionment with the realities of living in a modern Muslim society: 'For the Muslims of China, who have always been a small minority amongst the Han Chinese majority and who have survived for centuries isolated from the rest of the Islamic world, often experiencing intense periods of persecution, the idealistic expectations they have of Islamic countries can become the basis of considerable disappointment' (Armijo-Hussein 1999).

cousin in Linxia while she completed study at the *gongbei*. She explained to me that she had come to the *gongbei* because she had heard of Ma Yufang's international connections and hoped that through studying there she could be chosen to study overseas in Iran. One evening when I was visiting her at home, she brought out a collection of precious Sufi texts in Persian. She also talked about how most people (including her parents) don't have the education or language skills to understand either Arabic or Persian and thus cannot comprehend more complex aspects of Islamic philosophy. So for her, the 'special knowledge' of the Sufis is comparatively deep compared with 'ordinary people'. She softly told me how much it would mean to her to really grasp the ideas in these texts more deeply, and perhaps one day she might actually be able to. She spoke of her great respect for Ma Yufang and at the same time a certain degree of fear. She had hardly spoken to him directly herself, and the idea made her visibly nervous. In April 2012 she left China to study in Iran. I spoke to her in July while she was there, and she explained that she would be there for at least three years and wanted to continue on to university there. Her goal was to study abroad and return to China to teach language in a mosque or Islamic college.

One of her friends, Ma Xiulai, was 16 and was also studying at Guo Gongbei during the same period. She had finished middle school and was living with her aunty and uncle and their three children in Linxia while she studied at the *gongbei*. She too spoke to me of her hopes to study in Iran through the exchanges that Guo Gongbei offered and then come back to China to teach. She particularly wanted to focus on religious knowledge such as Islamic history and jurisprudence. In April she too departed to Iran with her classmates and like Zhang Yufang explained to me that she hoped to continue on to university study there.

Ma Yunhu (18), a young *chujiaren* mentioned earlier, expressed to me his desire to follow these students and study overseas in the future. He spoke of being very committed to the celibate life and to the continuation of his religious learning. He also said to me that 'Ma Yufang always encourages us to be committed to our study, and wants to support the most committed students to study in Iran, as this is where he studied. He is very well-respected in the community for doing so, and I know if I ever had the opportunity to learn in an Islamic country, I would take it. It is not guaranteed, but it's possible'. Ma Xiaobin (23) was another young *chujiaren*, originally from Linxia, who had studied at Guo Gongbei but was now studying in Iran. He had a brother studying English in college and a sister in junior high school. His parents were government employees. His specific focus was on contributing to Islamic education in China, as he explained: 'I am in college (in Iran) to learn the language, Persian literature, and the Qur'an. After this I want to become an *imam*, regardless of whether that is in a mosque or at Guo Gongbei. As long as I can make a contribution to the dissemination of Islamic culture, what the job is, is not so important. Although there is a strong religious atmosphere in study and life in this country, my knowledge compared with that of my family is richer. But I don't want to use my rank or position to teach them, I want to influence them by example.' Learning and studying was of primary importance to many young *chujiaren*, regardless of whether they committed to the celibate life in the end or not. Another student, Ma Yong, explained that for many *chujiaren* that he knew, 'after going to Iran to study, they have to look at their own situation, but the best thing is to keep studying, and accumulate more knowledge. They can then decide if they want to become *chujiaren* or not, that is not definite, but if they must return home then they will. Because the leader sent us out, if he needs us to return, we must return'.

Throughout the examples of male students, female students, and young *chujiaren*, the underlying motivations are similar. They each have aspirations to study at Guo Gongbei because they know it could lead on to study in Iran. Iran, in turn, is seen as a site of sacred importance in Islamic history. It is also a place where they can practise and improve on their Persian, which in turn could enhance their ability to understand Sufi texts. These are all important factors in their own charisma-generating practice.

Philip Taylor has written that pilgrimage has often been 'profoundly implicated in the constitution' of political authority, ethnicity, caste, class, national identity, cultural structures, and gender (Taylor 2004, p. 14). In this case, pilgrimage for study overseas generated forms of religious capital for the current and future leadership in Guo Gongbei and in turn strengthened their charismatic authority. Chen Yiming, the founder of Guo Gongbei, stressed the search for new knowledge by way of travel—both throughout China and to the Middle East. Nowadays, many students and *chujiaren* come to Guo Gongbei because of the charismatic inspiration of past and present leaders, a charisma that is strengthened in part by their experience studying in locations highly valued in Islamic history.

For young Muslim students and *chujiaren*—potential future teachers and leaders within both the Qadiriyya community and elsewhere in China—overseas experience studying in a Muslim-majority country was highly valued in the constitution of their own religious authenticity and authority. Furthermore, this study was seen to not only contribute to personal cultivation but to a sense of pride and national identity as Muslims in the Chinese context. While the *gongbei* was a distinctively Sufi site, its practices did not demand that students necessarily follow the life of a celibate and/or that they study specifically Sufi texts. Fundamentally, Guo Gongbei aimed to encourage and enable study and learning for individuals (both at home and abroad) in order to improve levels of religious knowledge amongst the Muslim community as a whole. This was distinctive in the region—as they were the only Qadiriyya *gongbei* site to do so.

REFERENCES

Alles, E., L. Cherif-Chebbi, and C.-H. Halfon. 2003. Chinese Islam: Unity and Fragmentation. *Religion, State and Society* 31 (1): 7–35.

Armijo-Hussein, J. 1999. Resurgence of Islamic Education in China. *ISIM Newsletter* 4: 1.

Armijo-Hussein, J. 2006. Islamic Education in China. *Harvard Asia Quarterly* 10 (1): 15–24.

Bourdieu, P., and J.B. Thompson. 1991. *Language and Symbolic Power.* Cambridge: Harvard University Press.

Eickelman, D.F., and J.P. Piscatori. 1990. *Muslim Travellers: Pilgrimage, Migration, and the Religious Imagination.* Berkeley: University of California Press.

Erie, M. 2016. *China and Islam: The Prophet, the Party, and Law.* Cambridge: Cambridge University Press.

Gladney, D.C. 1999. Making Muslims in China: Education, Islamicization and Representation. In *China's National Minority Education: Culture, Schooling and Development,* ed. G.A. Postiglione, 55–94. New York: Falmer Press.

Gladney, D.C., and Q. Ma. 1996. *Local and Muslim in China.* Hilton Hawaiian Village Hotel, Honolulu.

Jaschok, M., and H.M.V. Chan. 2009. Education, Gender and Islam in China: The Place of Religious Education in Challenging and Sustaining 'Undisputed Traditions' Among Chinese Muslim Women. *International Journal of Educational Development* 29 (5): 487–494.

Lipman, J. 1997. *Familiar Strangers: A History of Muslims in Northwest China.* Studies on Ethnic Groups in China. Seattle: University of Washington Press.

Liu, Z. 1971. *Tianfang Dianli (Norms and Rituals of Islam).* Reprint, Hong Kong: Hong Kong Muslim Propagation Society.

Ma, Y. 1997. *Linxia Guo Gongbei Jianshi (A Brief History of Guo Gongbei)*. Guo Gongbei Committee.

Meri, Y. 2010. *Pilgrimage and Religious Travel*. http://www. oxfordbibliographies.com/view/document/obo-9780195390155/obo-9780195390155-0061.xml.

Robson, J. 1965. *Mishkat al Masabih (A Niche for Lamps)*. Vol. 1. Lahore: Sh. Muhammad Ashraf.

Stewart, A. 2017. *Chinese Muslims and the Global Ummah: Islamic Revival and Ethnic Identity Among the Hui of Qinghai Province*. Abingdon: Routledge.

Tan, C., and K. Ding. 2014. The Role, Developments and Challenges of Islamic Education in China. In *Muslim Education in the 21st Century: Asian Perspectives*, ed. S. Buang and P. Ghim-Lian Chew. Abingdon: Routledge.

Taylor, P. 2004. *Goddess on the Rise: Pilgrimage and Popular Religion in Vietnam*. Honolulu: University of Hawai'i Press.

Werbner, P. 2003. *Pilgrims of Love: The Anthropology of a Global Sufi Cult*. Bloomington: Indiana University Press.

CHAPTER 7

Contentious Charisma

Despite the recognised and supported contribution of Guo Gongbei to Islamic education by the local government in Linxia, it is still subject to ongoing critiques. It must be noted, as was mentioned early on, that most Sufi orders in Gansu (and elsewhere) do not have celibate clergy. For some Muslims (Sufi and non-Sufi) in the surrounding community, the Qadiriyya practice of charismatic authority generated and determined by celibate practitioners is simply 'unorthodox' Islam and should be abolished. For state representatives, a charismatic system of authority that exists on the basis of the 'mystical' (and thus 'undocumented') process of 'divine permission' (*kouhuan*) is seen as potentially unstable and a threat to more secular and democratic forms of governance.

This chapter explores these discourses in more detail. I do this through a presentation and analysis of voices—those of local state representatives, Muslim academics, Sufi practitioners, and Muslim students. For the purposes of clarity, I divide these contestations into four sets of metacultural categories, detailed below. This broader discussion of the organisation of charismatic authority leads into the conclusion where I return to Weber's prediction about the transformation of charismatic authority and ask how it applies in this instance. If charisma 'cannot remain stable' will it become 'either traditionalised or rationalised, or a combination of both' (Weber and Runciman 1978, p. 244) as Weber theorised?

© The Author(s) 2018
T. Cone, *Cultivating Charismatic Power*,
https://doi.org/10.1007/978-3-319-74763-7_7

ORTHODOXY AND METACULTURE

Talal Asad stressed that orthodoxy 'is not a mere body of opinion but a distinctive relationship—a relationship of power' (Asad 1986, p. 14). Accordingly, he argued that the anthropology of Islam ought to understand 'the historical conditions that enable the production and maintenance of specific discursive traditions, or their transformation—and the efforts of practitioners to achieve coherence' (Asad 1986, p. 17). Put another way, following Bourdieu (Bourdieu 1984, p. 471), one could ask: what historical conditions lead or force people to become explicit, discursive or reflective about their practice? What are the conditions in which 'doxic' (taken-for-granted) or implicit practice becomes explicit commentary?

In the context of this Muslim community in Northwest China, as elsewhere in the Islamic world, an ongoing anxiety about maintaining orthodoxy has led Muslims to become reflexive and explicit about their practice. This maintenance of orthodoxy in the Chinese context is directly related to concerns about their perceived 'low-*suzhi*' status as a minority group within a non-Muslim majority country. As mentioned in the introductory chapter, the cultivation of a *qingzhen* habitus was an important way to combat this—a *qingzhen* habitus that relied on a sound understanding of the 'orthodox' rules of the 'tradition' of Sunni Islam. As such, practices seen as being 'unorthodox Islam', such as the celibacy of the Qadiriyya Sufis, were seen to only increase this anxiety. I understand this reflexive discourse about practice as a kind of 'metaculture', to borrow from Greg Urban. Metaculture is, Urban writes, 'culture that is about culture', operating 'as a distinct [...] layer of circulation articulating in various ways with the cultural plane' (Urban 2001, p. 281). Matt Tomlinson comments that this metaculture is:

> a cultural product, but one that reflects on, or comments on, aspects of culture, and as such it is necessarily comparative. Comparisons can be made along axes—themselves culturally shaped and calibrated—such as oldness and newness, effectiveness and ineffectiveness, and success and failure [...] metaculture is not a static reflection, not just an act of categorisation after the fact of expression; it is creative and consequential, functioning as an accelerative force propelling other cultural products into circulation (Tomlinson 2009, p. 19).

In the following discussion, four sets of metacultural categories underpin each set of contestations. The first set of contestations are centred around the metacultural categories of 'orthodoxy' and 'unorthodoxy'. The second set revolves around the metacultural categories of 'integrity' and 'corruption', the third around 'unity' and 'disunity', and the fourth around the categories of 'stability' and 'instability', specifically in relation to concerns at a governmental level.

Rhetoric of Tolerance

In 2012, the relationships between various Islamic factions (*paibie*) in Linxia were often described as having achieved, while not mutual understanding, at least a degree of mutual 'tolerance and respect'. Professor S. explained that 'yes, [in the past] there was a conflict between different groups, especially between the Yihewani and the *menhuan*, and between Yihewani and Salafiyya. It was a very serious conflict in the 1980s, and it lasted about ten to fifteen years. But at last people gave up. Because they felt that there was no use having conflicts between each other. I couldn't bring anyone from Yihewani to Salafiyya or take someone from *menhuan* to Yihewani, so, the people said, it's useless—useless to criticise others, you cannot change anyone's belief or affiliation. So people gradually gave up criticizing. Nowadays the government says of course we encourage harmony, peace, so in this situation people say, okay, good, we cannot change anyone's belief, why spend our strength to criticise others, trying to change others, we can't do it, useless. But in their heart, Yihewani say okay, they tolerate but they don't agree. Even *menhuan* don't agree with Salafiyya, Salafiyya criticise *menhuan* and Yihewani—so now [there is] just tolerance'. With regard specifically to the Linxia region, Zhao Yufang explained:

> There are many different ethnic groups, and besides this, we have different factions (*paibie*). As well as Gadelinye (Qadiriyya), there are Hufuye (Khu-fiyya) and Kuburenye (Kubrawiyya). Also, as well as the four main Islamic teachings, there is one called *santai*, and other teachings, which all exist in Linxia. The policy now is very good. People do not interfere with each other. By following the policy, and promoting the policy, this also helps. Before this, division between factions were very serious. So, for example, the Tibetans did not talk to people from other nationalities. Those are all old ideas, which have diminished now. We all believe in what we choose. I won't say any word about yours and you do the same. Through good propaganda (*xuanchuan*), there won't be any unnecessary conflicts. Now it is much more stable.

This 'propaganda' references what Fenggang Yang has described as a 'red-stained' religious market in China. This 'red-stain' references official Communist ideology and is 'reflected in the rhetoric of the clergy, theological discourses, and practices. For example, the authorities required the clergy to teach believers to 'love the country and love the religion' (*aiguo aijiao*), where loving the country precedes loving the religion [...] This is a mantra that the clergy in the approved religious organisations must chant to gain legitimacy in the eyes of the authorities' (Yang 2012, Chapter 5, para. 3). In Fig. 7.1, a banner hangs outside Guo Gongbei, displaying this very message: 'Love one's country, love one's religion, join forces [in the name of] progress.'

Zhao explained his own role in supporting this rhetoric of unity amongst groups in relation to his activities as a well-known Chinese/Arabic calligrapher:

Fig. 7.1 A banner hanging outside the *gongbei*. It reads, 'Love one's country, love one's religion, join forces [in the name of] progress'

I'm a CPPCC member of Linxia (Chinese People's Political Consultative Conference). I'm also in the Calligraphy and Painting Association. Also, I'm a member of both the Writing Association and General Secretary as well as a member of the Gansu Calligraphy Association. We get along very well. Not like in the past [when] we distinguished ourselves from one another very clearly. Decades ago, I thought there must be a medium between different ethnic groups and religious groups. In the calligraphy of Chinese and Arabic, most of them are mixed with each other, ethnic groups and religious groups are tied more tightly together. People should be together as well. The calligraphy that I depict also shows the importance of unity. They also pay more attention to it. People didn't communicate with Han people twenty years ago, which caused some conflicts. Then, through the good effect of education and promotion of policy, the old concept diminished, only very few people who received little education had this kind of idea. Not only in religion, people in art like us, communicate with other religious groups people and established a stable relationship. In April, I founded the Linxia Hui Autonomous Prefecture Arabic Language, Calligraphy, Painting and Art Research Institute (*Linxiazhou Awen shuhua yishu yanjiuyuan*). I tell people that their old attitude needs to change, and we need to view things differently under the new age. This work should be propagated. The development of culture and ethnic groups needs to be tied together.

Concerning the new (*xinjiao*) and the old religion (*laojiao*) of which Gladney spoke, Zhao Yufang explained: 'we called it like that twenty years ago, but now we don't do so. Twenty years ago, the new and old religions argued with each other, but now, we don't do that. We just do what we are asked to do.' Within this circulating rhetoric of tolerance, however, are a myriad of contestations. Contrary to Zhao Yufang, Ma Zhiqiang—a master's student who had been conducting research amongst the Hui in the Northwest regions—saw the relationship between the *menhuan* and other groups in a less positive light and used the terms *xinjiao* and *laojiao* to discuss the divides. He explained, 'The *menhuan* and *xinjiao* (Yihewani) relationship is very poor (*hen cha*), because *xinjiao* (Yihewani) and Salafiya oppose the *menhuan*, and oppose worshipping at tombs.[1]

---

[1] The Qadiriyya were distinctive from other Sufi orders in worshipping at tombs. According to Wang Huizhen, this was a practice to which other Sufi orders have had objections, for they believed this practice went against the regulations that Muslims shall prostrate only to Allah. Da Gongbei's interpretation however is that in doing so they are paying religious homage to the spirit of Allah as it is embodied in a human body (Wang 2009, p. 24).

Now they do not interfere with each other, but the feeling [between them] is not good. *Xinjiao* religious adherents will usually go only to their mosques to pray, *menhuan* religious adherents will go only to theirs. The differences between *laojiao* and *xinjiao* are actually not that great. The conflict between them, actually, is that *xinjiao* excludes some elements of *laojiao* that are *hanhua*, that is, elements that have received an influence of traditional Han characteristics.'[2] Here I adopt the metacultural categories mentioned at the beginning to further elaborate on various contestations in circulation, beginning with those of 'orthodoxy' and 'unorthodoxy'.

'Unorthodox' Practice Within the Qadiriyya

Criticisms about the Qadiriyya have historically, and still today, centred around their practice of Islam which has been seen as unorthodox due to what some see as a deeply syncretic form of Islamic practice, evidenced in their practice of celibacy, their use of incense, the ornately decorated Chinese-Islamic architecture of their *gongbei*, and their belief in miracles. In 1990, Dru Gladney described this syncretism with reference to language: 'through religious terminology familiar to the Hui in China, Confucian moral tenets, Daoist mystical concepts, and Buddhist folk rituals infused with new Islamic content pervade Qadiriyya Sufism' (Gladney 1996, p. 45).

While many Muslims are themselves aware of the influences of Buddhism and Daoism, debate has circulated within Chinese academic circles as to what extent the practices of the Qadiriyya can be seen to be influenced by Buddhism and Daoism. In particular, which practices came from within the stream of Qadiriyya practice itself and which came into being through

[2] Ma Zhiqiang further explained: 'They [other groups] think *xinjiao* is more pure. In fact *xinjiao* oppose *laojiao* and made some reforms. In fact many practices are "alien" and not the content of Islam. For example, when people die, in *laojiao* and *menhuan* they normally use the Qur'an to secure the "salvation" of the deceased person; however, the reforms in *xinjiao* use money to secure salvation. In fact, no matter what kind of salvation, neither is the original teaching of Islam, but an "alien import" (*yihua*). Worshipping a tomb (*gongbei*) is definitely not okay, because in Islam and Christianity it is the same: you can only worship one God. In China, the *gongbei menhuan* are only a small part. The majority are *laojiao* or *xinjiao*. Of course, the Christian and Islamic God, in [terms of the] concept they are different. But in [terms of] belief, you can't worship people or animals, besides God, so that's why people often say, "*ren zhu du yi*" (*tawhid*), our words of faith, meaning "you cannot worship a master, only God."'

the particular habits of the Chinese founder, Qi Jingyi. Wang Huizhen has postulated that 'as the Sufi orders themselves were a result of sinicized Islam, it (the Qadiriyya) has been inevitably influenced by traditional Chinese culture [...] By the time Islam spread to and developed in China and the al-Tariqah (Sufi order) came into being, Buddhism had been well developed and had gone through its own process of localisation. Therefore, Buddhism as it was found in China could easily mix with Islam' (Wang 2009, p. 22).

The practice of being a *chujiaren* in the context of the Qadiriyya has already been discussed with reference to Buddhist monasticism. Wang also argues that the notion of *chushi* or detachment from the world is mutually shared by Qadiriyya and Buddhist practitioners. Similarly, he cites the influence of Daoism, identifying that both Daoist philosophers and the Qadiriyya draw on the theory of Yin and Yang (*yinyang*), the five elements (*wuxing*), and the theory of Tai Ji and the Eight Diagrams (*bagua*). Professor L. however believes that 'if we carefully study the Qadiriyya *gongbei* system history, then the answer is no—they were not subject to the influence of Buddhism and Daoism [...] the so-called impact is just the conflating of two facts which are arbritrary'. Another Chinese researcher, Ma Yuxiu, has also questioned the assumption that the *chujiaren* system of the Qadiriyya can be attributed to either Buddhism or Daoism, arguing that there isn't sufficient evidence to suggest this directly. In particular, Ma argues that rather than the idea of celibacy being a resulting influence of Buddhist monasticism, it eventuated due to the influence of marriage-banning practices within some branches of the Qadiriyya order in the ancient Arab world (Ma 2008, p. 82).

Celibacy

In contrast, a leader at Dongchuan Mosque (a Jahriyya Sufi site based in downtown Lanzhou) had no hesitation in pointing out that the Qadiriyya had been deeply influenced by Buddhism and Daoism and that this subsequently rendered their practice of Islam 'unorthodox':

> The ultimate goal of the four *menhuan* is this: they all seek to eliminate selfish desires, but the way of every school is not the same; these four factions are not only produced in China—they are derived from the Arab world. In the Arab world there are already four different schools of thought. Through practice they raise their level and achieve their purpose. However, when they spread

to China they were subject to the influence of Chinese culture, especially the Qadiriyya, who were deeply affected by Chinese Daoism. It is the biggest difference between them and the other three *menhuan*. For example, they attach importance to becoming a *chujiaren*, using a praying mat (Buddhism, *putuan*), this is something from Daoism, there is also incense, this is also in Daoism. They also do not attach importance to the five pillars, although they observe them, they do not pay serious attention, more of a passive response. Actually inside Sufism, in Islam, there are also people who do not marry, but that is voluntary, nor is it advocated by Islam. But in the Qadiriyya they have this rule, if you want to be a *laorenjia*, to be a *dangjiaren*, you must be a *chujiaren*, so in their *menhuan* they have many *chujiaren*. This is very much like Daoism, because the leader of a Daoist group (*zhangmen*) must also be a *chujiaren*. In fact, their approach does not meet the requirements of Islamic law, or conform with the mainstream of Islamic practice. It will not be accepted as orthodox (*zhengtong*) Islam.[3]

Cyril Glassé notes that the Prophet Muhammad did not encourage celibacy or continence in marriage: 'In Islam, sexual relations are not considered to be only a step in procreation, tolerated because of the need to continue the species. The pleasure of sexual relations does not have a negative connotation; rather it is considered to be a Divine Mercy—even sacramental—and thus completely legitimate within social rules' (Glassé 1989, p. 357). Furthermore the Prophet, as well as many Sufis, 'gave evidence of drawing spiritual inspiration from earthly love' (Glassé 1989, p. 357). The well-known Sufi Ibn Arabi once said: 'The most intense and perfect contemplating of God is through women, and the most intense union [in the world] is the conjugal act' (Glassé 1989, p. 358).

Professor S. also attributed the tradition of celibacy to the influence of Buddhism and Daoism. As he stated, 'of course it's an influence—there is no such principle in Islam. In Islam, it's not necessary to not marry in order

---

[3] The Jahriyya leader also asserted the superiority of the Jahriyya over both the Khafiyya and Qadiriyya orders in terms of their differing adherence to the practice of *jiaocheng* (*Shariah*) and *daocheng* (*tariqah*): 'A true Sufi, an orthodox Sufi, will emphasise following *daocheng* and *jiaocheng*; Jahriyya (Zheherenye) characterise these more closely together. For *jiaocheng*, *daocheng* both are valued, both are done well. *Jiaocheng* is the basis of *daocheng*, it is like a tree growing from its roots, first you have roots, then you grow up, then a flower results. Khafiyya put more emphasis on *jiaocheng*, they have many rules about *wugong* (five requirements), and many auxiliary requirements (*fugong*). Jahriyya also have auxiliary requirements, but each requirement must be based on the Five Pillars (*wugong/jiaofa*) [...] each must correspond to God's command, there must be a good reason to do each.'

to be close to the saint. I think even the saint himself is married'. A young student from the *gongbei*, Ma Zhengjun, commented in confidence to me one day, 'I think it's not good [that they don't marry], this is contrary to the teachings of Islam. I prefer Huasi Menhuan (which is Khafiyya) because they are more in line with Islamic teachings (*Shariah*). If Sufism is contrary to Islamic doctrine, then it's not orthodox Sufism (*zhengtong de sufei*)'.

Ornate Decorations and Use of Incense

Ma Yufang at Guo Gongbei and Zhao Yufang, a *chujiaren* at Da Gongbei, both acknowledged the use of Buddhist and Daoist language and termi-nology in their practice and also in the ornate illustrations of their temple walls. But for them, this did not detract in any way from the legitimacy of their practice of Islam. It was natural, inevitable, that they had taken on some elements of local 'Chinese' custom and language—after all, this was the context in which they lived and in which Sufism had sought to gain traction. Ma Yufang stressed that though terminologies may be similar, their meaning was grounded in the Islamic context (such as 'Dao' in Daoism as discussed in Chap. 3). On the walls of the *gongbei*, well-known symbols and animals in Chinese culture more broadly demonstrated the explicit value connections the Qadiriyya were making with local culture. Usually inside a mosque, no representations of Allah, humans, plants, or animals are allowed. However Ma Yufang did not see this as a 'strong rule' in the Qur'an and explained that the creatures and objects depicted on the walls of the *gongbei* had been chosen for their shared resonance with Islamic values—such as eternity, knowledge, strength, and blessing (Fig. 7.2).

For Zhao Yufang, borrowing from and sharing amongst other traditions was not inherently problematic. He explained that 'we study mainly the work of predecessors and sages. Then there are some ancestors who wrote something, such as Ma Tengyi, he was an apprentice of Qi Jingyi, the Grand Master. Their writings are some of the best, they are from our *menhuan*. In addition to the people in our *menhuan*, we read some of the works of Liu Zhi'. When I remarked, 'Liu Zhi's work contains the *bagua* idea, as well as *taiji*. From this perspective, do you think Chinese Islam has received the impact of Chinese culture? Or Daoism, Confucianism and the like?' Zhao Yufang replied, 'The Qadiriyya *menhuan* think these are shared, they do not belong to a single sect or nation. But other *menhuan* do not think so, they think it is something from the Han, and Islam cannot use it, they do not recognise it'.

Fig. 7.2   Close-up of a decoration in Guo Gongbei depicting a dragon on a bell shape. In China, dragons are a symbol of power, strength, and good luck. They can also symbolise auspicious powers, including control over water and weather

In specific relation to the use of incense, Matthew Erie noted a conflict that occurred in 2000 between a Gedimu mosque in Linxia and the Da Gongbei complex of the Qadiriyya (a neighbouring tomb to Guo Gongbei) over the use of incense. This was related to a criticism the previous year by the same cleric who questioned the orthodoxy of *sujūd* (prostration by touching forehead to the ground) for the entombed saint—a practice which he believed should be reserved for God alone (Erie 2016, p. 130). This same cleric, after having spent time in Egypt studying Islamic law, argued that the burning of incense had been 'tainted by Buddhist and Daoist religious observances' (Erie 2016, p. 130). Erie notes that the Da Gongbei complex defended the use of incense, arguing that it was in line with Islamic law. This in turn developed into a physical confrontation between members of the mosque and the tomb complex. The dispute was resolved by Qi Jiequan, a Naqshbandi-Mujaddidi Sufi shaykh who met with the young Gedimu cleric, accusing him of 'harming ethnic unity'. Qi Jiequan staged a *jiangjiang*—a scriptural debate—and collected evidences from Islamic law and theology (both Persian and Arabic sources) to defend the use of incense (Erie 2016, p. 130). Erie notes that as a result tensions were reduced.

Miracles

As elsewhere in the Muslim world, the notion of miracles was also a cause of contention. In relation to the Qadiriyya, they further undermined their legitimacy, being viewed rather sceptically by some Muslim elites. In a discussion with Professor L., I asked him if he believed in the miracles espoused by followers of the Qadiriyya or thought they were possible. He replied:

No. He (Ma Yufang) said they want to reach this level, a little level lower than Qi Jingyi, but Qi Jingyi is an *Ahong* (*imam*), just an *Ahong*, not the greatest leader in Islamic history in China, just the leader of a Sufi group, he doesn't know Chinese culture well, perhaps he doesn't know Chinese [language] well. Yes, they said sometimes they have miracles, but I don't believe them. Most of them, I don't believe. This is the *menhuan*, they are saying it themselves. In traditional Islamic philosophy (*jiaoyi*), we call that *bid'a* [heresy]—sometimes I just think it's superstition. The greatest miracle is the Holy Qur'an.

Professor S. explained that in Islamic principle, miracles are possible—though he had never seen any: 'I personally haven't experienced any miracles. In Islamic principle, miracles are possible. Some people in the past performed miracles but I think sometimes some people claim to believe in miracles to make their master important or unique. I know there is some *shaykh* in Pakistan, himself he didn't say anything about his miracle, but his disciples said they saw so many miracles of their master. I just asked—give me one example. He said once, "I met him in the yard, and I said '*salam*' to him, and he went this direction and I went to his room. And in his room the master was sitting on his seat, despite having gone elsewhere." So it is a miracle. He said, and also others said many things about him. But I think maybe it is true, maybe it is not true.'

INTEGRITY AND CORRUPTION

In an earlier chapter I quoted Aunty, who talked about the possibility
of the present leader performing miracles. She replied that he could not
at the moment, but in the future there might be a possibility; however,
society 'was not the same as it was in the past. The disciples now face
many temptations, although they can commit to their beliefs, they are
not as pure (*qingzhen*) as the disciples before'. As has been explored
in the previous chapters, charismatic authority relied on the perceived
embodiment of charismatic power. The importance of this perception and
level of expectation was crucial to the integrity, viability, and cohesion of
the charismatic order. Several threats to this integrity were mentioned to
me—including a perceived 'increasing materialism'.

Ma Yufang commented to me on this issue and emphasised the role of
the Islamic faith in guiding the individual away from 'vulgar notions' that
would in turn lower their personal quality or *suzhi*:

> The *chujiaren* of today have a personal choice to live outside of the family,
> the views of others are not imposed. Now the thinking is relatively chaotic,
> materialistic, everyone, everyday, is thinking about how to earn money, how
> to have a more luxurious car, how to have more lovers. But after we leave
> the family, we put these vulgar notions behind us, and pursue the realm of
> life beyond this world (*houshi*). Indeed, no matter how much money you
> have, how high an official position, one day you will give everything away.
> Do you remember when Saddam was the monarch of his country? In less
> than a blink of an eye he became a prisoner. None of this is based on the
> individual's will, but the will of Allah. The President of the United States now
> looks famous, but after he retires will he not become just another common
> person? All the fame and fortune has nothing to do with him. Belief in God,
> faith that Muhammad is the messenger of Allah, a man who has such a kind
> of belief is a model. If there is no such faith, if you talk like normal people
> do, you have fallen according to the standards of this person, you have failed
> to reach a certain standard. A well-known Iranian scholar said, "one is not
> a person with a human form but with no heart; one is not a person with
> human appearance but no human spirit." So if you do not have the human
> mind, then your behaviour is futile. The Qur'an strictly refuted the view that
> people of this kind spread. They have eyes that do not observe, they have a
> brain that does not think, and ears that do not hear. Then this person is like
> an animal, and even more contemptible than an animal [...] We believe that
> the Islamic religion is the world's best and most civilised religion [...] To be
> excellent people, if you study the core of the world's great religions in order

to make a comparison, you will find, Islam is not under the various rules and restrictions of this world, but beyond this world. For your own soul, to have clear specifications to discern between the righteous and the wicked. Without these words, a good man is not rewarded, nor are the wicked duly punished. What fairness would this world have?

Ma Yufang's concerns here call to mind a number of 'traditional self-images' of Islam often invoked in order to combat threats of moral pollution (e.g. the threats of materialistic wealth and sexual desire).[4] These are the *finality of Islam*—that Islam contains all the moral and religious truths necessary for all humanity; that of *Islam in History*, in which Islam will be ultimately triumphant in changing the whole world into *dar-al-Islam* (the sphere of Islam); and that of the *idealisation of Muhammad and early Islam* (Watt 1989). The young Persian teacher at the *gongbei* spoke privately at one stage about his own perceptions of some of the *chujiaren* within various Qadiriyya *gongbei* and also stressed the impact of materialism on their 'moral fibre':

I have started preparing to find a good master/teacher. I want to make the first contact with these people, and look at their modes of worship, see what their level is like. But now it is difficult to find a good teacher like this, because many people are becoming more secular, and chasing material things. A disciple (*chujiaren*) should not endorse this behaviour, because a disciple should see through all of this after he makes a decision. But now I have seen *chujiaren* who like to pursue material things more than us, they like to buy expensive things. If a disciple's purpose is to follow God, he does not chase after material things, this is a true *chujiaren*, this is legitimate (*hefa de*), if not, he is not legitimate (*bu hefa de*). Linxia has some *chujiaren* who are relatively frugal (*jiejian de*), for example the *dangjiaren* at Taizi Gongbei. But some of his thoughts are a little conservative (*baoshou*), especially in accepting new things and in initiating education.

The importance of a 'good master', someone who was *hefa de*, was also of concern for some Muslim leaders in the community who sought to gain the sanction, the *kouhuan* of a Sufi authority. However, speculations

---

[4] Alexander Stewart has also noted amongst the Muslim community in Qinghai criticisms that the Chinese state have 'embraced a myopic obsession with material aspects of development, which they implicate in encouraging rampant selfishness and immorality' (Stewart 2017, p. 4249).

also circulated about the integrity of *kouhuan* itself. In the report by Ma Hucheng about the situation of *menhuan* in Gansu, the argument is put forward that conflicts within *menhuan* are on the rise and are mainly centred on the struggles for 'three authorities': religious authority, authority over the *menhuan's* properties, and authority in management, with religious authority being the key issue. The author says, 'The lack of a well-designed system to pass on religious authority and heritage has left ample room for all parties to desire power. Dominant groups and individuals often provoke controversies in an attempt to seize religious authority. In order to obtain the proof of authority, they often manipulate the shaykh's *kouhuan* and forcefully promote their own views through families' (Ma 2011, p. 61).[5]

As a result, some Muslim leaders had felt the need to go outside of China to seek this 'divine permission', as Professor L. explained:

> Some leaders, just like the man who passed away, that *Ahong*, he visited India three times, and when he was alive he wanted to visit a fourth time. He asked me to help him get a passport, and I don't have the power to help them—as you know, a passport for a Muslim from this area is difficult. I asked him why do you go there? He's Qadim, he said he wanted to go visit Imam Rabbani, "I want to get *kouhuan* [permission]." Maybe some of us want to become a new Sufi master, but they don't have the permission. You know if you want to be a leader/master, you must get permission from another teacher, even one word, even *tafsīr* [exegesis of the Qur'an]. Just like my Grandpa, he had this permission. When he was born, the master of Khafiyya/Naqshbandiyya in China visited his home, and he gave a name to my grandpa. My grandpa was a Sufi master, as you know, he changed his mind [and was known] as Yihewani. So I understand. He's [the *Ahong* who passed away] in Linxia. He doesn't have official permission from a Sufi master so he wants to visit again to get the permission. Even if you are Yihewani, Khafiyya, Jahriyya, Huasi Menhuan, Zhangmen, even if you belong to Naqshbandiyya—they all want to reveal the Sufi [ideas] once more [...]

[5] Professor L. informed me that there had been a case recently in the Dongxiang area where a Jahriyya *gongbei* had temporarily closed down because the master had passed away, and the sons could not decide who should take over. Another foreign PhD researcher (whom I knew in Lanzhou) was travelling through that region earlier in the year and had mentioned that there had been a series of protests in the streets outside this *gongbei* when he was there.

Professor L. also told me that at a Qadiriyya *gongbei* in Guanghe County (a densely populated Muslim area between Lanzhou and Linxia), rather than the next in line being elected by *chujiaren*, the decision is made by an elder. In Da Gongbei and Guo Gongbei, the *dangjiaren* is also a scholar (an *imam*), whereas in other Qadiriyya sites an elderly leader is not necessarily an *imam* and does not necessarily understand Islamic knowledge. As he explained, 'Of course, the "quality" of the *dangjiaren* [*dangjiaren suzhi*] is different in different regions. The Qadiriyya system is in Linxia, Ningxia, Haiyuan, and Lingmingtang in Lanzhou. A few of them share commonalities, but they are all individual'.

Another complaint that I heard from younger disciples and students was that many *chujiaren* who had left the *gongbei* to study overseas did not return. They had ended up getting married and leaving the celibate life. The Persian teacher told me in confidence that 'Actually, Guo Gongbei sent some disciples out to study, and a good number of them got married over there. These people are not a good influence in the *gongbei*, and caused some people to complain to the *dangjiaren*'.

One *chujiaren* had acknowledged to Professor L. struggling against feelings of desire, feelings that would sometimes 'invoke envy and required personal restraint'. Several younger men spoke to me of their changing conceptions of what being a *chujiaren* meant as they got older. Ma Xiaobin was a 23-year-old *chujiaren* from Linxia studying at Guo Gongbei. He had recently been studying in Iran but was home at the *gongbei* to visit his family and prepare for celebrations:

I'm 23 years old. I grew up in Linxia. I have a brother, a sister, and my parents are government employees. I am now studying in Iran. I made a decision to become a *chujiaren* when I was 12, because I grew up in a family with an Islamic background, my family often took me to the *gongbei*. I liked the environment and atmosphere, and I thought to dedicate one's whole life to God would really help the cause of the religion. At the time, I was relatively young, and in fact, had no real concept of what a *chujiaren* meant [...] Now I have grown up, I have a more profound understanding of the concept of [being a] *chujiaren* and I see the responsibilities and requirements of the *chujiaren* get harder and harder, while others can go with the flow. My brother is in college and is a student of English, my sister is in junior high school. I go to school in Iran where there are female students and female friends, and some are very interested in Chinese culture and Chinese, so I will introduce them to it. As for marriage, I have not considered it just yet, I will go with the flow. At the right time, marriage is also possible, although we have the idea of a *chujiaren* in the *gongbei*, but all things are not absolutes, Islam pays more attention to providing a freedom of choice.

While there seemed to be a circulating feeling of embarrassment about *chujiaren* who were once committed but had then 'never returned', Ma Yufang tried not to frame this negatively to me. He talked about it as just a matter of choice: 'in this age they can choose, but in my age this was not the case. Now once they are married, they will no longer be a *chujiaren*. But we would not blame them for making such a choice—that is their freedom.'

'TOO MANY GROUPS': UNITY AND DISUNITY

In Northwest China, Ma Yufang saw the existence of the Sufi *men-huan* as fundamental for cohesion in the Chinese Muslim community—fundamental because of the leadership that it offered. 'Without the *men-huan*', he explained, 'Islam will be easily destroyed [...] The reason why the Islamic world is a mess is due to the lack of leadership. Because of it, everyone says they are leaders (and you have disunity).' A leader of the Jahriyya order in Lanzhou also described a sense of unity generated by the Sufi *menhuan*—but only by his faction. He criticised other factions (Qadiriyya, Khafiyya, and Kubrawiyya) for not having unified leadership and offered an account of why he believed the Jahriyya were more united:

Official statistics say that there are more than 20 million Muslims in China. But in fact there are about 100 million Muslims.[6] The rulers have been most concerned with the Jahriyya, because this sect has particularly strong cohesion, very united. Nationwide, Jahriyya only has one leader. Other *paibie* [factions], have many *laorenjia* [leaders], therefore inside one *menhuan*, there are a lot of older people vying for power, and financial resources, competing spheres of influence, even fighting. As such, there is no cohesion throughout *menhuan*, there is disunity. The future development is worrying. When their mode of transmission is not standardised, they give birth to many branches, finally distorting the original teachings. It is not a continued/ inherited tradition. But in the Jahriyya, he (Ma Mingxin) preached that there is only one way. Now people read the classics [*nian de*], they cultivate

---

[6] This idea that China includes over 100 million Muslims dates back to the early twentieth century, when the Republican government (with no demographic evidence) claimed falsely that there were nearly 50 million Muslims in the country (Pillsbury 1981, p. 35).

in the same way as people did in the first generation, no change has been passed down, no-one among them introduced change, just like the doctor has a prescription, and it never changes. Allah gives the Five Pillars to every Muslim, these cannot be changed, if we modify the process of inheritance, that would have changed the appearance of Islam, so it is not like it is now. There are many versions of the Christian Bible, but the Qur'an is the same all over the world. This shows that, the Bible has been tampered with in the process, but the Qur'an is not considered to have been tampered with previously.

This leader was clearly dissembling, given that within the history of Jahriyya, there were many schisms over leadership that resulted in a number of branches and sub-branches (Gladney 1999, p. 123). For others outside of the Sufi *menhuan*, the existence of so many different factions (*paibie*) within the Muslim community—and thus so many different leaders—was seen as a great source of disunity. Ma Zhiqiang, a Muslim student in anthropology, explained that:

> Once I used to belong to *xinjiao*, now I don't look for a group, because I think Islam is one, you should act according to Islamic teachings, this is a qualified Muslim. If every person belongs to a different group, this isn't good for the development of the religion or development of the people, this is what I think for myself. My view is, I wish to undertake practices in accordance with the Qur'an and the Hadith, this is the content of Islam that will never change. My view is that many people consider themselves as 'Salafiyya', also people often say 'three teachings' faction, but I don't think it is good, there are more and more groups, the development of Islam is becoming more and more chaotic. Now there are many *menhuan* and *paibie*, everyone fights with each other and this is detrimental to the development of Islam. Through my own efforts, I want to dispel misconceptions about Islam.

Professor L. too agreed that there were 'too many *paibie*', and he spoke idealistically of returning to a time before the existence of factions. He also echoed Ma Yufang's concerns over a 'diminishing morality' and the influence of Han materialism. His answer to this was that Sufism, at the heart of Islam and Islamic philosophy, should be drawn upon to re-establish a sense of unity within the Islamic community in China. It should not be promulgated through the *menhuan* institutions, or thought to 'belong' only to them, as it were. Sufi texts should be studied by all groups, and 'groupings' and 'divisions' should be lessened, if not eradicated completely. As he explained:

> Why do Yihewani and many groups need to develop Sufism? Because they live in a Chinese society, a rapidly changing society, and as most *Ahong* said, there is no character—no soul. The girls, like in other parts of the world, go on the street and have a lack of morality. Muslims are not independent in this society, they are strongly influenced by the Han society, so they don't find a good way, the good way of Confucian [morality]. But where is the Confucian [ideal]? We can't find it. The Chinese government builds a Confucius Institute, but where is Confucius in China? That's a political question. So the Chinese Muslim scholar thinks about what things can solve this problem, these difficult issues. So nowadays we need Sufism [...] We hope that society changes to be as good as we imagine—but we have to go back to Liu Zhi, to Qadim's way. Why? Qadim [was] before Jahriyya, and Huasi Menhuan. [At that time] there were no *pai* (*menhuan*/groups/factions). Last week in my lecture I talked with the young generation about this. At that time there were no different groups. We were the same—both Muslim and Chinese—we must go back to that time, to Shaanxi school, to a time when there were no *pai*.

Professor L. argued that Sufism in China was now 'awakening' or 'regaining consciousness' (*suxing*). Many of the young educated generation were, in his opinion, against the *menhuan* and also against the current leaders of the *menhuan* as they were seen to be only interested in monetary gain. This was in contrast to the perceptions held of the first Sufi leaders in China, such as Ma Mingxin of the Jahriyya or Ma Laichi of the Khufiyya, who were idealised as leaders of integrity. Many of the young educated generation believe that if Islam is to develop in China, the first step is to 'return back' to Sufi philosophy and knowledge. But, crucially, in a more 'universal form', not in the form of the *menhuan*. 'Nowadays', he explained, 'Chinese Muslims, especially in Northwest Gansu or Ningxia, they think about how [to develop Sufism...] I call this the *second movement*. The centre of the second movement must come from Chinese Muslim Sufis.'[7]

---

[7] Professor L. questioned the historical given that 'Sufi' texts were only ever studied by the Sufi *gongbei* and that other groups were always 'against' the Sufis: 'Before the Cultural Revolution', he explained, 'most Muslim people here in Gansu, or even in Ningxia or Qinghai, they didn't know details, they only know *menhuan*. But when Prof. Ma Tong wrote this book [History of Sufi *menhuan* in Northwest China], maybe some people knew more about

This call to 'revive' Sufism and to use it as a means of morally grounding, reinvigorating, and uniting the Muslim community is similar to the way in which Sufism was called upon as a means of spiritual renewal or revival in the Indonesian context. The expectations amongst the Indonesian elite in the mid-twentieth century were that changes in the education system and Muslim modernist reform would rid Indonesia of its more mystical and devotional—Sufi—practices. But as Julia Howell has demonstrated, the contrary has occurred. What she describes as 'Sufi devotionalism' is flourishing in both rural and urban areas and has been taken up by 'even members of the national elite […] These new aficionados are reinterpreting Sufi thought as a source of inspiration for contemporary religious practice and are even becoming involved with long-established Sufi institutions (the Sufi orders, or tarekat)' (Howell 2001, p. 702).

A leading neo-modernist intellectual in Indonesia, Harun Nasution, argued that the ethic of Sufism—of worldly asceticism—needed to be developed in order to 'create a community that was made up of hardworking individuals with low consumption and high productivity' (Cone 2002, p. 62). According to Nasution, mysticism in the early Islamic centuries 'was an individual affair, stressing the individual pursuit of exoteric knowledge. Such an approach, he felt, provided the basis for the construction of the economically rational, self-directed, follower of Islam' (Cone 2002, p. 62). Notwithstanding the dramatically different socio-political climate within which the Chinese Sufi community exists as compared to Indonesia, it is of interest to note here the similar thread in thinking that occurred between these two Muslim intellectuals with regard to the role of Sufism and Sufi philosophy in Muslim society more broadly. It also points to a

it […] For Khafiyya, they belong to the Naqshbandiyya order, and Jahriyya also belongs to Naqshbandiyya, also as you know Humen in Guanghe […] We belonged to Khafiyya. At that time they don't know, [that we are] doing [following] Sufi, but after even [reading Ma Tong], as you know, even in Ma Tong's book, he wrote Yihewani never do [practise] Sufi[sm]. Do you agree with this?' I replied, 'No, I don't think so'. Contrary to the sharp lines drawn historically between the various Islamic groupings, Professor L. offered evidence to the contrary: 'Yes, until today, just like the *Ahong* who just passed away, just like many leaders of Khafiyya or Jahriyya, still today, maybe they are sure, they can say, Yihewani they never do Sufi, Yihewani against Sufi. But, when we do research [among] the Yihewani, when we check their textbooks, I was very surprised. When we go back in history, the history shows that Yihewani teach and learn from these Sufi books and also they do worship, they do something just like the Sufi does.' Indeed, the Han Kitab texts generated during the Qing Dynasty were infused with mystical (Sufi) ideas (Murata and Chittick 2000; Murata et al. 2009; Murata 2017).

global process of what Erik Ohlander has described as a 'repopularization of Sufi thought [...] evidenced in the vigorous and wide-scale publication and consumption of Sufi texts, especially translations and popular editions [...] churned out in great numbers by publishers both major and minor in the Arab World, Turkey, Iran, Pakistan and Indonesia' (Ohlander 2011, p. 429).

STABILITY AND INSTABILITY: THE RATIONALISATION OF CHARISMA?

In 1928, Linxia was the site of frequent conflicts between local Muslims and Nationalist Army forces. These conflicts damaged or destroyed much of the Muslim area of town known as Bafang. During the Hehuang Event, the commander of the 17th Army Division of the Republic of China, Governor Zhao Xiping, ordered his army to rob the property of Guo Gongbei and to kill the students. An entry in a local history of Guo Gongbei recounts:

> He arrived in the west city of Hezhou [Linxia] in person and ordered the artillerymen to fire on the western suburb of the *gongbei*. Suddenly fires emerged, smoke thickened, and Guo Gongbei and the adjacent Da Gongbei, Taizi Gongbei, Dataiye Gongbei, Gujia Gongbei and other Islamic grand buildings were burned to the ground. During this time, the stone tablet, gold plaque, imperial edict and yellow satin letter given by the Emperor Kangxi, notices issued by the royal court and famous calligraphy and paintings, curios, jade articles and other precious historical relics were all burned into dust. Then, he compelled the soldiers to rob and burn the so-called 'Chinese Mecca'—Bafang, the gathering zone of Muslim people, 7 or 8 miles in circumference. This area was all burned to dust, causing over 40,000 people to become homeless, and resulting in a tragedy of Hui-Han revengeful killing (Ma 1997, pp. 15–16).

In 1932, the Da Gongbei master Zhang Zhengchuan and his disciple, Ma Shiming, both began to reconstruct Guo Gongbei according to the original appearance. In 1958 however, in the early years of the People's Republic of China, anti-feudal and anti-religious campaigns expanded. These revolutionary cleansing campaigns targeted Buddhism, Daoism, and Islam, and many clergy were penalised for being landlords or promoting revolutionary or reactionary values (Yang 2012, Chapter 4, para. 6).[8] Consequently, Guo Gongbei along with other *gongbei*, mosques, and Buddhist and Daoist temples in the region were all shut down. Ma Shiming (the leader of Guo Gongbei at the time), other celibate disciples of the *gongbei*, and religious staff at other religious sites were reportedly 'criticised and imprisoned, or moved to other villages' (Ma 1997, p. 17). In 1959, 'Linxia city took the opportunity of digging an artificial lake to raze Guo Gongbei to the ground' (Ma 1997, p. 17). At that time, the bones of the Sufi teachers buried there (Chen Yiming and his disciple Muhammad Mahamudi) were moved and buried on the 'northern hillside' with other disciples. After the Maoist decades ended, the Communist Party of China gradually implemented new national religious policies. Subsequently, in the spring of 1985, the government returned the original land base of the Guo Gongbei tomb. Ma Shiming took charge again, and together with donations of money and time of a management committee and disciples, the *gongbei* was reconstructed on the original ruins. The bones of Chen Yiming and Muhammad Mahamudi were moved back from the northern hillside and were buried in the tomb pavilion (what is now the worship hall in the *gongbei*). In 1988, after four years of construction, the shrine was finally completed (Ma 1997, p. 18).

---

[8] According to their own historical records, when Guo Gongbei was first built in 1719, the disciples obtained double salaries from the Qing Dynasty. However when the Republic of China was established, they depended on their own income, which at the time came mainly from farming. The lands they ploughed were sometimes donated by the disciples; some were given as a gift by the family of a *chujiaren*; and some were bought by the *gongbei*. Until 1949, the *gongbei* had a total of 54 mu (3.6 hectares) of cultivated land, mainly consisting of dry lands in several villages in the Linxia County. The income generated from the land was used to cover repairs of the *gongbei's* architectural facilities, to cover the living expenses of the permanent residents (*chujiaren*), to cover some living expenses for students who were studying there, and to cover expenses for annual March and September birthday or death anniversary events in the *gongbei*. However, after the reform and opening up policy (*gaige kaifang*) in the 1980s, the land was collected by the state as publicly owned property and as a result their revenue sources were greatly reduced. Since that time and until today, Guo Gongbei exists on funds provided by the local government which cover living expenses for those at the *gongbei* and on donations by religious adherents (Ar. *Niyyah and Zakat*) that help to cover miscellaneous expenses of the *gongbei*. There have also been some wealthy disciples in the past who donated all of their property to the *gongbei* prior to their death. In addition, the *gongbei* has also occasionally received some small donations from domestic and foreign governments and/or religious groups and organisations (Ma 1997, p. 36).

These historic incidents, relating specifically to Guo Gongbei, highlight the tensions that have existed within China with regard to the management of religious practice. While today Guo Gongbei is allowed to operate, the Chinese Communist Party also continues to enforce atheist propaganda through the education system and mass media (Yang 2012, Chapter 1, para. 2). This balancing act raises important questions about secularism and secularist states, as Fenggang Yang has noted: 'That religion can survive and thrive under atheist Communist rule raises important theoretical and practical questions. How much can the state control the growth or decline of religion? [...] To what extent can a secularist state promote secularisation?' (Yang 2012, Chapter 1, para. 2). I frame this particular contestation around the notions of stability and instability with specific regard to the governance of the Sufi *menhuan*.

In discussing this, I refer to insights from a report written by scholar-official Ma Hucheng (mentioned earlier). This report, originally written in Chinese (and then translated into English), is titled *The Historical and Present Situation of Islamic Menhuan in China* and appeared in a selection of papers from a three-conference series on Muslim minorities in Northwest China published by the Institute for Global Engagement. It is important to note that this report represents part of an ongoing effort by the government of China to gain greater control over Islamic institutions at every level (Wang 2016, p. 577). As such, the report makes no claims to scholarly analysis, but rather contains a series of recommendations that would effectively give the state more control over the Sufi communities of Gansu. It is thus reflective of a much larger process regarding the control of religious spheres by the state, one that includes not only other Muslim institutions but also other religious groups, such as Buddhist and Christian organisations (Yang 2012, See Chapter 4).[9]

In the report Ma Hucheng provides a profile of the formation, growth, and evolution of *menhuan* and their function throughout history. The report also puts forward strategies for 'religious work' and identifies 'major problems' within the present *menhuan*. The tone of the report is reasonably

---

[9] Here it is important to note that the relationship between the Chinese State and religion is not a strictly 'control-and-resistance' paradigm. While it is 'true that the balance of power rests overwhelmingly with the state [...] state policy is not simply imposed, and religious organizations and individuals have participated in constructing and modifying official ideological positions on religion and the policies and regulations governing religion' (Dunch 2008, p. 156).

negative, painting a picture of the *dangjiaren* (termed the 'Hierarch' in the report) as complicit in practices of exploitation: 'The feudal rule of the Hierarch over his followers is manifested in various ways, including spiritual control, slavery and economic exploitation. In order to enforce such rule, each *menhuan* has a set of strict regulations that are established by usage. For example, in order to achieve spiritual control, the shaykh of a *menhuan* is declared as the medium between his followers and Allah. Without the shaykh's word (*kouhuan*) no one in the *menhuan* is able to enter heaven' (Ma 2011, p. 55).

It concludes with a section titled, *Religious Work to Complete Regarding Menhuan: Suggestions and Strategies*. The first recommendation in the report is that the 'Hierarch' (the *jiaozhu*, or *dangjiaren* of the *menhuan*), as the seat of ultimate religious and secular authority in the *menhuan*, should be abolished. The second recommendation is that the hereditary systems of succession and/or the giving of *kouhuan* (divine permission) that elects him, should also be abolished in favour of more democratic and bureaucratised election processes:

> *Abolish the succession of the Hierarch while preserving the succession of religious heritage*[...] In the process of passing on a *menhuan's* religious heritage, either the local government's Department of Religious Affairs should preside over the signing of all relevant agreements and documents, or the event should be approved by the local government. In all agreements and documents, there should be clear specification that the successor is only to conduct teaching of his *menhuan's* religious doctrines, and that he should not in anyway interfere with the *menhuan's* secular affairs, such as appointing *akhunds* and giving *kouhuan*. Otherwise, the government will not recognise the successor's qualification as a *menhuan's* leader, and the previous leader will not be allowed to give *kouhuan* over the succession of religious heritage by the successor (Ma 2011, p. 74).

The report, thus, is about control over religious institutions by state institutions. Ma goes on to mention in the report 'signs of progress', namely, that 'the process of assigning akhunds (*ahong* or *imams*) is moving toward a system of appointment through public consultation' (Ma 2011, p. 58). This shift to more democratic processes is certainly true for Guo Gongbei, which (since 1985) has had a management committee that delegates duties, responsibilities, and decision-making processes. The *imam* (*Ahong*) is also elected through public consultation with religious adherents.

In relation to charismatic leadership in the sense of Weber discussed earlier, what is desired here is the transformation of the election process of the *Hierarch* (*dangjiaren*) so that it is no longer wholly 'charismatic' and thus 'unstable'. Weber described charismatic authority as being strongly opposed to rational and bureaucratic authority. However, charisma can and still does remain a part of bureaucratic organisation. They are not necessarily so opposed as Weber seems to imply. Indeed, the CCP and multitudes of seemingly 'rational' systems of authority and leadership rely on the charisma of their leaders to function. As Mayfair Mei-hui Yang reminds us, even though modernity encouraged the separation of religion and state politics as two distinct spheres, 'the sovereign powers of past state orders all had their ritual capitals, court and state rituals, and cosmologies that embedded earthly political orders in the realms of the sacred transcendent' (Yang 2008, p. 9). Through the transformation of an intimate, secretive, and 'mystical' process into a seemingly more open, meritocratic, and transparent one—more closely aligned with the election processes common within mosques in Linxia—the government could 'rationalise', in one sense, the charismatic organisation process. Clearly however, the local or state government could not wholly replace the 'charismatic' organisation of the *menhuan* with a wholly 'bureaucratic' organisation because each system is inherently always going to contain elements of both.

Several other recommendations are made in the report that tell of a number of other related anxieties about the Sufi *menhuan*—in particular, the ways in which they could contribute to greater political instability in China through international networks and internal proliferation. Specifically, these recommendations include the desire to prevent new *menhuan* from emerging in an effort to curb internal religious conflicts, to prevent further divisions and differentiations within *menhuan* themselves, to prevent *menhuan* from contacting and establishing relations with international Islamic organisations in an effort to curb extremist influence, and to prevent *menhuan* from transforming into political groups (Ma 2011, pp. 74–75).

These recommendations and the concerns underpinning them reflect very strongly an underlying attitude by the Chinese government that has never completely disappeared. Lipman has noted that during the Qing Dynasty, the Sufi networks were often viewed with great suspicion due to their 'bizarre ritual practices' and 'propensity for sedition'—suspicions similar to those faced by Daoist and Buddhist groups (Lipman 1997, p. 69). Nowadays, these suspicions clearly remain. While the Sufi *gongbei* sites are currently classified as 'legal', Ma Hucheng even goes so far as to suggest that they are 'cults' and should be 'illegal'[10]:

> *Prevent the formation, development and expansion of cults (heterodoxy) within menhuan*[...] Once any trace of these cults is found, the government should eliminate them as soon as possible, instead of simply leaving them alone for the sake of temporary stability. We cannot and should not allow these religious heretics to endanger our society (Ma 2011, p. 75).

The question is to what extent these present 'recommendations' can and/or will be implemented in the case of the *menhuan* in China. A study by Abbink (2003) looked at similar efforts made in Southern Ethiopia to replace charismatic authority with a bureaucratic system of rulers and legalities (Abbink 2003). He found that the process 'was neither complete nor successful, because the sources of legitimacy of leadership and authority remained firmly within the local societies and were ill understood by outsiders, including State authorities' (Abbink 2003). This report concerning *menhuan* in China was motivated by a need to 'understand more deeply' the nature of leadership and succession within the *menhuan*, in order that greater control could be wielded. But clearly it is not just a straightforward matter of data-gathering: 'Although these policies are already very clear', Ma asserts, 'some people still consider them as being impractical and difficult to implement [...] The current focus of our religious work is on the management of individual *menhuan* who have had certain problems, but this rarely considers the overall situation' (Ma 2011, pp. 64–65).

This chapter has responded to the question—why is charisma contentious? I have done this by framing the many voices involved in the discourse around sets of metacultural categories that emerged in the analysis—that of 'orthodoxy' and 'unorthodoxy', 'integrity' and 'corruption', 'unity' and 'disunity', and 'stability' and 'instability'. These 'categories' I must emphasise are not to be thought of as 'static reflections', but rather, following Tomlinson, as concerns that constantly propel others into circulation. They are concerns, I have argued, that continue to

---

[10] 'Cults' was the published translation, but the term *xiejiao* could also be translated as heterodox.

circulate about the practice of Sufism, and specifically Qadiriyya Sufism, in China today. Firstly, Qadiriyya Sufism is seen as 'unorthodox' Islam due to the syncretic influences of Buddhism and Daoism and the resultant practices of celibacy, use of incense, belief in miracles, and Chinese-Islamic architecture and decoration. Secondly, the charismatic authority of their *chujiaren* (celibate practitioners) is subject to questioning by those who see the impact of materialism and the desire for marriage as thwarting their religious sophistication. This in turn is impacting the level of trust placed in the election process of *kouhuan*. Thirdly, while Guo Gongbei maintains that the leadership of the *menhuan* is vital to unity and cohesion within the greater Islamic community, others feel that there are simply 'too many factions', one voice even suggesting that Sufism be the means by which a sense of unity be re-established. Finally, the system of religious succession and the role of the leader within Sufi networks (such as Guo Gongbei) is subject to great suspicion at the level of local government, and recommendations have been made that this somewhat 'secretive' process be replaced with a system of 'democratic' election.

REFERENCES

Abbink, J. 2003. Local Leadership and State Governance in Southern Ethiopia: From Charisma to Bureaucracy. In *Tradition and Politics: Indigenous Political Structures in Africa*, ed. O. Vaughan. Trenton: Africa World Press.

Asad, T. 1986. *The Idea of an Anthropology of Islam*. Washington: Center for Contemporary Arab Studies, Georgetown University.

Bourdieu, P. 1984. *Distinction: A Social Critique of the Judgement of Taste*. Cambridge: Harvard University Press.

Cone, M. 2002. Neo-Modern Islam in Suharto's Indonesia. *New Zealand Journal of Asian Studies* 4 (2): 52–67.

Dunch, R. 2008. Christianity and "Adaptation to Socialism". In *Chinese Religiosities: Afflictions of Modernity and State Formation*. Berkeley: University of California Press.

Erie, M. 2016. *China and Islam: The Prophet, the Party, and Law*. Cambridge: Cambridge University Press.

Gladney, D.C. 1996. *Muslim Chinese: Ethnic Nationalism in the People's Republic*. Cambridge: Harvard University Press.

Gladney, D.C. 1999. The Salafiyya Movement in Northwest China: Islamic Fundamentalism Among the Muslim Chinese? In *Muslim Diversity: Local Islam in Global Contexts*, ed. L.O. Manger. Surrey: Nordic Institute of Asian Studies.

Glassé, C. 1989. *The Concise Encyclopedia of Islam*. London: Stacey International.

Howell, J.D. 2001. Sufism and the Indonesian Islamic Revival. *The Journal of Asian Studies* 60 (03): 701–729.

Lipman, J. 1997. *Familiar Strangers: A History of Muslims in Northwest China.* Studies on Ethnic Groups in China. Seattle: University of Washington Press.

Ma, Y. 1997. *Linxia Guo Gongbei Jianshi (A Brief History of Guo Gongbei).* Guo Gongbei Committee.

Ma, Y. 2008. Gadelinye Menhuan Chujiaren Zhidu Tanxi (A Discussion of the Monk System of the Qadiriyya Menhuan). *Journal of the Second Northwest University for Nationalities, Department of Philosophy and Religious Studies, Central University for Nationalities, Beijing, China,* 1.

Ma, H. 2011. The Historical and Present Situation of Islamic Menhuan in China. In *Muslims and a Harmonious Society: Selected Papers from a Three-Conference Series on Muslim Minorities in Northwest China: Gansu Province, 2008, Shaanxi Province, 2009, Xinjiang Autonomous Region, 2009.* Arlington: Institute for Global Engagement.

Murata, S. 2017. *The First Islamic Classic in Chinese: Wang Daiyu's "Real Commentary on the True Teaching".* Albany: State University of New York Press.

Murata, S., and W.C. Chittick. 2000. *Chinese Gleams of Sufi Light: Wang Tai-yu's Great Learning of the Pure and Real and Liu Chih's Displaying the Concealment of the Real Realm.* Albany: State University of New York Press.

Murata, S., W.C. Chittick, and W. Tu. 2009. *The Sage Learning of Liu Zhi: Islamic Thought in Confucian Terms.* Cambridge: Harvard University Asia Center for the Harvard-Yenching Institute.

Ohlander, E.S. 2011. *Sufism.* The Oxford Handbook of World Philosophy. UK: Oxford University Press.

Pillsbury, B. 1981. The Muslim Population of China: Clarifying the Questions of Size and Ethnicity. *Institute of Muslim Minority Affairs. Journal* 3 (2): 35–58.

Stewart, A. 2017. *Chinese Muslims and the Global Ummah: Islamic Revival and Ethnic Identity Among the Hui of Qinghai Province.* New York: Routledge.

Tomlinson, M. 2009. *In God's Image: The Metaculture of Fijian Christianity.* Oakland: University of California Press.

Urban, G. 2001. *Metaculture: How Culture Moves Through the World.* Minneapolis: University of Minnesota Press.

Wang, H. 2009. *Linxia Da Gongbei Menhuan xingcheng yu zuzhi yunxing moshi yanjiu (Organization and Formation of Da Gongbei Menhuan in Linxia).* Masters, Northwest Minorities University. http://www.cnki.net/KCMS/detail/detail.aspx?QueryID=0&CurRec=19&recid=&filename=LXSK198806009&dbname=CJFD7993&dbcode=CJFQ.

Wang, J. 2016. Islam and State Policy in Contemporary China. *Studies in Religion* 45 (4): 566–580.

Watt, W. 1989. *Islamic Fundamentalism and Modernity.* London: Routledge.

Weber, M., and W. Runciman. 1978. *Max Weber: Selections in Translation.* Cambridge: Cambridge University Press.

Yang, F. 2012. *Religion in China: Survival and Revival Under Communist Rule.* Oxford: Oxford University Press.

Yang, M.M.-H. 2008. *Chinese Religiosities: Afflictions of Modernity and State Formation.* Global, Area, and International Archive. Berkeley: University of California Press.

CHAPTER 8

Conclusions

In *Muslim society* (Gellner 1981), Ernest Gellner took the neo-Weberian view that modernity, as a form of progressive rationalisation, would, in Muslim societies, result in the shift from what he called 'low Islam' to 'high Islam', that is, from 'traditional' and 'ecstatic' forms of religion associated with rural populations (such as forms of Sufism) to so-called 'modern' and 'rational' forms of religion associated with urban populations and scriptural adherence (see also Gellner 1992, p. 11). In China, this tired and reductionist view of Sufism has been articulated in very similar terms:

> As social civilisation progresses and the cultural level of all followers of *menhuan* increases, their sense of democratic values is greatly strengthened. The number of people blindly supporting the upper class of *menhuan* and their theories of mysticism is in decline, while the number of those who are capable of rational thinking is increasing. (Ma 2011, pp. 53–58)

However, Sufism is not simply 'a religion of the common people' nor is it 'irrational' or associated only with those of the so-called lower class. In *Embodying Charisma*, Pnina Werbner and Helene Basu importantly strived to bridge the gap between the 'false dichotomies' of 'high' and 'low', 'orthodox' and 'popular' Islam that much scholarly literature has imposed upon the study of Sufism (Werbner and Basu 1998). Like Werbner and Basu, I also argue that Sufism is 'a single, total, symbolic reality' (Werbner and Basu 1998, p. 4) and one that is at the heart of Islam itself. As such, the desire expressed in the report discussed in *Chap. 7*—to change the system

© The Author(s) 2018   189
T. Cone, *Cultivating Charismatic Power*,
https://doi.org/10.1007/978-3-319-74763-7_8

of charismatic succession practiced within the Sufi networks—may prove difficult to realise. As Ma Hucheng identifies in his report—'handling the Hierarch (election of the *dangjiaren*) tradition requires dealing with the masses and respecting their choices in religious belief; this can never be handled carelessly and hastily' (Ma 2011, p. 70). In 1987, Gladney argued that the Sufi *gongbei* continue to be vital to the local communities, the 'religious masses', that surround them (Gladney 1987, p. 517). This is still very much the case. The religious site of Guo Gongbei serves many important roles in the local community. For the students and *chujiaren*, the *gongbei* was an enabler of education and travel. For the families I came to know, generation after generation carried out their weekly worship at these tombs and on special occasions would travel to many Qadiriyya *gongbei* in different locations over a period of several days. The charismatic power at the heart of this site, and at the heart of the network of *gongbei* sites like it, was a very real phenomenon—for practitioners and adherents alike.

CHARISMA IN THE CHINESE SUFI CONTEXT

The charisma at the heart of this particular case study of Islamic leadership was generated and maintained in a number of important ways. Mauss once said that 'at the bottom of all our mystical states there are body techniques which we have not studied, but which were studied fully in China and India, even in very remote periods' (Mauss 1979, p. 122). Accordingly, he postulated that there were 'biological means' through which one could enter a 'communion with God' (Mauss 1979, p. 122). Unlike the majority of studies on charisma in Sufism, which have been reductive in painting Sufi spiritual power as either a product of social or economic relations or as merely a kind of doctrine, in this study charismatic or spiritual power in the Sufi context has been taken seriously—that is, I have attempted to understand it as the practitioners themselves have done—as a real phenomenon. In doing so, the body has been understood as the main focus of the disciplinary dimension of the Sufi ritual, and I have built on the work of Mauss (1979 [1935]), Werbner (1998, 2003), Lizzio (2007), and Kugle (2012) in their emphasis on spiritual power and charisma as an embodied property. In particular I have drawn on Kugle's notions of being *through*, *against*, and *in* the body in exploring the relationship of the ego and the body in the production of charisma. Throughout each part of the discussion, this study has been underscored by Bourdieuan notions of habitus, bodily hexis, implicit pedagogy, and religious capital. In my analysis of discourse in the final chapter, I again drew from Bourdieu in aligning his notion of doxic practice with Urban's notion of metaculture to aid in understanding the ways in which 'culture comments upon culture' and the conditions that produce explicit commentary about what once was, or still is, implicit, or doxic, practice.

Previous studies of Sufi charisma in anthropology have focused on the context of hereditary lineages and amongst Qadiriyya orders in other parts of the world (Afghanistan, Iraq, Kurdistan, Northern Caucasus, Pakistan, and Indonesia) where the spiritual genealogy or lineage has been overwhelmingly hereditary. The consonantal root of the word *baraka* (Sufi spiritual power) in Arabic—'B-R-K'—means 'to be made to bend your knee' and includes specifically 'the way the camel is made to kneel for mounting. The verb is thus receptive—one receives blessing on bended knee—and submits to patriarchal authority. Built into the root, therefore, is the implicit sexual transmission of *baraka* which is passed patrilineally from generation to generation' (Zussman 1998, p. 90). This study offers a distinctive counterexample. It is a case study of a Qadiriyya order of a Sufi charisma that does not rely on blood ties.

The linguist Fritz Goerling has posited that while *baraka* is a central concept amongst Muslim communities worldwide, its precise meaning varies somewhat depending on the history of the cultural group in question. He found, for example, that amongst Muslims in West Africa, there was a shift of meaning from the primary meaning of blessing to mere power itself. So while *baraka* literally means 'blessing' or 'grace', Muslims have been known to use the term much more broadly to refer to qualities of spiritual grace, personal force, unique power, charisma, luck, and success. This study has explored how *baraka* is constituted in a particular locale and in so doing responds to recent theoretical interests in the 'local' and 'embodied'. I have argued that in the Chinese Sufi context, this *baraka* or charisma was a bodily capability, a physical manifestation of the 'spiritually realised' person (Lizzio 2007, p. 33). It was translated as either *jixiang* (lucky and auspicious) or *zhanguang* (to touch a light) and was described as a particular quality that only very few people could cultivate and only very few would ever 'meet with'.

This charismatic power was cultivated primarily through a set of bodily disciplines which emphasised the development of the individual along a three-stage path (*sancheng*), each necessary for the development of the next. Within this was a foundational set of bodily practices that were seen as being *qingzhen*. These included adherence to the five pillars of Islam, physical cleanliness, the correct preparation of food, and sexual abstinence. An important part of this stage was also developing a sound knowledge of the Qur'an and Hadith and learning the languages of Islam (Arabic and in this context Persian as well). In the second stage they emphasised the practice of the 'eight dimensions' (*bawei*) and *gongxiu* (which included the study of texts, silent meditation, and *dhikr*). Achieving mastery over these practices enabled one to be given 'permission' to attain a certain religious stature (*gei kouhuan*—'to exchange/give by way of mouth/speech') and to be let in on the 'secret' and 'protected' knowledge passed only through word of mouth and only to be received by those who were deemed 'ready' (*kouchuan xinshou*, 'transmitted orally, received in the heart'). Finally, there was a belief in the possibility for miracle-making (*shenji*), which was reliant on mastery of both the cognitive and physical elements just described. As miracles were proof of charismatic power in the saints of the past, so too were miracles expected of the current leader. The existence or achievement of the embodiment of charisma was acknowledged by others in the form of their expectations—they may not have necessarily 'seen' evidence of this charismatic power but they nonetheless had 'expectations' that the 'extraordinary' could happen again (Goossaert 2008, p. 5).

    This bodily charisma was socially reinforced and strengthened by a number of other important practices that have been discussed—including narrative and naming, emulation, social proximity and distance during public ritual, and education and mobility. Drawing on Bakken's work on the exemplary model, I argued that the capabilities, habits, and qualities of person stressed in the stories told about the saints, and the specific meanings of the generational names, served to generate a particular kind of charismatic exemplar. Miracles were a repeated theme in both textual and oral narratives and included the abilities to tame animals, heal illnesses, change the weather, shift matter such as rocks and iron, predict the future, and appear after death. The habits of living in silence, in seclusion and 'accumulating knowledge', were emphasised in the cultivation of these miraculous powers. Finally, deference to the saints that possessed these traits was made implicit in the very names that were given to new members in the genealogy. Qi Jingyi and Qi Daohe's naming system was built around both the individual meaning of a character and the combined meaning of all ten names. As a *chujiaren* of the Qadiriyya, one's very name was not only a link with the ancestors but a way of embodying particular values—values such as *dao* (truth), *yong* (perpetuity), *shi* (nobility), and *fang* (fragrance). Charisma was further strengthened through the daily emulation of exemplary practice. Students lived and studied alongside the *dangjiaren* and other *chujiaren*, and it was here that processes of 'implicit peda-gogy', of unconscious inculcation, were at their strongest. Through their emulation of various elements of daily practice (the five daily prayers, strict cleaning ritual, lengthy recitations), students took on elements of the charismatic habitus. Religious adherents, too, sought to emulate and benefit from the exemplary model of the *dangjiaren* in various ways. They emulated his quest for knowledge in going to the *gongbei* to speak with him about religious teachings and by taking classes at the *gongbei* held for members of the community. Religious adherents set up dedicated spaces in their homes to commemorate the saints of Guo Gongbei; some practised meditation during the night; some went out of their way to perform an annual journey to key Qadiriyya *gongbei* sites in the region. Some felt they could gain from the charismatic power of the deceased saints by venerating their tombs and offering prayers to Allah through them; others felt they could draw on this power by coming into contact with the *dangjiaren*. For many students and adherents alike, stories of the miraculous capabilities of past Sufi saints played an important part in the deference paid to the current leader, for they all knew how committed he was to his own project of miracle-making and that his belief in the possibility of such miracles was real.

Public rituals also played an important role in the strengthening and reinforcing of charisma in relation to social proximity and distance and the alteration of these practices with the sacred and profane. Several theorists have contended that a leader's social distance from followers influences their perception of the leader and, consequently, determines the attribution of charisma. In the context of Guo Gongbei, I described this as a kind of 'conspicuous invisibility' (Harms 2013), either a notable absence and/or certainly a very limited involvement by the *dangjiaren* in particular public rituals—most notably weddings, Friday prayers, and funeral procedures. During some rituals, the *dangjiaren* and *imam* maintained distance from particular practices that could have been seen as 'profane'. I described a wedding event typical of the region, during which the expected absence of the *dangjiaren* served to demarcate and reinforce the boundaries around his celibate status. The *imam* who was involved maintained a social distance too—most notably from the 'sacrilegious' activities of *nao dong fang* and *shua gongpo*. In the local funeral, the *dangjiaren* was often present during initial blessings and in the commemorations that followed the burial, most notably as a source of good luck and a symbol of religious authority, but interestingly it was the *imam* who conducted the formal part of the service. This delegation of ritual responsibility and the social distance that resulted contributed to his charismatic appeal. In the final example of the commemoration event for Chen Yiming, most notable was the affective response that occurred amongst adherents who sought proximity to the charismatic source. In shaking or kissing Ma Yufang's hands, or placing hands, head, or a kiss on Chen Yiming's tomb—many were visibly moved. In this context, public rituals—through conscious acts of distancing and conscious allowances of proximity—were an important means of generating and sustaining charismatic power.

Finally, pilgrimage for study overseas generated important forms of religious capital and in turn strengthened their charismatic authority. Here I traced the history of travel in the cultivation of Sufi saints in Guo Gongbei and the ways in which travel in Islam involved spiritual or temporal movement (Eickelman and Piscatori 1990, p. 2). Nowadays, many students and *chujiaren* come to Guo Gongbei because of the charismatic inspiration of past and present leaders, a charisma that is strengthened in part by their experience studying in locations highly valued in Islamic history. For young Muslim students and *chujiaren*—potential future teachers and leaders within both the Qadiriyya community and elsewhere in China—overseas experience studying in a Muslim majority country was highly valued in the constitution of their own religious authenticity and authority. Within this discussion I also provided a background to Islamic education more broadly in China as a means of contextualising the role that Guo Gongbei is playing in responding to contemporary concerns. Study overseas was seen to contribute not only to the individual charismatic cultivation of students and *chujiaren* but also to a sense of pride and national identity as Muslims in the Chinese context. While Guo Gongbei was a distinctively Sufi site, its practices did not demand that students necessarily follow the life of a celibate or that they study specifically Sufi texts. Fundamentally, Guo Gongbei aimed to encourage and enable study and learning for individuals (both at home and abroad) in order to improve levels of religious knowledge amongst the Muslim community as a whole. Guo Gongbei was distinctive in this encouragement of religious educational travel as it was the only *gongbei* site in the region to do so.

CHARISMA: CONTROVERSY AND IMPLICATIONS

These practices of Islamic leadership, however, were not without controversy. The charismatic authority that was supposedly granted by the successful embodiment of this charisma continues to be challenged by voices both within the Chinese Muslim community and by state representatives outside of it. In this study these contestations were framed around a series of metacultural categories or underlying concerns. First that of 'orthodoxy' and 'unorthodoxy': the practice of celibacy, their use of incense, their belief in miracles, and the ornate Chinese-Islamic architecture of their *gongbei* spaces are all held up as evidences of an Islam that is problematic—in part for its syncretic absorption of Buddhist and Daoist cultural elements. Second, 'integrity' and 'corruption': as explored in *Chap. 7*, concerns around issues of personal 'quality' or *suzhi* amongst the Hui are also in circulation regarding the Sufi leaders. The impacts of materialism and desires for marriage are seen by some as undermining the integrity (the *suzhi*) of the *chujiaren* and the possibility of their authentic spiritual advancement. This in turn is having an impact on the trust people have in the election process of *kouhuan*. Third, 'unity' and 'disunity': while Guo Gongbei maintains that the leadership of the *menhuan* is vital to unity and cohesion within the greater 'Islamic community', others feel that there are simply 'too many groups' and this is not conducive to a sense of unity within the 'Islamic community'. Finally, 'stability' and 'instability': at the level of local government, the system of religious succession and the role of the Hierarch within Sufi networks (including Guo Gongbei) is subject to great suspicion, and recommendations have been made that this somewhat 'secretive' process be replaced with a system of democratic election. But given the long, complex, and deeply embedded history of Sufi systems of succession—to what extent can changes be made and a process of 'rationalisation' occur?

Of perhaps broader significance for the government are the increasing levels of contact between the leaders of international Islamic denominations and organisations. These very real and direct connections with the global community can also be related to a broader increase in Muslim activism within China. In 2009, Gladney argued that 'no matter what conservative leaders in the government might wish, China's Muslim politics have now reached a new stage of openness. If China wants to further participate in the international political sphere of nation-states, this is unavoidable. With the opening to the West in recent years, travel to and from the Islamic heartlands has dramatically increased in China' (as cited in Ashiwa and Wank 2009, p. 198). Certainly, an increasing number of Chinese Muslims now go on pilgrimage to Mecca, and many are also involved in major projects in the Middle East and Africa, some able to utilise their Arabic language skills. With the recent launch of the One Belt, One Road initiative in May 2017—a hugely significant global economic and diplomatic trade programme—these collaborations and connections are bound to increase and strengthen, bringing with them new opportunities and potential challenges for China's Muslim community.[1]

It was noted earlier that many Sufi orders in China trace their origins to Iran (Wang 2014, p. 78). Today, the site of Guo Gongbei maintains a particularly strong relationship with the country and has a well-established system of sending *chujiaren* and students there to study. At the same time, Iran now provides over 30 per cent of China's energy needs and is also an important centre for manufacturing in the Middle East, producing with its Chinese partners motor vehicles and machinery for the Middle East and African markets (Burman 2013, Chapter 9, para. 20). In this practice the institution was demonstrating what Voll has described as the role of Sufi sites in processes of 'glocalisation'—that is, the role of many Sufi sites throughout the contemporary world in simultaneously fostering a local identity, while drawing on association with a global community (as cited in Bruinessen and Howell 2007, p. 298). These long-standing cultural affiliations and exchanges, and the significant geo-political partnerships now built upon them, contribute also to state-level anxieties mentioned earlier. As Edward Burman has argued 'local factionalism and even terrorism, or legitimate political protest, must now be set against the new geopolitical ambitions and energy needs of China' (Burman 2013, Chapter 7, para. 41). Ma Hucheng has noted in particular a concern that 'as our nation's *menhuan* search for their roots overseas, if any connection is established between *menhuan* and extremist religious groups, then *menhuan* not only will become followers and lose their own independent and self-sufficient position, they also will bring the disaster of international political struggles to our country and damage our efforts to conduct diplomatic missions' (Ma 2011, pp. 74–75). However, as Gladney notes (citing the late Imam Shi Kunbing of the oldest mosque in Beijing), 'with so much now at stake

---

[1] Jacqueline Armijo provides an interesting discussion on the many and varied cultural implications of the developing economic ties between China and the Gulf (Armijo 2013).

in the Middle East, the government cannot risk antagonizing its Muslim minorities' (Gladney 2004, p. 313). In such a globalised economy, China must sustain a balancing act between its management and control tactics on the one hand and its demonstration of respectful recognition and tolerance on the other. One of the most pressing concerns in this regard, in terms of both internal and external pressure, is the treatment of its Muslim Uyghur population in Xinjiang, an issue that was highlighted earlier (Gladney 2008, p. 200).

The symbolic and practical role of Sufi sites such as Guo Gongbei in the wider geo-politics of these economically and politically significant relationships cannot be discounted. Moreover, the impacts of these ongoing exchanges in terms of cultural change within the Chinese Muslim community will be interesting to watch. Ma Qiang has described recently the impact of globalisation on the development within Chinese Islam of new factions (*xin paibie*), of denying factions (*wu paibie*), and of mixed factions (*hunhe paibie*), noting that 'New intellectual trends and activities in the Arab world and in South and Central Asia have powerfully influenced Chinese Islam, including the Tabligh movement, reformism in religious law, the Taliban movement, and Sufi thinking [..]' (Ma 2012). While it is beyond the scope of this work to examine these influences further, I conclude with a series of related questions. Will there be a gradual transformation of the curriculum within the Islamic education system as some desire? If so, what role will the Sufi institutions play in these changes? Will the 'second movement of Sufism' that Professor L. spoke of develop into something more tangible and distinctive within the Chinese Muslim community? If so, how will increased geo-political interdependence and educational exchange with Iran and other countries in the Middle East impact these transformations?

EPILOGUE

One afternoon in November 2011, I was guided by an older Hui woman into Taizi Gongbei, collecting and lighting incense sticks on the way. She looped her arm in mine and took me to each tomb site, helping me to place the incense sticks in the urns in front. I then sat with her as she listened to a recitation occurring in the worship hall. Here, the *chujiaren* sat over copies of the Qur'an. Their quiet voices generated a low hum. They swayed back and forth a little, and every now and then they would gently kiss the text. At one point one of the speakers became very emotional in his recitation and began to cry as he called out the words. After this recitation had concluded and the *chujiaren* had dispersed, my friend took me by the hand and led me down the short road to Da Gongbei, collecting more incense sticks as we went from the stalls near the gate. After saying *salam* as we entered, she helped me light the sticks and place them one by one in the appropriate urns. Finally, we went to Guo Gongbei and I stood to the side as she went into the tomb enclosure for private prayer. These daily and affective practices within the charismatic space of the *gongbei* have both temporal and spatial importance. These practices are part of a discursive and embodied tradition that relates these individuals to both past and future through the medium of the present (Asad 1986, p. 14). They also connect them with a transnational community—a transnational community with whom ties extend beyond the realm of a shared religious history. These charismatic sites—and the charismatic power at the heart of them—serve an arguably ever-increasing importance in the maintenance of strategic relationships within the contemporary geo-political scene.

REFERENCES

Armijo, J. 2013. China and the Gulf: The Social and Cultural Implications of Their Rapidly Developing Economic Ties. In *Asia-Gulf Economic Relations in the 21st Century: The Local to Global Transformation*. Berlin: Gerlach Press.
Asad, T. 1986. *The Idea of an Anthropology of Islam*. Washington: Center for Contemporary Arab Studies, Georgetown University.
Ashiwa, Y., and D. Wank. 2009. *Making Religion, Making the State: The Politics of Religion in Modern China*. Stanford: Stanford University Press.
Bruinessen, M.V., and J.D. Howell. 2007. *Sufism and the 'Modern' in Islam*. Library of Modern Middle East Studies. Vol. 67. London: I.B. Tauris.
Burman, E. 2013. *China and Iran: Parallel History, Future Threat*. Stroud: The History Press.
Eickelman, D.F., and J.P. Piscatori. 1990. *Muslim Travellers: Pilgrimage, Migration, and the Religious Imagination*. Oakland: University of California Press.
Gellner, E. 1981. *Muslim Society*. Cambridge: Cambridge University Press.
Gellner, E. 1992. *Postmodernism, Reason and Religion*. London: Routledge.
Gladney, D.C. 1987. Muslim Tombs and Ethnic Folklore: Charters for Hui Identity. *The Journal of Asian Studies* 46 (3): 495–532.
Gladney, D.C. 2004. *Dislocating China: Reflections on Muslims, Minorities, and Other Subaltern Subjects*. London: C. Hurst.

Gladney, D.C. 2008. Islam and Modernity in China: Secularization or Separatism? In *Chinese Religiosities: Afflictions of Modernity and State Formation*. Oakland: University of California Press.

Goossaert, V. 2008. Mapping Charisma in Chinese Religion. *Nova Religio: The Journal of Alternative and Emergent Religions* **12**(2):12–28

Harms, E. 2013. The Boss: Conspicuous Invisibility in Ho Chi Minh City. *City and Society* **25** (2): 195–215.

Lizzio, K. 2007. Ritual and Charisma in Naqshbandi Sufi Mysticism. *Anpere E-Journal for the Anthropological Study of Religion*, 1–37. http://www.anpere.net/2007/3.pdf

Ma, H. 2011. The Historical and Present Situation of Islamic Menhuan in China. In *Muslims and a Harmonious Society: Selected Papers from a Three-Conference Series on Muslim Minorities in Northwest China: Gansu Province, 2008, Shaanxi Province, 2009, Xinjiang Autonomous Region, 2009*. Arlington: Institute for Global Engagement.

Ma, Q. 2012. Quanqiuhua beijingxia de Zhongguo Yisilanjiao yanjiu jidai jiaqiang (The Urgent Need to Study Islam in China in the Context of Globalization). *Zhongguo minzu bao*.

Mauss, M. 1979. Body Techniques. In *Sociology and Psychology*, 95–123. London: Routledge and Kegan Paul.

Wang, J. 2014. The Opposition of a Leading Akhund to Shi'a and Sufi Shaykhs in Mid-Nineteenth Century China. *Cross-Currents: East Asian History and Culture Review* 12. http://cross-currents.berkeley.edu/e-journal/issue-12.

Werbner, P., and H. Basu. 1998. *Embodying Charisma: Modernity, Locality, and Performance of Emotion in Sufi Cults*. London: Routledge.

Zussman, M. 1998. Baraka: Grace, Healing and Political Legitimacy in the Middle East and North Africa. *Yearbook of Cross-Cultural Medicine and Psychotherapy* **99**: 87–101.

GLOSSARY

bagua　八卦. Bagua refers to 'the eight trigrams'. These refer to a 'Chinese conceptual diagram of the cosmos, consisting of all possible combinations of three unbroken (yang) and broken (yin) lines […] An octagonal building would represent the Eight Trigrams in its architecture' (Lipman 2000, p. 565).

baraka　白拉克提. Meaning 'blessing' in Arabic. In Islam, it refers to a quality, power, or force that emanates from Allah and can be transmitted to human beings or objects. Muhammad, Prophets, and persons thought of as holy are seen to possess *baraka*. In some contexts, *baraka* can be acquired by touching a shrine or the tomb of a saint (*wali*) or the Black Stone in the Ka'bah. A *baraka* from God initiates a Sufi order (*silsila*).

bawei　八维. A code of conduct in the Qadiriyya order that shaped daily practice. Referring to the practices to 'eat little, drink little, sleep little, speak little, always clean, always memorize (recite), always fast, and always be quiet' (Ma 1997, p. 23).

chujiaren　出家人. This is the term used to specifically refer to the disciples of the Qadiriyya order. It literally means, 'those who have left the home or family'. I have translated it in places as disciple rather than monk, but otherwise use the Chinese term throughout. Other terms also used as equivalents include *qinglian ren* 清廉人 (honest person), *qin lian ren* 勤练人 (practiced person), and *ji jiao ren* 记教人 (one who teaches remembrance).

© The Author(s) 2018
T. Cone, *Cultivating Charismatic Power*,
https://doi.org/10.1007/978-3-319-74763-7

dangjiaren 当家人. The name of the spiritual master of the Chinese Qadiriyya order. It is equivalent to shaykh or *mawlā* in Arabic (also referred to as Hierarch in some English translations). In China, amongst non-Sufi Muslims, the equivalent word is 'ahong' (阿訇). While other Chinese Sufi orders generally use the term *jiaozhu* 教主 or *changjiao* 常教 (leader of the order) with the same meaning as a *shaykh* in Arabic, the Qadiriyya order prefer the term *dangjiaren* (literally, to be like a family person, to act as the leader of family). Other terms also used by Qadiriyya: *daozu* (道祖), *baba* (巴巴), *halifa* (哈里法) (from the Ar. *khalifah* meaning 'head of state'), *laorenjia* (老人家), *taiye* (太爷).

dhikr Alternatively spelt *Zikr* in Arabic. It is often translated as 'remembrance' or 'invocation' and is a ritual prayer common amongst Sufi orders. The *Dhikr* is essentially a 'remembering' of God through the frequent repetition of his names or of short phrases or prayers. It can be silent or vocal.

Gedimu 各底木. From the Arabic *qadīm*, meaning old, ancient, old tradition. This term refers to those Hui who follow the 'old' tradition (as opposed to Sufism or the Yihewani). Today, as in the past, the Qadīm are the majority group amongst the Hui. In the early history of Islam in China, the Qadim 'evolved by absorbing Shi'a Islam within the Sunnī mainstream and Sufism was tolerated. They adopted the tenets of the Hanafi school of law and developed a clerically-based organisation centred on the local Muslim community' (Wang 2001, p. 37).

gei kouhuan 给口唤. A method to exchange sacred knowledge in the Chinese Qadiriyya order. It literally means 'to exchange/give by way of mouth/speech'.

gongbei 拱北. The term is the Chinese transliteration of the Persian word *gunbad* or *gunbaz* meaning 'dome'. The term is used to refer to the 'tombs of Sufis (esp. Sufi saints but also other prominent religious figures) in China' (Wang 2001, p. 38). They are often the base for a Sufi order and their activities. Turkic Muslims in NW China refer to tombs or shrines as *mazar*.

gongxiu 功修. Literally meaning 'meritorious actions of cultivation'. In the context of Qadiriyya Sufi ritual, it refers to specific cultivation practices dictated by the *sancheng* or 'three stages'.

Hui 回. Hui is the name used for one of ten Muslim minorities in China, of which the Hui are the majority. The Chinese word 'hui' 回 is formed by two panels or circles, one embedded in the other. According to

Zhou Chuanbin and Ma Xuefeng (Ma and Zhou 2009, p. 3), Muslim theologians of China have argued that the inner one represents the earth and the outer the sky. Some also suggest that the shape of the word could represent the shape of the Holy Mosque of Mecca. The word also has the meaning of 'return', which connotes both the foreign origin and the religious goal of Chinese Hui Muslims.

imam   With diacritics in Arabic is *imām*, Ch. Ahong (阿訇). Prayer leader in Muslim community.

Jahriyya   哲赫林耶. Zhehelinye, from the Arabic word *jahar*, to 'say', 'express something aloud'. This Sufi group is a branch of the Naqsh-bandiyya. It was founded by a Chinese *hajji* who, after his return from Mecca and Yemen in the eighteenth century, sought to reform particular Sufi practices (such as the veneration of Islamic saints). Adherents of this order recite the *dhikr* loudly (thus called by some the 'voice-raising group') and move the body and head about during religious service (Wang 2001, p. 135).

jixiang   吉祥. Used by the Chinese Qadiriyya as an equivalent to the Arabic word *baraka*. It means 'lucky/auspicious/propitious'.

Khafiyya   虎非耶. Hufeiye (Ch), from the Arabic *al-khafiya* meaning hidden or secret. This Sufi group is a branch of the Naqshbandiyya and evolved in the seventeenth to eighteenth centuries under the influence of a number of Chinese *ḥājji* who went to Mecca and also studied in Yemen and Bukhara. Its *dhikr* recitation tends to be conducted in a low tone or silently (Wang 2001, p. 52).

kouchuan xinshou   口传心授. A method to exchange sacred knowledge in the Chinese Qadiriyya order. It literally means 'transmitted orally, received in the heart'.

Kubrawiyya   库不林业. Kubulinye (Ch), from the Arabic *al-Kubrīya* meaning grandeur or glory. This Sufi group originated in Iran and came to China in the fourteenth century through Central Asia. The Kubrawiyya is characterised by long periods of meditation and *dhikr* chanting. It is mainly found in Gansu Province (Wang 2001, p. 62).

menhuan   门宦. The 'leading or saintly descent groups' of early Chinese Sufi leaders (Gladney 1996, p. 41). Also understood as 'orders'. The four main *menhuan* in China are the Qadiriyya, Khufiyya, Jahriyya, and Kubrawiyya. These are then sub-divided internally into smaller *menhuan* and branches.

Qadiriyya   嘎德林耶. Gadelinye (Ch), from the Arabic *qadar* meaning fate, destiny, or power. This Sufi group derives its name from the founder

'Abd al-Qādir al-Jīlānī. It was introduced into China in the seventeenth century. It is distinctive from the other four Sufi orders active in China due to its absorption of Daoist and Buddhist practices and ideas. Its clerics are also celibate (Wang 2001, p. 34).

qingzhen 清真. The Chinese term literally means 'pure' and 'true'. In the Chinese context, it is an important signifier of the Chinese Muslim identity—demarcating a particular set of practices, relations, and objects deemed to be 'Islamic'.

Salafiyya 赛来菲耶. Sailaifeiye (Ch), from the Arabic *al-Salafiyya*. In China this Islamic group developed after separating from the Ikhwani movement in 1937, as a result of returning *ḥājji* who had been in contact with the Salafiyya movement in the Middle East. In its doctrine, the Salafiyya 'only accept the authority of the first three generations of Islamic leadership (Muhammad, his Companions and their immediate disciples)' (Wang 2001, p. 95).

sancheng 三乘. Three vehicles/stages that are central to the Sufi path of self-cultivation. The three stages are *Licheng* (礼乘/Sharī'ah/Propriety/islam/*li* 礼), Daocheng (Ṭarīqah/the Way/īmān/*dao* 道), and Zhencheng (Ḥaqīqah/the Real/iḥsān/*zhen* 真) (Murata et al. 2009, pp. 82–86).

suzhi 素质. *Suzhi* refers to the quality of a person and marks 'hierarchical and moral distinction between the high and the low' (Kipnis 2006, p. 297). It has become an important concept in a 'national eugenicist discourse' in China that is concerned with '(re)producing citizens of the highest mental and physical quality' (Gillette 2000, p. 80).

wudian 五典. This refers to the five cardinal relationships adhered to by the Qadiriyya: compliance with God, compliance with the prophet, compliance with the parents, compliance with the country, and compliance with its governor (*shun zhu*/顺主, *shun sheng*/顺圣, *shun qin*/顺亲, *shun guojia*/顺国家, *jiqi zhizhengzhe*/及其执政者) (Ma 1997, p. 25).

wugong 五功. The five pillars of Islam: prayer (*li*, 礼), religious service (*nian*, 念), fasting (*zhai*, 斋), paying alms (*shishe*, 施舍), and pilgrimage (*chao*, 朝).

Yihewani 依赫瓦尼. From the Arabic *al-Ikhwan al-Muslimun*, meaning 'Muslim brotherhood' or 'association'. At the end of the nineteenth century, influenced by Wahhabi ideals from the Middle East, Hui reformers returning to China introduced the ideas of the Ikhwani movement. Yihewani doctrine emphasises the adherence to 'true Islam' (practice based on the Qur'ān and Ḥadīth) and 'the purging of customs not in accordance with *Sharī'ah* law. It also opposes China's Sufi orders and suborders' (Wang 2001, pp. 127–128). Today, this group is found mainly amongst the Hui in Northwest China.

zhanguang 沾光. Used by the Chinese Qadiriyya as an equivalent to the Arabic word *baraka*. It means 'to bask in the light or to benefit from association with somebody or something'.

REFERENCES

Gillette, M.B. 2000. *Between Mecca and Beijing: Modernization and Consumption Among Urban Chinese Muslims.* Stanford: Stanford University Press.

Gladney, D.C. 1996. *Muslim Chinese: Ethnic Nationalism in the People's Republic.* Cambridge: Harvard University Press.

Kipnis, A. 2006. Suzhi: A Keyword Approach. *The China Quarterly* 186: 295–313.

Lipman, J. 2000. MA TONG, A Brief History of the Qadiriyya in China (translated from the Chinese and introduced by Jonathan LIPMAN). *Journal of the History of Sufism* 1–2: 547–576 [Zarcone, T. and Buehler, A., editors. Simurg Press].

Ma, Y. 1997. *Linxia Guo Gongbei Jianshi (A Brief History of Guo Gongbei).* Guo Gongbei Committee.

Ma, X., and C. Zhou. 2009. Development and Decline of Beijing's Hui Muslim Community. Chiangmai: Silkworm Books.

Murata, S., W.C. Chittick, and W. Tu. 2009. *The Sage Learning of Liu Zhi: Islamic Thought in Confucian Terms.* Cambridge: Harvard University Asia Center for the Harvard-Yenching Institute.

Wang, J. 2001. *Glossary of Chinese Islamic terms.* Richmond: Curzon Press.

APPENDIX

HUI WEDDING SERMON

Who fulfilled the words of *sunnah*—if married—is a qualified parishioner/ convert. If the woman was reluctant to marry the man and the man sincerely accepted, this shows that a virtue of Islam is freedom of marriage. We are opposed to arranged marriage, or adulterous marriage [...] As Muslims we should always learn *īmāni* (faith), always read. For a long time if you do not learn the words of *īmāni*, then you will not keep up with things. Technology is now so well-developed, we have made aircraft, cannons are a very easy thing, but how to make an individual? This shows that people are among the most exquisite of all things. Man and woman come together in order to create people, this is the most important. Just like after a purchase there might be an electrical malfunction, marital relationship problems also occur. It is not good if there is chaos in marriage, caused by conflicts between the husband and wife. As the use of electrical products should follow precautions, between husband and wife there are also precautions. It is possible to add some humour, but to say anything at all, for example, 'I do not want you, you go back to your family.' You are absolutely not able to say these words of divorce. Although divorce in Islam is allowed, it is always a last resort. The fight between a husband and wife is uncivilised behaviour, and it is best not to do so. I hope after you get married you will get along, and be civilised.

© The Author(s) 2018
T. Cone, *Cultivating Charismatic Power*,
https://doi.org/10.1007/978-3-319-74763-7

COMMEMORATION CEREMONY SPEECHES

Speech Two from Government Representative

Today Guo Gongbei holds a commemoration ceremony for Chen Taizu (Chen Yiming). This is an important celebration for all Muslims. On behalf of the United Front Work Department of CPC Central Committee, the City Bureau of Religious Affairs and the City Islamic Association, I warmly congratulate the leaders and congregation of Guo Gongbei for supporting the party's religious policy to love the country and love religion, uniting to advance bravely the Three Represents (NB: the duty of the Chinese Communist party in 2001, namely: to represent productivity of an advanced society, forward the progress of advanced culture and the fundamental interests of the people to focus on the promotion of national unity), supporting closely the advancement of national unity and constructing a harmonious society. They have made their own contributions to the advancement of national unity, social stability and the culture of society. I take this opportunity to give good wishes to the leaders of Guo Gongbei and others, a wish that they can enhance learning, that they enhance the learning of the party's ethnic and religious policies, and that they can support laws and regulations to strengthen education. Recently Guo Gongbei in this respect has done very well. In the last three years, Guo Gongbei has made a tremendous contribution to the development of Islamic culture. Unity and harmony is the core premise of everything we do, to do a good job in ensuring the unity of our work and to carry out other activities, to improve relations between the masses, to strengthen relations between different ethnic groups, to mutually respect and support each other.

Speech by Guo Gongbei Leader

It is autumn in Hezhou; in this beautiful and fruitful harvest season, we hold a grand gathering, like the celebration held for Chen Taizu (Chen Yiming), we also commemorate the completion of Guo Gongbei. At this point, on behalf of Guo Gongbei, I stand with *dangjiaren* of other *gongbei* at this celebration. Imams from various mosques, leaders who have come to participate in this ceremony and friends, I give you warm welcome and sincere greetings. Today we feel very honoured to have so many distinguished and prestigious guests, today a brand new Guo Gongbei has finally been completed successfully. Its solemn magnificence is not only the pride of Hezhou's Muslims, it is also the pride of China's Muslims. Today, it embodies the efforts of many of us, especially all of the staff of Wang Yongjun (local governor), dutifully taking great efforts in brick-carving and intricate wood-carvings. Simultaneously, for care and support in the construction process, I give sincere thanks to the parishioners who have made a donation [...] Our Guo Gongbei originates from Islam. Sage Chen Yiming is the 29th generation descendant of the Prophet, such learned wisdom cultivated from heaven to earth. He came to China across the sea and to Little Mecca—Hezhou. Due to the actions of our leader Chen Yiming to defend the country, the name Guo Gongbei is conferred in the Qing Dynasty as an edict for Guo Gongbei to protect the country, 'To serve the country and protect the people.' However, due to historical reasons, after the revolution, there was a ban. Guo Gongbei has since made important contributions to the development of Islamic religion. Since the Third Plenary Session, the Party's national policy implemented in 1986 meant that after hardships and trials, Guo Gongbei could be rebuilt. After years of trials and hardships, Guo Gongbei could be built safely. After the rebuilding Guo Gongbei is exquisite with wood and brick carvings, contributing wonderful workmanship to China's Islamic architecture. I wish to thank all of those who donated money and materials in the process of rebuilding efforts. May Allah give them good fortune in this life.

INDEX

© The Author(s) 2018   211
T. Cone, *Cultivating Charismatic Power*,
https://doi.org/10.1007/978-3-319-74763-7